LEVON HELM: ROCK, ROLL & RAMBLE

The Inside Story of the Man, the Music and the Midnight Ramble

**By
John W. Barry**

Levon Helm: Rock, Roll & Ramble: The Inside Story of the Man, the Music and the Midnight Ramble.
By John W. Barry
ISBN 978-0-578-30605-6 (paperback)
All rights reserved. No portion of this book may be reproduced in any form, shape or manner without the express written consent of the author.
Copyright 2022 © by John W. Barry

john@rockrollramble.com

Cover and back cover design by Mike Dubois. happylifeproductions.com

Cover photo: Levon Helm at the Mountain Jam music festival, Hunter Mountain, Hunter, New York, on June 6, 2010. www.mountainjam.com. Photo by Dino Perrucci. www.dinoperrucciphotography.com
Back cover photo by Chris Howe.

Website: rockrollramble.com. Conceived and designed by Tony LoBue.

DEDICATION

This book is dedicated to Chris Howe, a pivotal member of Team Levon. Without his support and encouragement, this book would have never seen the light of day. Thank you, Chris.

CONTENTS

Dedication		iii
Foreword		vii
Preface		ix
Chapter One:	An Opportunity to Fight Back	1
Chapter Two:	The Barn	32
Chapter Three:	Jimmy Vivino and an All-Star Baseball Team Playing Football	53
Chapter Four:	Barbara O'Brien	65
Chapter Five:	Tony LoBue: 'He Was Who I Thought He Was'	75
Chapter Six:	Justin Guip	88
Chapter Seven:	Larry Campbell	95
Chapter Eight:	The Midnight Ramble	105
Chapter Nine:	Team Levon	149
Chapter Ten:	The Grammys	184
Chapter Eleven:	Arkansas	192
Chapter Twelve:	Canada: 'It Sounded Like Going to the Moon'	213
Chapter Thirteen:	Woodstock, Saugerties and Ulster County	221
Chapter Fourteen:	The Second Coming of The Band	247
Chapter Fifteen:	The Movies	254
Chapter Sixteen:	Muddy	268
A Final Word:	From Red Rocks to Turkey Scratch	275
Acknowledgements		291
More Acknowledgements		295
Thank You		301

FOREWORD

Levon was a friend of mine and he also played drums.

Levon was an incredible musician and singer, I loved playing with him, but he was an even better friend and human being.

Peace & love

Ringo

PREFACE

You don't have to look too far in New York's Hudson Valley for physical manifestations of an aspiration that binds together all of humanity—the pursuit of freedom.

The prominent role that the region north of New York City played in the American Revolution is memorialized far and wide, from the burning of Kingston by the British on October 16, 1777; to the ratification of the U.S. Constitution by New York State, which occurred on July 26, 1788, in Poughkeepsie.

"The British viewed New York City and the Hudson River Valley as key strategic locations," according to the National Park Service. "After evacuating the patriot stronghold of Boston in March of 1776, the British concentrated on New York as a base of operations. In July of 1776, shortly after the signing of Thomas Jefferson's Declaration of Independence, a huge British fleet of nearly 500 ships and 35,000 men—the largest single armed force in America until the Civil War—appeared off New York."

The Hudson Valley played a pivotal role in the American Revolution as a transportation and supply route.

And the City of Kingston in February 1777 welcomed delegates to a Provincial Congress, for the crafting of the first New York State Constitution. The Convention of the Representatives of the State of New York worked on the state constitution for two months inside the Ulster County Courthouse. The document was approved on April 22, 1777, and provided for the election of a governor, lieutenant governor and members of a senate and assembly. New York held its first elections in June of 1777. On October 16, the British arrived in Kingston.

"Looking upon Kingston as a 'hotbed of perfidy and sedulous disloyalty to King George the Third and His Majesty's Parliament,' the British punished Kingston for hosting the revolutionary state government, and for generously providing Washington's army with wheat and other food supplies," according to the National Park Service. "Under the command of Major General John Vaughan, the British troops moved into Kingston's Stockade area and set fire to every building, largely succeeding in burning the city to the ground...Kingston paid a large price for its role in the American Revolution."

But, "With many of Kingston's Dutch buildings made of stone, numerous buildings were simply gutted and not completely destroyed by the fire...Reconstruction was slow and painful," and, "As the years passed Kingston slowly rebuilt..."

Freedom maintained a firm foothold in the Hudson Valley, which played a pivotal role as the fledgling nation worked to secure its future.

Nearly two centuries after the British burned Kingston, and just a few miles west of the city in the Town of Woodstock, plans were set for a different kind of American revolution. These plans would crystallize in mid-August 1969 with the Woodstock Music and Art Fair. Yeah, it was held about 60 miles away from Woodstock in Bethel, Sullivan County. But the planning for Woodstock took place in the Town of Woodstock, and the defiance around which that famous festival unfolded in the name of freedom has been entrenched in the spirit of that town, that name, that legacy, ever since.

"Freedom," bellowed Richie Havens, during his opening set at the Woodstock festival on Friday, Aug. 15, 1969. "Freedom."

With the utterance of a single word, over and over, the 1960s counterculture had unleashed its battle cry. The world has never been the same since.

The Town of Woodstock is where Levon Helm found himself in the 1960s, prior to his band, The Band, playing the Woodstock festival. Levon settled in Woodstock and called it home for the rest of his life. And many of the folks I interviewed for this book said they knew no one who better exemplified, illustrated, embodied and underscored the concept, idea, notion, practice and pursuit of freedom, than Levon Helm.

The freedom that Levon embraced and defended revolved around the personal freedom to, pretty much, do whatever the fuck you want, because of your own personal choice, and consequences be damned as principle triumphed. Many of us would never, could ever live life this way, so we turned to Levon, as a beacon casting a warm glow of freedom far beyond the music he made with The Band and as a solo performer.

We turned to Levon because he walked the walk when it came to exercising personal freedom, for better or worse. And you didn't have to look any further than his Midnight Ramble house concerts to witness a guy living his life and sharing his artistry on his own terms.

One angle on all of this crystallized on May 3, 2012, two weeks to the day after Levon died, when Amnesty International released the song, "Toast To Freedom." The new tune was released in honor of the 50th anniversary of Amnesty International, which in 1962, "evolved from a one-year campaign to free political prisoners—the inspiration of the British lawyer Peter Benenson, outraged by the injustice he saw worldwide—into a global movement fighting for justice, freedom and human dignity," according to a press release announcing the song.

"Toast To Freedom" was written by Carl Carlton, a German songwriter, guitarist and vocalist who spent a considerable amount of time, over years, at Levon Helm Studios.

I can vividly remember hanging around Levon's on a random, cold, Sunday afternoon, and in walked Carl with a writing pad and pen. Scrawled at the top of a page were some lyrics that I was, at the time, very honored to read after Carl shared them with me:

"How delicious is the winning of her kiss/Bind her love to eternal bliss/She's the greatest power in the universe/Freedom."

These are the opening lines to "Toast To Freedom."

A longtime fan of The Band, Carl found himself at Levon Helm Studios in Woodstock by way of Dockside Studio in Maurice, Louisiana. Carl in 1999-2000 was working there with Sonny Landreth and he shared the music he had made with his band, the Songdogs. Someone mentioned Levon's name in the context of Carl's music and, the next thing he knew, Levon had been invited down south to Dockside Studio to join in on the recording.

After working with Sonny Landreth, Carl ended up working on three of his own albums at Dockside, and Levon joined in each time.

The first time he came down, Levon was talking in a hoarse whisper following his radiation treatments for cancer of the vocal cords. But, Carl said, "He was always outside with my children, Jessica and Max, and my dog Buddy. Levon taught my kids how to play American football. It was great times; lovely, big dinners."

Carl expanded his relationship with Levon by bringing the Songdogs to Levon Helm Studios, to record their fourth album in Woodstock.

A longtime supporter of Amnesty, Carl sometime later found himself in Dublin, Ireland, with his close friend, longtime music industry executive, activist and entrepreneur Jochen Wilms. Bill Shipsey, the founder of Art for Amnesty, Amnesty International's global artist engagement program, was also on hand. Carl and Jo had just returned from a trip to Woodstock, where they had spent time at Levon Helm Studios, enjoying the Midnight Ramble.

Talk turned to Carl writing a song for Amnesty's 50th anniversary, and when a location for recording the song was discussed, the answer was obvious—Levon Helm Studios in Woodstock, New York, would be the perfect place.

"It's the Levon spirit, it's the Woodstock spirit, it's my family here," Carl said during an interview at Levon Helm Studios. "I didn't give it a second thought. Woodstock is a symbol of freedom. Levon is so free, creating the Midnight Ramble, just being, just doing what he does best. Levon stands as the equivalent of freedom for me. He doesn't come at you and teach you how to be free—he just lives it."

Carl embarked on the project with Jo Wilms, who along with Bill Shipsey served as co-executive producer on "Toast To Freedom." And the song evolved into a collaboration between Carl and Larry Campbell—the Grammy winning producer, musical director, multi-instrumentalist and vocalist for the Levon Helm Band—following Larry's work on the tune during the recording process.

"Toast To Freedom" was produced by Bob Clearmountain, who has worked with Paul McCartney, David Bowie and Bruce Springsteen. Carl and Larry served as co-producers.

The whole "Toast To Freedom" project was a bit of a mind-bender for me.

Twenty-six years before the release of "Toast To Freedom," on June 15, 1986, my teenage mind was blown when Amnesty International's

"Conspiracy of Hope" tour rolled into the old Giants Stadium, in northern New Jersey's Meadowlands Sports Complex. The dozens of acts included the reunited Police, U2, Peter Gabriel, Joni Mitchell, Joan Baez, Jackson Browne and Miles Davis.

I attended the hours-long show with my closest friends from high school. We arrived at about 8:30 a.m. to tailgate in the parking lot and left towards midnight, if my memory serves me correctly.

It was an epic experience that unfolded nearly a year after the Live Aid concerts in London and Philadelphia. So the concert held to raise money and awareness for political prisoners had a lot of momentum from the concerts held to raise money and awareness for those starving in Africa.

And as the son of first-generation Irish-Americans—all four of my grandparents were born in Ireland and immigrated to the U.S—the Amnesty International logo, a candle surrounded by razor wire, held special meaning for me. This was because the oppression suffered by the Irish in the six counties of Northern Ireland, at the hands of the British, was a constant topic of discussion in my house while I was growing up.

Fast forward more than 25 years and there I was, a fly on the wall during the week-long Amnesty recording session at Levon Helm Studios, for "Toast To Freedom." Adding gravity to the whole scene was the presence at Levon's of Amnesty International Executive Director Larry Cox. The entire situation was overwhelming, to say the least.

Performing on the song at Levon's were Keb' Mo'; Donald Fagen of Steely Dan; and Carl Carlton and the Songdogs. Representing Levon Helm Studios on the tune were Levon, Larry Campbell, Larry's wife, Teresa Williams, and Levon's daughter, Amy Helm. All were members of the Levon Helm Band.

Levon Helm Studios Chief Engineer Justin Guip worked on the recording. And numerous performers later added vocals to the track, including Warren Haynes, Carly Simon, Ewan McGregor, Kris Kristofferson, Rosanne Cash and Angelique Kidjo.

"Levon was one great soul," Wilms, who attended many of Levon's Midnight Rambles, said in the Amnesty press release. "I am so grateful we got to work with him, his outstanding band and team in his barn in Woodstock. He was an inspiration and our muse. The song 'Toast To Freedom' is dedicated to Amnesty International, but in a certain way is now a 'Toast To Levon' and a celebration for him as well."

And now for a slight detour.

On July 28, 2010, Levon played Radio City Music Hall in New York City with Willie Nelson, and I remain very grateful to this day to have joined the Levon Helm Band's entourage for that show. After arriving that afternoon, I wandered around one of the world's most famous venues and opened a random door to find myself gazing into the house, with thousands of empty seats, and the Levon Helm Band running through sound check on stage as lights with an orange glow illuminated the empty theater. It was a moment I will never forget.

There was a narrow ledge affixed to the wall, stage right, that was clearly not accessible to the public during a performance, but I somehow managed to get to it through that door. The ledge climbed higher and higher and I just walked up it until I reached the first balcony. I sat down, looked around and soaked it all in.

Nearly two years later, on March 4, 2012, I found myself sitting in an orchestra seat at Radio City as the guest of Jo Wilms, at a benefit performance for Amnesty International. Jon Stewart, Stephen Colbert, Mumford & Sons and Russell Brand were among the headliners. Monty Python's Michael Palin, Eric Idle, and Terry Jones appeared by way of pre-recorded videos. But it was Coldplay, who if I'm not mistaken closed the evening, who stole the show with a romp through their hit song, "Every Teardrop is a Waterfall."

I'm getting chills writing about it now because toward the end of the song, Coldplay lead singer Chris Martin bounded off the stage to his right and ran up the very same ledge that I had commandeered on the afternoon of that Levon Helm-Willie Nelson show two years prior. Things were a bit different for Chris Martin that night, of course, what with the lighting rig and full-blast confetti canyons on the ledge, and the crowd going nuts, beneath falling confetti and streamers, as he climbed to the first balcony, just as I had done on that afternoon in July 2010.

So yeah, I can say without hesitation that Chris Martin of Coldplay once followed in my footsteps.

And now I raise my glass and say to you, here's to Coldplay, here's to Amnesty International, here's to Jo Wilms, Carl Carlton and Larry Campbell; here's to Levon Helm, his band and his team; here's to Woodstock, New York; here's to the Midnight Ramble and all it represents.

This is MY toast to freedom.

Like millions of people, I'll never forget the first time I heard Levon Helm sing.

The year was 1983 and I was sitting on the floor of the dining room in the house where I grew up, on Renee Lane in Bardonia, New York. My sister Eileen had purchased the soundtrack to the film "The Big Chill" on LP and I wanted to hear "Gimme Some Lovin'" by the Spencer Davis Group.

The record on the family turntable kept playing and things finally got around to a song I had never heard before, by a band I had never heard of before. The tune was "The Weight" and the band was The Band. I was 13 or 14 and I had never heard of Levon Helm. The aching in "The Weight" left me bruised. Levon's voice offered hope. That chord progression, Levon's voice, the whole thing left me in a trance. I had no need for words or descriptions or analogies. Hearing "The Weight" for the first time and hearing Levon sing for the first time were all about emotion and feelings and sensations and a sizzling desire to hear more.

Twenty-one years later, I found myself face-to-face with Levon Helm inside his home-recording studio on Plochmann Lane in Woodstock, New York. I was a staff writer for the *Poughkeepsie Journal*, he had launched his Midnight Rambles and I was there to interview him for a story.

Not long after, I began hanging around Levon Helm Studios more and more. Discussions emerged regarding Levon writing a second book. I was convinced that I was the guy to help him get the job done.

Levon was not the kind of guy who was partial to a structured interview schedule. So thanks to Levon's manager, Barbara O'Brien, a plan emerged for me to hang around with my digital recorder, capturing in an unrehearsed, impromptu manner Levon's thoughts on his past and his present. At the heart of it all were his stories, those all-consuming, epic, compelling, engaging, poignant, thoughtful, weathered, sad, cautionary and hilarious stories. The next thing I knew, I was a fly on the wall in his kitchen after the Rambles; in the studio during recording sessions; on road trips; and just about everywhere in between. Through it all, I got to know the guy from Turkey Scratch, Arkansas, pretty well.

As I look back on the time I spent with Levon and the many hours I spent at Levon Helm Studios, I have no need to speak any words or offer descriptions or serve up analogies—just like that moment when I heard Levon sing "The Weight" for the first time. Those years, those moments, the stories Levon told around his kitchen table after the Midnight Ramble, and the music he made just inside the front door of his home during the Midnight Ramble, remain suspended in time. And they will be forever framed by emotion and feelings and sensations—and a sizzling desire to hear more.

This book is not a chronology of Levon Helm's life. *This Wheel's On Fire*, which Levon wrote with Stephen Davis, captured that in fine form.

Levon Helm: Rock, Roll & Ramble tells the story of Levon's Midnight Ramble house concerts, which ran from 2004-2012 and ignited his once-in-an-era comeback, the glory of which he shared with us all. This book also offers insight into those places that shaped Levon's life—Arkansas, Canada and Woodstock, New York; and those things he held closest to his heart—his family; his friends; his dog Muddy; and Team Levon.

This story would not be complete without a look at two things that sculpted Levon Helm as an artist: his film career and the Grammy Awards he very proudly won as a solo musician, long after his career with The Band. Underscoring everything is Levon's enduring passion for music.

One last thing to mention is that much of this book unfolds in the present tense. And I know that's exactly how those who grew close to Levon, regardless of whether they knew him directly or simply enjoyed his music as a member of the audience, would like to remember him—in the present tense.

The story that unfolds on the pages that follow began as a collaboration between Levon Helm and myself. In his absence, I worked very hard to finish the tale we set out to tell. I hope I did this story the justice it deserves.

And now, as Levon himself might say, "It's show time."

—John W. Barry

CHAPTER ONE

An Opportunity to Fight Back

Leave what you can and take what you like was pretty much the policy at the potluck table inside the garage at 160 Plochmann Lane, Woodstock, New York, most Saturday nights beginning in 2004.

And you never knew what you might find.

There could be cheese sandwiches in plastic baggies, chili in a crock, brie and crackers, lasagna in a pan, spaghetti in a pot, pizza in a box, a dozen individually wrapped soft tacos in a basket, apple pie, chocolate layer cake or cupcakes with orange frosting and rainbow sprinkles.

There were many aspects of Levon Helm's Midnight Ramble house concerts that underscored the grassroots, we're-all-in-this-together nature of one of the most compelling musical events ever held. But the potluck table inside the garage on the ground level of the home recording studio operated by the former drummer, vocalist and mandolin player for The Band, whose coal-fired spirit, stubborn determination and artistic edge lit dark paths across generations, seemed to stand out.

The potluck table dated back to the earliest Rambles, when Levon was broke, in bankruptcy, recovering from cancer of the vocal cords and on the verge of losing his home to foreclosure—after rebuilding it in the wake a devastating fire. But as the world around him collapsed, Levon's vision for the Midnight Ramble crystallized around an idea he had been kicking around for decades. And on May 18, 2004, during an appearance inside U.S. Bankruptcy Court, on Main Street in Poughkeepsie, New York, Levon's fortune began to turn.

A longtime fan of The Band, Westchester County attorney John O'Neill and his wife, Irene, made many road trips to Levon Helm Studios for the Midnight Ramble. Not long after his first trip to The Barn, John became the attorney for Levon Helm Studios, and his duties in this role ran deep.

Among his many duties, John secured permission for the use of songs on Levon's three comeback albums, *Dirt Farmer*, *Electric Dirt* and *Ramble At The Ryman*. He negotiated deals with concert promoters and guest musicians for shows at numerous venues, including the Beacon Theatre in Manhattan and the Ryman Auditorium in Nashville. John negotiated deals with multiple parties for *Ain't in it for My Health,* the documentary about Levon. And he secured copyright protections for Levon's recordings and intellectual property.

One of John's first legal endeavors was working with Orange County, New York, attorney Mike Pinsky, in representing Levon and his wife, Sandy, during their bankruptcy case.

Levon and Sandy had filed for bankruptcy multiple times previously, and this time around their case started out as a Chapter 7 liquidation case. John and Mike, however, got it converted to a Chapter 11 reorganization bankruptcy.

"We had some skirmishes with the bank, which probably just saw this as wanting to delay things more," John said. "Levon was apprehensive. After the fire, the medical bills, it was looking bleak. He wasn't happy about the financial predicament he was in, but this was where he was, at the end of the rope in terms of the bankruptcy process."

Despite all that was unraveling around him, Levon remained hopeful. John recalled him saying, "I'm a rock and roll musician. If this doesn't work out, we'll start over and we'll do something else."

And there were glimmers of hope. As the bankruptcy cases unfolded, the Rambles were under way and work on Levon's first album in years, *Dirt Farmer*, was in its infancy.

In advance of a pivotal bankruptcy hearing in Poughkeepsie, Levon, Sandy, John and Levon's soon-to-be-manager, Barbara O'Brien, met up at the restaurant inside the nearby Poughkeepsie Grand Hotel. They were gearing up for a hearing in which the judge would either approve or deny the reorganization plan proposed by Levon and Sandy.

"He sort of wandered off to the restroom and he seemed to me to be troubled over what was going to happen," John said. "He had been in other bankruptcies that had failed. I went back to remind him, I said, 'I don't want you to worry. I'll tell you when it's time to worry.'"

They headed to court and, John said, "We were able to convince the judge that the business plan had a reasonable probability of succeeding and was preferable to the uncertain prospects of a liquidation. We told this judge that the revenue generated from the Midnight Rambles, as well as sales of *Dirt Farmer*, an album in preparation for imminent release, would generate revenue sufficient to fund the reorganization. We advised the judge that, thanks in part to favorable media attention, the Midnight Rambles had quickly grown from a modest beginning to an event that sold out most Saturday nights.

"The judge agreed with our arguments and entered an order confirming the plan of organization. The effect of the confirmed plan was to restore to Levon and Sandy control of their businesses and properties, including The Barn, which generated income critical to fund the plan. The plan permitted the refinance of an onerous first mortgage that had financially strangled the Helms. The plan also provided for payment of the allowed claims of other creditors over time."

Based on traveling shows he saw while growing up in Arkansas cotton country in the Mississippi Delta, the Midnight Ramble resurrected Levon's career, allowed him to recover his financial footing and set the stage for three Grammy-winning records. As he had done decades earlier with The Band, Levon with the Midnight Ramble triggered a seismic shift through the rock and roll paradigm.

"There never will be anything like it again," said Levon Helm Band guitarist Jimmy Vivino, who is well-known for his work on late-night television with Conan O'Brien. "There's no doubt about that."

And all Levon did this time was turn the knob on his front door and invite fans into the home he and Sandy shared.

With the Midnight Ramble, Jimmy said, Levon, "built it to this thing where people just wanted to see him. There were no expectations. What an idea—to just have people come to your house."

The Midnight Ramble allowed Levon to redefine the music industry on his terms—and the response was strong.

"Hearing the music and watching Levon with the smile on his face, when he was playing those songs, I would look around and think this is the best place in the world to be," said Radio Woodstock (100.1 FM/WDST) Program Director and Morning Host Greg Gattine. "Right at this moment, there isn't any other place in the world that I would rather be, than with Levon Helm."

Woodstock artist Mike DuBois crafted the designs for Levon Helm Studios merchandise and designed the album covers for Levon's *Dirt Farmer* follow-up, *Electric Dirt*, as well as *The Midnight Ramble Sessions Vol. 3*. Mike also attended a lot of Midnight Rambles.

"It was an emotional experience, and you knew it was an experience you could only get there," Mike said. "It really elevated your spirit, like being in a Southern Baptist church on Sunday, and that was due to the authenticity of Levon's intention. He was very sincere in his intention of wanting people to have a great time and expressing emotion through music. He naturally did it. He didn't try. We were experiencing a pure energy transfer of Levon's spirit and soul—that smile of his, that laugh. He really loved making people happy. He loved a good laugh. He was tenacious about having fun."

When Levon hatched plans for the Midnight Ramble, he wasn't working with any record company, large or small. He hadn't released a record in decades. And cancer of the vocal cords had left him unable to speak, never mind sing. Levon's voice was at the heart of his career as a musician. And this was how he had earned his living since a teenager, when he launched his career as the drummer for the rockabilly band Ronnie Hawkins and the Hawks.

That was in the late 1950s. By the start of the new millennium five decades later, the private jets, the Corvettes, and the sold-out concert halls were mere memories of fame and fortune come and gone for the guy who had grown up in poverty in Turkey Scratch, Phillips County, Arkansas.

"We were just about at the end of our rope financially," Levon said. "So the Midnight Ramble was going to be one big rent party or go out with a bang. We were going to have one more tear 'em down night or two, and all of a sudden, the thing started getting legs of its own and people started wanting to come and pay to get in.

"That was just about the time when the shit was ready to hit the fan. All of a sudden, you're sick and you can't work and you haven't been able to work and the bills don't stop and they're still coming in. You've got your hands full trying to get well, and then to have the other stuff heaped on top is certainly an unfair way to go. Those radiation treatments, after a while, they can get ahold of you. It's a little bit raw. The bankruptcy part—that was just getting ready to cloud over and really rain—that don't scare you after all that radiation."

Joined by his daughter Amy, Levon traveled daily from Woodstock to Sleepy Hollow in Westchester County, for radiation treatments at a satellite location operated by Memorial Sloan Kettering Cancer Center in Manhattan. It was that Sleepy Hollow, the community due north of Tarrytown and the Hudson River's Tappan Zee Bridge that inspired author Washington Irving to write "The Legend of Sleepy Hollow," with its notorious Headless Horseman.

Levon and Amy traveled to Sleepy Hollow five days a week and then some until Levon hit his magic number of 28 treatments.

"Just the trip down and back was where all the time went," Levon said. "The ride is about an hour-and-a-half, hour and 45 minutes. Once we got there, it would only take half-an-hour, 45 minutes, and most of that's just waiting, waiting your turn. The actual treatment itself was over in two or three minutes. At the time, I didn't share much with anyone because I couldn't really talk. I'd write Amy notes and whisper to her and Sandy. But I just kind of got by myself and did it that way.

"Those trips with Amy were bonding. It sure did keep me from getting dramatical about it. Amy was in New York but she would come up and stay at her mom's in Woodstock and be around to go with me. I don't think she missed a damn trip. She came with me every time. I tried to get her to give herself a break and she'd say, 'No. We don't want to break our good luck.' I tried to tell her after a while, 'I can do this.' She'd say, 'No, I'll just ride down with you.' Amy went through all that with me. She sure did. I'm happy she was strong enough to do that. It's a sad thing—not everybody can handle that kind of adversity."

As we all do when faced with calamity, Levon learned much from the reactions of those around him.

"Some people stick their head in the sand and some people want to know everything and Amy wanted to know everything about it, so, you know, it was great that she could do that; and it did make us a whole lot tighter," he said. "It was a period of just, maybe it will, maybe it won't, you know? The sad part about it is, so many people that were down there—I would see every day—were there by themselves. Their families couldn't take it. They couldn't stand it. Amy was the soldier of all of us. And of course, you couldn't just throw down in front of her."

Once at Sloan Kettering, Levon might duck into an alcove in the waiting room, just to have some time for himself. But it was an aquarium that left the biggest impression on him and raised his spirits as he geared up for his treatments.

"Before you get to the desk and go around the hallway, back to the departments, there is one big aquarium. It is beautiful and it goes from the floor to the ceiling. And there are all these ocean fish, wild looking fish; and they're all in there, swimming around. It's really a good idea, boy—a hell of an idea. It's like sitting in front of a fireplace.

"They are really great people. A couple times, I said to a couple of nurses, 'You think this is working?' And they'd say, 'No doubt about it.' And after 28 of those radiation treatments, they gave me a little thing, a little certificate, congratulating me. Once those radiation treatments ended it was, shit, it had to be two or three years before I was talking again. It's amazing what the body could take. If it don't kill you, it makes you stronger, you know."

"Amy got me into Musicians On Call and we would go down to Sloan-Kettering and play the day room and a lot of the kids, they'd be too sick and wouldn't feel like coming down. So we would put on the gowns and the caps and go upstairs and the nurse would say, 'Come on, they want to come up, they want to play one song.'

"Then you go in and start playing one thing, and the kids start moving around, and they've forgotten how sick they are for a few minutes. We did it for the kids and we started doing it just for people in general. We still played the day room for the kids, but doing it and seeing some of the older folks, for me, it was kind of like a payback.

"It was also a celebration of just how much strength there is, because that's what got me through— music; music and the power of prayer, having people pray for me. I'm not surprised how music helped me recover, because it's music; that's the power of music. Through my trials and errors over the years, I've seen it do some wonderful things. It's the language of heaven. God and religion and all of it manifest itself through music and the more I can have, the better I feel.

"There was never any thought of not trying to sing again—not with music; you just can't do that. If you've got a shot at making some more music, you've just got to do it. It's like canceling a show, you know. You've got to have a real good reason to do something like that. It just ain't right. It's not just you—it's all the other players. Anytime you can have that kind of fellowship and mutually create a sound that is at least a joyful noise, you just can't resist it. It has to be done.

"Rick Danko, God bless him, when Rick lost his son, he had a show to get to. He said he just had to have it, you know. I did the same thing when he passed. I had a show that night. I'm glad I did.

"Rick and I did duo shows together for a couple of years' period there, where we would do acoustic stuff. Of course, that was Rick. Rick liked to do that kind of shit, you know? I'd go along with him. But I always wanted to have a bunch of us.

"The crowd really enjoyed those shows Rick and I did together. They really did. You won't find anybody that didn't like Rick. If you were a player and you went to a Rick Danko show, you could bet one thing, you were going to be part of it. He was going to get you up there and have you sing one or two. Rick knew how to include people in a show just about as good as anyone. You know, give them his high harmony part, give them his vocal part and find another one. 'Sing my part, sing my part,' he'd say. 'I'll do something else.' He and Richard Manuel, he and Richard, boy, that's what gave me so much confidence back in the old days. I just didn't think anybody could out-sing Richard. Richard would do 'I Shall Be Released' or something. It's all over, you know."

As Levon continued to recover, support emerged from his fellow musicians.

"Steve Jordan did those Rainforest Alliance shows, and not long after those radiation treatments, on every one of those shows, Steve Jordan would put me into the house band and make me second-chair drummer. That's the kind of guy Steve Jordan is and boy did that feel like staying in the game. So I got to play on some of the songs and Ricky Skaggs was also on those shows. Of course, I've always admired Ricky and his band, Kentucky Thunder—there's not a better band. They're like The Chieftains or Los Lobos. They're like the Ozark Mountains. They're there. They're part of it.

"At those shows, I couldn't really talk, but I could whisper to Ricky and he's one of those guys who's fun to laugh with. Before he would leave, he would write down his number and hand it to me and tell me he was praying for me and if I needed to talk to him or needed anything, to give him a call."

With the radiation behind him, Levon turned to mother nature for respite.

The pond—he called it the creek—and the woods on his 18-acre property just minutes from downtown Woodstock offered their own treatment. Levon would stand on the edge of the pond, lift his head and let the warm Woodstock breeze pass through the pine trees to soothe his ailment in its own way.

"I had a full schedule," he said. "It just took all your energy just to deal with it, and that was the most relief I could get, to sit down on the creek there, get out in the water, and get water on your face and stuff. I was down there just about every day. I would always make sure to keep the sun at my back so it didn't shine on my neck."

The radiation treatments scorched Levon's neck.

"I couldn't stand it," he said. "It was awful, like a third-degree burn, raw. It starts off and you don't notice it. And then it finally starts to get a little bit pink and then, just as they got ready to stop the radiation treatments, I mean, it really turned into a burn. I'd take a Kleenex and I would dab it, and all that burn would just come off, stick to that Kleenex. They gave me all kinds of salves and creams, every one of them burned—the only thing that gave me any relief was pure aloe. You cut one of those leaves off and split it open, put it against your neck and boy, it was like putting ice cubes on it. Oh, God. There's nothing better than aloe—pure raw aloe."

"Music played a big part in my recovery," Levon said. "I played it and listened to it—and you can always dream it. That was what I always enjoyed, going back and reminiscing. I kept busy trying to think up some of the old stuff for *Dirt Farmer*.

"Somebody told me that even if you didn't really sing or play, that if you did it in your mind, those same mechanisms of muscles and nerves fire on each other; the thought of it wakes all that up."

The seeds for Levon's comeback and recovery were planted in a band called the Barn Burners, which at various times featured Jimmy Vivino of late-night television fame; Amy Helm; and vocalist and harmonica player Little Sammy Davis, among others.

"Anytime the Barn Burners would play, I would be off mic, but I would be doubling Sammy and be singing in unison with him," Levon said. "We went out and played and it was just—I think it was good for us to get out and play around a bit, travel a little bit, get that going again. It's just a wonderful thing you get to do. You get to blow into town—it's almost like playing the hero. You get to divert the crowd's attention for a couple of hours if you do it right, handle it right and do it for your heart, then ride out. That's the best part of the day for all of us. I can forget my little transgressions, too."

Saxophone player Erik Lawrence, who also played in the Barn Burners with Levon, when he was wasn't singing because of the cancer, asked him, "Don't you miss singing?" Levon, according to Erik, responded, "Only when I'm working with my daughter."

Levon Helm only wore clothing made in the U.S.A. He loved sushi and Popeye's chicken. He loved the pound cake made by Sandy's Aunt Joyce. He loved his dogs. And he loved college football.

On the drive from Woodstock into Manhattan for performances, he would admire the architectural detail of those beautiful buildings that embody old New York.

Warren Haynes of Allman Brothers Band and Gov't Mule fame first performed with Levon during a 1993 Band tour, for which the Warren Haynes Band served as the opening act for a handful of shows. He would in later years perform with Levon at Levon Helm Studios, the Beacon Theatre in New York City and the Mountain Jam festival in New York's Catskill Mountains.

"Levon's drumming was as organic as it gets," Warren said. "His feel was impeccable. All the times that I played with him, I found it to be so easy, like drinking water; one of the easiest feels to lock in with that I've ever experienced, with any drummer."

Warren said Levon's dual roles, as drummer and vocalist, left a big impact on the musicians with whom he performed.

"His drumming influenced his singing and his singing influenced his drumming," Warren said. "It was all a part of the same thing. Singers depend on drummers to make them comfortable, and when a singer is playing with the right drummer, it's really easy to sing—and obviously Levon understood that in spades. When he was singing, he was dictating the pocket, and when someone else was singing, he understood as a singer how to make it feel as natural and comfortable as possible."

Warren said that run of Warren Haynes Band shows, opening for The Band, was a "thrill."

"Everything about it was exciting to me—playing with them, opening up, getting to hear them live and hanging out. That whole run of shows was really fun."

As for interacting with Levon on personal and musical levels, Warren said, "With both of us being from the South, and having gone north for personal and musical reasons, we were like old friends from the first conversation we had. The first time we played music together, it was as easy as could be. Playing together was a blast—just sharing something with a kindred spirit means everything.

"His attitude, from knowing him before he was sick and knowing him after he got sick—he just always exuded positivity. He never seemed to let anything affect him or get him down. He was just one of those people who affected everyone in a very positive way. When you were out with Levon, you felt better because he was so exuberant and excited to be doing whatever you were doing."

Levon Helm looked at tractors the way some of us might marvel at a Porsche or a Lamborghini. He enjoyed the writing of Ralph Waldo Emerson. Standing in a field of corn, he would hold raw kernels in his hand like they were rubies or sapphires, gazing at them as though he were a gemologist studying diamonds with a diffraction spectroscope.

"Levon was my mentor," said Brian Parillo, a drummer who was on hand at Levon Helm Studios for the launch of the Ramble. "He could teach you how to treat people. He had an approach on life that was uncompromising on his ideals. He stayed true to himself, always. He was who he was. He liked to drive really fast. He had a real generous soul."

And Levon Helm loved having a horn section in his band.

"Every time we played a big festival and The Band was afforded a budget, there would always be four horn players coming in," said Randy Ciarlante, drummer in the second incarnation of The Band.

And this, of course, transferred over to the Levon Helm Band. A horn section, Levon said, was "The icing on the cake."

"That's what I notice from the crowd—you can see them smile when those horns light up. It's like hitting that cowbell—that will get a grin out of 'em, especially when we do some of the old, old stuff, The Band stuff. That stuff, if it don't have the horns, it just don't remind you enough of the way it was. Without the horns, it's not really like a full show. It's like a dress rehearsal. Everybody don't have to be there. But with the horns, all the lights go on."

Said Paul Berry, Levon's lifelong friend from Arkansas, "He always, always wanted to have a horn section, since I've known him. 'Horns make people happy,' is what he would say."

And Levon Helm loved a good story.

"He had a gift for storytelling, a profusion of down-home metaphors that created amusing anecdotes," said Randy Ciarlante.

Sometime in the 1960s, Levon and Paul Berry stayed up late listening to Beethoven's Symphony No. 9—which includes the composer's "Ode to Joy"—on Paul's state-of-the-art stereo system, using headphones.

"When we got through, you should have seen the look on Levon's face," Paul said. "The first thing he said was, 'I'll never play or sing "Roll Over Beethoven" again.' He was so overcome by the beauty and the complexity of a symphony performed on that scale."

In the 1970s, Levon joined Paul and his wife, Mary, for a night on Broadway to see *The Wiz*. He enjoyed the show so much he returned to see it again with Amy.

Levon's favorite Christmas songs were "Fairytale of New York," by The Pogues with Kirsty MacColl, and "Run Rudolph Run," by Chuck Berry. He loved the music of Bobby Osborne and his dear friend Mavis Staples. When someone died, Levon didn't like to say they were buried. To this old dirt farmer, they had simply been planted.

The 1990 "Wall" concert that Roger Waters of Pink Floyd fame staged in Berlin, Germany, featured a range of musicians and bands, including the second incarnation of The Band. And Waters during a 2020 interview for this book shared some of the perspective he gained that night, on his guests from Woodstock, New York.

"When I put on 'The Wall' in Berlin, they couldn't have been more idiosyncratic and delightful," Roger said.

That 1990 concert was also on Roger's mind 22 years later, when he performed at an all-star concert, at the Meadowlands Sports Complex in New Jersey, that paid tribute to Levon. The "Love for Levon" show at the Izod Center, formerly known as the Brendan Byrne Arena, was held to raise money to pay down the nearly $1 million mortgage that remained on Levon Helm Studios after Levon's death.

Among the performers featured at the extravaganza were Levon's old friend, Joe Walsh of The Eagles, playing "Up on Cripple Creek" with jamband pedal steel guitar player Robert Randolph; Allen Toussaint delivering a driving "Life is a Carnival;" and country star Dierks Bentley performing "Rocking Chair."

Roger performed with My Morning Jacket. And he sang a duet with Amy Helm, with Larry Campbell playing fiddle, on "Wide River to Cross" from *Dirt Farmer*. It was a story Roger told about Levon, however, that stole the show.

Clutching a red baseball cap in his hands, Roger told the crowd about The Band playing his "Wall" concert in Germany in 1990. After the show, Waters ended up back at the Intercontinental Hotel in Berlin, where he ran into the guys. Levon approached Roger, told him he liked his style and gave him his red baseball cap, the very hat that Waters held before the crowd at the Meadowlands, 22 years later, in October 2012.

During the 2020 interview for this book, Waters recounted that story from the Intercontinental Hotel and then said, "I can't stop smiling, you know. We're talking about Levon Helm and I can't stop smiling. He was such a fucking ray of light."

Cross the Lone Ranger with George Bailey from the Frank Capra film, *It's a Wonderful Life*—a rock star riding the range, always pushing over that next rise on the ridge, crippled by desperation, firing back with determination—and that was Levon Helm.

According to the members of the Levon Helm Band, the man from

Turkey Scratch paid his musicians well. And according to Randy Ciarlante, Levon could be quite mischievous.

"Lavon was definitely a playful disruptor," said Randy, who, like some, called Mark Lavon Helm by his given middle name. "The more things got out of hand, the funnier it got for him—and us."

One of Randy's favorite Levon Helm band configurations emerged in the late 1980s, with Randy on drums; Jim Weider, guitarist in the second incarnation of The Band; multi-instrumentalist Paul Branin; bass player Frank Campbell; and piano player Stan Szelest, who had played with Levon decades earlier. The band became involved with a movie in which Levon was acting, the 1989 film *Staying Together* with Stockard Channing and Sean Astin, and the musicians were contracted to write music for the movie and appear on screen as the backing band. Levon portrayed a singing pharmacist.

"The process took about four weeks, and willingly being an accomplice to his impish behavior may have been the most fun I've ever had in my career," Randy said. "Second only to making music, Levon was impassioned about finding the good times in life."

But along with the fun, Levon could also have a sharp side, particularly when it came to defending his bandmates or standing up to record company executives.

"If we were having a hard time collecting our money, he would find a way of getting the master tapes we were working on, then negotiate," Randy said. "I saw him do that once—'Yeah. We've got the tapes.' He knew how the business worked. Those cats were into it from the beginning."

But still, Levon could be insecure.

"Levon got his voice back and all of a sudden the press was everywhere—TV studios and TV cameras and all this other stuff," said Erik Lawrence, who, in addition to playing with the Barn Burners joined Levon in the second incarnation of The Band and the Levon Helm Band.

"We were really pushing to play at the Beacon Theatre. They had come in with a legitimate offer—and Levon didn't want to do it. And he didn't want to do it because he had played at this seedy little place in Manhattan, this club, with the Barn Burners, and nobody showed up. It was heartbreaking to him. It was really demoralizing."

The Beacon shows eventually unfolded in triumphant grandeur, in March of 2007. And afterward, Erik said, Levon called him up and said, "Tell all the guys that this is the best band I've ever played with!"

But despite this success, Levon was extremely wary of performing at the famed Ryman Auditorium in Nashville that July.

"He didn't want to do it," said Tony LoBue, who managed the Rambles and was the webmaster for www.levonhelm.com. "He didn't want to do the Ryman for nothing. He was coming up with every excuse—'It's a Wednesday night; people in that area don't go out on Wednesday nights; I know those people, they're weekend people; Wednesday night is no good; nine o'clock is no good.' Everything in the world was wrong with it."

Levon eventually agreed. Then he changed his mind. Barbara O'Brien stepped in. Levon Helm Band Music Director Larry Campbell—a multi-instrumentalist and former member of Bob Dylan's band—explained to Levon just how deep his impact on the music world ran.

"Larry talked to him that night," Tony said. "And Larry's telling him, 'Levon, all these people at the Ryman, their careers were built on your music. You were their inspiration. You're going there as the guy who started all this stuff.'"

Levon ultimately played the Ryman, and Emmylou Harris and Sheryl Crow were among the notable names to sit in. A year later, Levon returned to the Ryman. Harris, Crow, Alison Krauss, and Robert Plant sat in. That 2008 show in Nashville set the stage for the 2011 release of the *Ramble At The Ryman* DVD and CD, the latter of which won the Grammy for Best Americana Album.

But as the accolades piled up, the insecurity remained.

Take, for instance, a recording session for *Electric Dirt,* Levon's 2009 release that won the first Grammy ever awarded in the Americana category. Levon was at the studio working with Larry and Justin Guip, former chief engineer for Levon Helm Studios.

"Justin and I were up in the control room, trying to get a vocal from Levon," Larry said. "He does one take and it's okay. Normally, the thing with Levon was, sing it through three times and by the third time, it's there. He does the one take, I say, 'Okay, cool, Levon, let's try it again.' He says,

'Yeah. I've got to go get a Coke. I'll be right back.' He goes in the house and we're sitting there. And it wasn't unusual to wait. When Levon says, 'I'll be right back,' normally that meant an hour later. We go in the house, there's nobody there. I call his phone, there's no answer. Justin and I went back and did something, overdubs, then we went home. The next day, we come to the studio, he's not around. And then the day after, he shows up and he comes out and he says, 'Okay, let's do that vocal'—right where he left off.'"

That scenario, Larry speculated, was driven by Levon's insecurity.

"I've heard stories about Levon being confrontational, but I never really saw that. When he was overwhelmed with a situation, if he was uncomfortable, he'd just leave the room—not really a healthy way to deal with stuff, but that's what he had to do. You got what you got with Levon."

As the foundation was laid for the Midnight Ramble, Levon Helm Studios, or The Barn as it is called for its design and feel, was scheduled to be auctioned off at the Ulster County Courthouse in nearby Kingston.

If not for the Midnight Ramble and the revenue generated by $150 tickets, a ticket price unheard of at the time, all would have been lost. But Levon never gave up. He never quit. He never backed down from his next at bat, even as he teetered on the brink of losing everything.

"Drummers don't make as much as singers do," Levon said. "It's more fun, but the pay scale is lower. Drummers should get more, to tell you the truth. Shit—he's got the hardest part of the thing to lift. It's slipper-ier over on his side. But people know that don't none of us get out alive. It just don't work that way. You're better off just to, you know, come on and man up. For me, the whole thing is an opportunity to fight back. If I can't fight back, I'm fucked. That's when I start ranting and drinking and paying fines and all kinds of stuff. I just can't sleep."

For the early Rambles, Barbara O'Brien asked those attending to bring a plate of food for the potluck table, just like you might ask someone to bring a side dish to a house party or a barbecue. And the tradition carried on, through times that were lean and flush.

The potluck table illustrated the spirit of community that defined the Midnight Ramble, far beyond the rock stars and celebrities who passed through the doors of Levon Helm Studios. That was the spirit that Levon brought out in folks—fans, friends and strangers. And it stretched beyond his property on Plochmann Lane.

"The Midnight Ramble meant business, for restaurants, hotels, everyone you talked to," said lifelong Woodstock resident Paul Shultis Jr., a contractor who oversaw the rebuilding of Levon Helm Studios after it was destroyed in a 1991 fire. Paul's grandfather, Ralph, built the original building.

"Yeah, great, he saved himself and he saved the building. But to him it was more, look what the rest of the community is getting out of it too. The Rambles were quite beneficial to the whole community. And that was really one of Levon's theories behind it, to be supportive of the community. I don't think he wanted people to come for the Ramble and leave. He wanted them to experience Woodstock—get them to come, get them to say they're going to come back."

The values and traditions that Mark Lavon Helm grew up on in Phillips County, Arkansas; all that defined him as a person; that which was at the core of his existence in Woodstock, regardless of whether times were good or bad, that's what drove the Midnight Ramble in Woodstock.

"The Midnight Ramble worked because of Levon's tireless work ethic," said Brian Parillo. "Levon made the Midnight Ramble. He was the reason it was so successful. He just went out and delivered, night after night."

The music was, every Saturday night, week after week, for eight years, once-in-a-lifetime. But everything really revolved around Levon as a person, Levon as a man, someone with values and an ability to inspire in others the same respect for ideals and tradition that he had.

Consider those Rambles when Levon's voice following his recovery from cancer wasn't firing on all cylinders and he sang one or two songs. On the rare occasion, he didn't sing at all.

In December 2010, Levon was admitted to Kingston Hospital on a Saturday afternoon, hours before a Ramble. Just before Levon would have come out to perform, Barbara told the crowd that he was in the hospital and wouldn't be performing with the band that night. The Levon Helm Band show would go on, minus Levon Helm. Anyone who wanted a refund, Barbara told the crowd, was welcome to see Levon Helm Studios office manager Geanine Kane downstairs at the merchandise table for a refund. Out of a sold-out crowd of more than one hundred fifty, only three people asked for, and received, their money back. That night, Levon's fans left happy, fulfilled, and satisfied—feeling like they had gotten their money's worth—without him even being in the room.

But the sold-out crowds kept coming. Fans were happy just to sit in the same room with the man they considered an old friend, someone who, with The Band and beyond, had seen them through good times and bad, with the stories he told in song of juke joints and Confederate generals and broken hearts and smoke-filled clubs and dancing down in the Mississippi Delta.

"When we'd go onstage, people were just yelling his name—it was just the sight of him," said Levon Helm Band vocalist, piano, keyboard and accordion player Brian Mitchell. "He's a compelling guy. There are certain people that you can't take your eyes off of when they walk into a room—and he was one of them."

But Levon's fans remained devoted to him as much for his music as what he accomplished off the stage—recovering from cancer; getting his voice back to speak and sing; clawing his way out of bankruptcy and keeping his home off the auction blocks; embarking on a comeback in every sense of the word, in rock music and in the grind of everyday life. To put it quite simply, he accomplished what he had set out to achieve.

"Levon was larger than life," said Jimmy Weider, a Woodstock native who grew up a fan of The Band and played their music in cover bands before taking over Robbie Robertson's guitar duties in the second incarnation of The Band. "Levon had a personality that would take over a room—very strong; one of the strongest willed guys I've ever met. But you wouldn't want him to get mad at you."

Said Randy Ciarlante, "And he got mad at us."

When Levon sang, you could feel your own heart aching in his voice. The conviction with which he sang gave you courage. His signature vocal tone was part growl, part roar, part plea for help and it served as a lightning rod for all of our troubles, not just for a few hours at a gig, but across generations. When Levon sang—with one turn of a phrase, one note, one lyric—he somehow managed to capture the despair we all feel, the hope that keeps us going and the resolution for which we never stop longing. He tapped into that terrifying sensation of solitude that every one of us has experienced, at those times in our lives when you feel like you haven't got a friend in the world.

But Levon also made you feel like he was right there with you, clinging desperately to any solid ground that remained, as his world fell apart in a manner that wasn't much different than the way in which your world might be falling apart.

Levon Helm had resolve. He did not give up. And he maintained that sparkle in his eye and that laugh in his gut through all the calamity. Levon Helm represented much of what we value in those we admire, and a lot of what we wished to be true of ourselves.

All of this resonated so strongly with his audience because just like you and me, Levon was forced to manage the madness of life and make sense of insanity. There was a bond of familiarity he shared with millions of people he never met. To quote Levon about Levon, "There was a guy who never met a stranger."

Here's a Coke, have yourself a chair, I'm glad to know ya.

"He was really a guy who lived by his own rules," Brian Mitchell said. "He stuck to his guns. Maybe he could have made more money if he had done this or done that, but he was a man of principles and it was always something I had the greatest respect for. He didn't do the easy thing. He did the thing that meant something to him. It's a testament to his love of the music. That's what it was really about. It wasn't about being a rock star. He was a musician—bottom line. And he always stuck with it. There's not a lot of guys who go from playing stadiums to blues bars. It was all about playing music for him and I think people really related to that, his audience. He played the blues bar just liked he played the Greek Theater or the Beacon."

Around 1985 or 1986, Paul Shultis was figuring out how he could help the family of a close friend who had recently died in a car accident, leaving behind a wife and two daughters. So Paul set out to organize a benefit concert to raise some cash for the family. The move illustrated the compassion that binds together many in Woodstock.

Paul enlisted the help of several musicians who lived in town, including The Band's Rick Danko, who performed with brothers Happy and Artie Traum, and harmonica player Sredni Vollmer. Eddie Kaercher, co-owner of the nearby Getaway Inn, showcased his musicianship while kicking off the event.

Paul also invited a local performer with global recognition who knew his grandfather well—Levon Helm. Levon, who was generous in lending his musical talent to local fundraisers, over the years played three benefits that Paul Shultis oversaw—one for that family of a friend, who had died in the car accident; another for the American Legion in Woodstock, but whose proceeds ultimately supported the Woodstock Little League; and a third, held at The Barn during the Ramble days, that raised $20,000 for the Woodstock School's music program.

"For a good cause, he was always there," Paul said.

Back in the mid-1980s, for the concert benefiting the family of Paul's friend, he and his team utilized a flat-bed trailer and built a stage out of wood in an open field behind what is known as the Watering Troff property on Route 212. The site later became home to the Gypsy Wolf Cantina Mexican restaurant, then the Dixon Roadside. Levon enlisted the Woodstock All-Stars, the band he was playing with at the time. Stan Szelest joined in. And Levon told Paul he would bring a friend who would play drums with him. Levon called him Mighty Max. The rest of us know him as Max Weinberg.

"I said, 'O.K.' I didn't know who Max Weinberg was," Paul said of the drummer for Bruce Springsteen's E Street Band.

A couple of days before the show, Paul and the gang were finishing the stage and, he said, "Levon and Sandy show up in a Buick station wagon. He does three or four doughnuts in the parking lot and says, 'How you boys making out? You gonna be ready for the show?'"

The day of the show arrives. Levon's guest shows up. And, Paul said, "I learned who Max Weinberg was."

Levon was well-known in New York's Hudson Valley for playing benefits to support his neighbors. And this approach to community-building was illustrated by the ties Levon maintained with the Bardavon 1869 Opera House in Poughkeepsie, the state's oldest, continuously-run theater, which is listed on the National Register of Historic Places.

Levon performed at the Bardavon with the Barn Burners, as well as at the Hudson River Arts Festival that the Bardavon staged on the City of Poughkeepsie waterfront.

And the Bardavon team, at the venue's sister theater in Kingston, the Broadway Theater at Ulster Performing Arts Center, welcomed Levon for a late May birthday concert in 2011 that benefited UPAC's Capital Campaign and the Rhinebeck Science Foundation.

Also at UPAC, Levon played a November 2011 benefit concert for victims of Tropical Storm Irene, which devastated communities in the Catskill Mountains. Together, the "Shelter from the Storm" concert at UPAC on Nov. 18, and a Ramble the following night at Levon Helm Studios raised $116,000 for victims of Tropical Storm Irene. The Levon Helm Band at UPAC was joined by Donald Fagen, Natalie Merchant, Graham Parker, John Medeski, Chris Wood and others. And both shows were presented by the Bardavon, Levon Helm Studios and Radio Woodstock.

Speaking of UPAC, the audience for Bill Maher's performance there in 2010 was surely unaware that Levon, a fan of Maher's, was watching from the wings. Maher proved to be especially captivating to Muddy that night, who was on hand at UPAC and enthralled by the shadows that Maher left on the black stage curtain behind him.

Maher and Muddy sealed their friendship that night in Maher's dressing room, when comedian and dog were horsing around, rolling around on the floor together.

In addition to his generous nature, Paul said making folks feel appreciated was important to Levon, regardless of the obstacles he happened to be encountering in his own life at the time, or the success he was enjoying. This approach to life was underscored when Paul and a group of others joined Levon in February 1997 for a trip to Roseland Ballroom in Manhattan, where Levon was to sit in with Sheryl Crow. The group arrives and Levon is directed backstage. Levon tells Paul and the group to join him, but is told they can't accompany him.

"Levon said, 'I'll just sit here with my friends—when we can all go down, we'll go down,'" Paul recalled.

Levon didn't like where the group was sitting, so he arranged for everyone to get better seats. The time came for him to perform, he left for the stage, performed and returned to the seats. After the show, the whole group was welcomed backstage.

"He never made you feel like he was better than you, or famous," Paul said.

Larry Campbell said Levon "had a complete lack of pretension—for better or worse, a complete lack of pretension.

"Levon couldn't possibly be anything other than what he was—and that's a rare quality—and I mean for better or worse, because in a lot of cases, that was to everyone's detriment, including his own. That honesty, it's completely alluring, completely compelling, because that's what we all want to be. We learn through life's experiences how to stifle that in ourselves and he seemed fearless in that sense. When you betray who you are, it's usually out of fear. You feel like you have to put on this pretense in order to accomplish or gain whatever you're going for. He didn't know how to do that—that's magnetic. He wasn't concerned with anything other than musicianship and music. The trappings of fame and stardom meant nothing to him. And that's the way he lived. He was only interested in who you were as far as what kind of person you were and what kind of musician you were. Anything else was insignificant. It was so refreshing to be in an environment like that.

"I had those eight years with Dylan—I was around entertainment stars all the time. It's so easy to lose perspective of why you're really doing this. Levon had no use for any of that stuff. And that was the basis of the Ramble—a place where music rules.

"He always remained just a simple guy from Arkansas. How he could live in Woodstock for 40 years or more and not lose an ounce of that accent? That was the physical manifestation of him not being able to be anything other than what he was. As far as being in touch with the basic necessities of what makes a happy life, that's the way he lived.

"The whole concept of the Rambles was making everyone feel welcome, making everyone feel they're a part of this and making everyone feel we're just here to have a good time and enjoy making music—and that's for the musicians as well as the audience, and that's a direct reflection of his soul. It was just an honest display of art in an era where those things were rare.

"Levon had been out of the public eye for so long—never forgotten about, but just not on the radar. But his time was coming. If we all played our cards right, if we stayed true to the music we were making and if we followed the path of music-making for its own sake, there would be an incredible amount of interest in his re-emergence, as long as it was coming from a completely honest place. It's one of those things I could just feel. All the right people were in place to make this happen. It was the purest musical situation I've ever been in. And how can you fail with that? Here is a guy who represented artistic integrity for so many people at one time, who had been off the radar for a while. If we all, together, build this thing that is based on artistic integrity, with him at the forefront, re-emerging from this absence, it has to succeed. As long as it was done with the right motives."

The Rambles started out as a rent party. They evolved into a final option to keep economic disaster at bay. And they culminated in triumph. Levon not only painted himself out of a corner, he generated a curtain call that lasted eight years—one more gig, with one more encore and it all kept repeating on a loop.

But to understand Levon, you have to understand The Band.

"The Ramble was an extension of what The Band was and what Levon brought to The Band," Mike DuBois said. "Without Levon, The Band would not have had that authentic Southern spirit behind it. He was the source of that and it carried through to the Rambles in Woodstock. They were as unique as The Band itself was."

Levon, bass player and vocalist Rick Danko, vocalist, piano player and drummer Richard Manuel, keyboard and horn player Garth Hudson and guitarist Robbie Robertson took notes and chords and voices and instruments and launched a musical moonshot. They started as the Hawks, backing Ronnie Hawkins from Arkansas. Then they backed Bob Dylan. And then they became The Band. The world listened closely as Levon and the guys, as The Band, took their first steps on the lyrical lunar surface and the ground fractured beneath the pressure of their musical moon boots.

"I don't think anyone could think of a more perfect band name for this group," said Dawes drummer Griffin Goldsmith, who along with his band has played at both Levon Helm Studios; and Big Pink, the Saugerties house where The Band lived and worked decades ago. "They define what it means to be in a band. They weren't the first to do it but they were seemingly one of the most influential. And I can't think of a band with more distinct characters. The relationships seep through. Upon first listen you can intuit that these musicians had played and grown immeasurably together—for better or for worse."

Warren Haynes credits his siblings with turning him on to the music of The Band.

"I had two older brothers who had great taste in music, and they had tons of great records, and I got to be force-fed all this great music thanks to them," said Warren, a guitarist, vocalist and songwriter. "Some of the music they had was The Band music, so I was exposed to it at a very early age. I was always drawn to Levon's voice, just based on how unique and full of personality it was."

Warren said the music of The Band, "made a huge impact on me. I think that music is among the rare music that is even better now than it was when it was made."

The Band created a new sound, a new feel that resonated in a new way for millions of critical, discerning and unforgiving music fans who, as the 1960s were ending, impatiently craved the next big thing.

And as the 1970s unfolded, The Band established a firm foothold as a singular musical ensemble that drew fans from all quarters. When they served as an opening act for the 1974 Crosby, Stills, Nash & Young stadium tour, said Graham Nash, "I would watch their set with great interest, of course."

But even though The Band was opening for CSNY, Nash remained in awe of them and, as a result, was too shy to approach any of the guys or chat them up.

"I should have, of course," he said. "I'm not particularly un-famous myself. But I was just too shy. They were too incredible a band in my mind...I mean, holy shit, they were The Band...They were incredible. That's why I didn't want to intrude on their life. They were the best band in the world apart from the Beatles, as far as I was concerned. I was just a fan."

Roger Waters said he was in Los Angeles the first time he heard "Music From Big Pink."

"Big Pink changed everything, completely, overnight," he said. "It was sonic. It was the sound that they made all playing together. It was the sound of the drums. It was what they created. It was just completely different than anything I had heard before and it was remarkable. They were great songs as well. When I heard that record, I went, 'Wow. What was that?' And it had a lot to do with the drum sound."

Roger was also taken with Rick Danko.

"His high harmonies, those high harmonies and his bass playing, the bass parts as well were very integral to the revolution that was 'Big Pink,'" Roger said. "What a great band they were."

Randy Ciarlante called The Band "the quintessential garage band."

"The Band's music, tempo-wise, sometimes fluctuated but it moved organically from verse to chorus to bridge," he said. "Richard, Levon and Rick stacked their vocal harmonies in a completely unique way. Their pitch and tone were immaculate, but more often than not, rhythmically, it was far from linear. The pockets were deep, the lyrics provocative, the melodies mesmerizing. Storylines came to life and you found yourself always taking the journey with them."

For one perspective on The Band from Levon's point of view, there is Paul Berry's story about the cover of the album *Before the Flood,* which chronicled The Bob Dylan and The Band tour of 1974 and featured a massive crowd, holding lit matches aloft in the dark, on the cover. According to Paul, Levon once said about that tour, "Bob sold the tickets, but we [meaning Bob and The Band] lit the matches."

As a young man, Gov't Mule multi-instrumentalist Danny Louis first heard The Band as his musical interests were shifting toward jazz. He had been enjoying Jimi Hendrix, The Doors, Santana and, "the whole Woodstock pantheon" he said. But regarding rock music of the late 1960s and early 1970s, he continued, "I was finding rock and roll not to be the be-all-hear-all-idiom that I wanted it to be. I thought it was losing its fire and rebelliousness."

Danny was finding the grit of rock and roll in Miles Davis and jazz. And then there was The Band.

"I heard 'The Weight,' I heard 'Big Pink' and it was a sensation," he said. "It was on the roots-ier end of the spectrum. I didn't understand that I was listening to a band that had three bona fide lead singers, incredible arranging and storytelling from a songwriting standpoint that was as good as anybody else. I didn't get that. I was a little too stupid.

"They didn't have a torch-bearing shredder as a lead guitar player, which all my favorite other bands did. They didn't have a particular front man that was the rainmaker in The Band, the way The Doors had Jim Morrison.

"I didn't understand how great that was. My friends who were really into the Dead were into The Band. My friends who were really into The Beatles were into The Band. But my friends who were really into Hendrix and John McLaughlin weren't into The Band and I was sort of more with that crowd at that time.

"And yet Dylan figured it out pretty quick. And friends of mine that were really into it were like, these guys are one of the greatest writing and recording and performing groups you're ever going to hear.

"The recordings were kind of loosey-goosey. I didn't get Garth at first. He was decorating at-will over everything. What he played in the first verse was different than the second verse and the third verse. But it wasn't too long before I wanted desperately to buy a Lowrey organ, instead of a Hammond B-3, so I could sound just like him. Rick's playing was like a Dixieland tuba player having a great time. All of that took a while for me to take in as a holistic musical force."

But *Stage Fright* hooked Danny. And so did *Northern Lights, Southern Cross*.

"When I heard 'Acadian Driftwood' and all that stuff, they were heroes then," he said.

The Band delivered rustic songs that quenched a thirst. They satisfied a vast, national aching and yearning, around which a generation of teenagers matured into adults.

"I wasn't a Band fan, but I heard their stuff," said saxophone and tuba player Howard Johnson, who performed with The Band on the live *Rock of Ages* record and at The Band's final concert, The Last Waltz. He also performed with Levon Helm and the RCO All-Stars and was an anchor of the Levon Helm Band and the Midnight Ramble.

Howard continued, "The lyrics, especially, were pretty unusual. They took this from that and that from that and put together some nice music. But the lyrics are what were outstanding. They weren't readily comprehensible, even. You had to put a little work into it and you couldn't come away and say, 'Oh, this meant that.' It's just its own thing out there."

Prior to being tapped by Band producer John Simon to put together a horn section for the *Rock of Ages* shows in 1971, "I wasn't very interested in doing anything with them," Howard said.

The Band's *Rock of Ages* record captured four gigs culminating on New Year's Eve 1971 at the Academy of Music in Manhattan. John Simon, who produced The Band's first two records, had played with Howard in Taj Mahal's band when Taj had a four-tuba ensemble. When The Band was looking for their horn section, John Simon contacted Howard.

"We went to the first rehearsals and we found out that everything was in the wrong key," Howard recalled.

According to Howard, legendary composer and arranger Allen Toussaint had written the horn arrangements while listening to a cassette on which the songs had been recorded. But the speed of the cassette player was a bit slow, so songs that had been recorded in the key of G played back in the key of F sharp. So the horn arrangements were written in the key of F sharp, when they should have been written in the key of G.

"When we got to the rehearsals, we realized all the tunes were in the wrong key for the horns," Howard said. "At that point, I just met the guys that day, including Levon, who, I thought he was rather formal, a well-mannered Southern gentleman, which kind of shocked me. When we realized the problem with the arrangements, they said, 'Well, let's get somebody to get in here to recopy everything in the right key. But for today's rehearsal, we'll play it in the key that you have it in.' Now, I was impressed at that point. When Simon called me about it, I said, 'Who are these guys? What are they doing? What are they knowing?' I just kind of held a lot of rock people under suspicion anyway.

"With Taj Mahal on that Fillmore circuit, we played with so many bands who were well known and had hits but who could not play by any standards I had. Yeah, they could get in the studio and make stuff perfect. But they weren't performers. And I wasn't trying to be some kind of elitist jazzhead, either. If they weren't coming up with it, I knew it. When these guys said they would do that—it's one thing to move your hand down a fret on the guitar. But it's another thing if you've got two keyboard players and they're playing in the key of F sharp instead of G. These guys have got to know something."

The *Rock of Ages* experience, the rehearsals and the performances showed Howard that The Band, "were just so good. I don't know many guys who are that proficient, who are not jazz players. Jazz players just get so much stuff they work out and usually, rock players, they kind of decide what they're going to play ahead of time and play that for the rest of their lives. These guys had a lot of flexibility. They didn't play the same thing over and over again. There was always some excitement to it. Being an old jazzer, I always appreciated that. I think it appealed to people on a level that they didn't quite even understand. It was a different enough thing and a famous enough thing to just get kind of swept up in it. They were innovators. They weren't bringing something totally new out in terms of the sound you heard. But the lyrics were more poetic than a lot of people think."

Levon's relationship with The Band legacy, however, was beyond complicated. And then there was his relationship with Band manager Albert Grossman.

"There weren't any real albums after the first two, first three," he said. "Everything else was 'Best of,' 'Live at You-Know-Where.' The Band was just a miserable fucking deal. The Band wasn't never no fun, shit. The Band always, you know, Albert always wanted to lock everyone in the room, have that stand-offish bullshit, like with Bob. 'You can't see Bob.' Fuck all that, you know? I don't want to be like that. Shit. There is a lot of arrogance to that bullshit. In fact, that's why I never could stomach that shit. That ain't me. No. Uh-uh."

As for Levon's drumming, Howard said, "I didn't pick up on it so much at first because I was familiar with that kind of playing and he did it very well. I didn't realize the impact he really had until we were playing in the RCO All-Stars. He sure did have a big beat, what they used to call a big beat. Amy's got that, too, with her drumming. She's a great singer too. I used to wait for 'Ain't That Good News.' She's just really got it going on."

Pulsing with Amy Helm's soulful serenade and Brian Mitchell's bleeding organ, the song "Ain't That Good News" was a staple of the Midnight Ramble that showcased Amy's gospel influences.

Soul music, rock, folk, gospel, Americana, instrumentals and lyrics that could leave you sobbing and smiling over the course of a few musical measures, that's what saved Levon Helm from ruin—songs and the intimacy with which he performed them. And just like millions of Americans faced with health care costs that grind your finances into dust, as illness gnaws at your bones, Levon prior to the Midnight Rambles was desperate for salvation.

Attorney Mike Pinsky offered a sharp perspective in a press release issued in October 2007:

"Levon and his wife, Sandy, successfully emerged from Chapter 11 bankruptcy in the second week of October of this year. Their case is now closed, with creditors being paid in full and with interest over time. One of the bankruptcy trustees in the Poughkeepsie court makes a practice of asking folks: 'What led up to your financial difficulty?' In Levon's case, the short answer to that question is several paragraphs long.

"It began roughly 30 years ago with the break-up of the original Band and with *The Last Waltz*, the Martin Scorsese rock documentary chronicling the untimely end of one of the most groundbreaking and influential acts in the history of modern music. After The Band reunited (without J.R. Robertson) came the tragic loss of lead singer, keyboardist and spiritual brother Richard Manuel in 1986. Richard Manuel's death devastated Levon.

"Stan Szelest (who had been a member of The Hawks even before Ronnie Hawkins and Levon recruited Richard, Rick Danko, Garth Hudson and Robertson) stepped in to play for the reunited Band in Richard's place in 1990. Because of Stan, also a close friend, Levon, Rick and Garth had started to move on after losing Richard. Then in 1991, Stan Szelest died and Levon's barn recording studio and home burned down.

"In the fire, Levon and Sandy lost almost all of their possessions, along with many of Levon's contracts and financial records. The insurance proceeds for the rebuilding of their home and Levon's studio were $100,000 short of what was needed. They went into debt and remortgaged their home. Conflicts over finances with management and professionals for the reunited Band eventually boiled over into litigation. Multiple lawsuits were filed against Levon, Sandy, Rick and Garth, leading to a default judgment eventually vacated as improper. In the meantime, Levon's royalty checks, then his primary source of income, were seized to satisfy that judgment and have never been returned.

"Levon, known to Band fans all the world over for that trademark Arkansas Delta howl, became hoarse and then unable to speak. He was diagnosed with cancer circa 1997. Then came cancer surgery, followed by a series of 28 radiation treatments in 1998. The cancer left him barely able to whisper. Unable to speak much less sing, outside jobs proved hard to come by. Then, in another hard blow, Rick Danko passed away in 1999."

But, the press release said, regarding Levon, "The Midnight Rambles...were the saving grace on his way back to physical and financial health..."

That press release was issued on Oct. 22, 2007. Eight days later, on Oct. 30, 2007, *Dirt Farmer*, Levon's comeback CD and first album in years, was released.

On Plochmann Lane in Woodstock, dawn was breaking. As the Midnight Rambles ignited Levon's bottom-of-the-ninth, two-out, full-count comeback, the release of *Dirt Farmer* gave it momentum and thrust. Two CDs followed—2009's *Electric Dirt* and 2011's live record, *Ramble At The Ryman*.

All three won Grammys and, as much if not more than Levon's time as drummer, vocalist and mandolin player for The Band, these records and the Midnight Rambles that inspired them defined who he was as a musician and a person. And far beyond The Band, the Midnight Ramble and these records framed the legacy that Levon left when he died of cancer on April 19, 2012.

CHAPTER TWO

The Barn

According to msbluestrail.org, the website for the Mississippi Blues Trail, an endeavor of the Mississippi Blues Commission funded partly by grants from the National Endowment for the Arts, National Endowment for the Humanities, Mississippi Department of Transportation and Mississippi Development Authority Tourism Division, blues guitarist Hubert Sumlin grew up in Mississippi and Arkansas, played in Howlin' Wolf's band and with Muddy Waters; and he played guitar on records by Chuck Berry and Willie Dixon.

Sumlin also shared stages with the Rolling Stones and Santana, according to msbluestrail.org. According to *Rolling Stone* magazine, the Rolling Stones paid for Sumlin's funeral when he died in 2011.

But it was sometime in 2000 or 2001 when Hubert Sumlin found himself in New Paltz, New York. The Ulster County college town sits about two hours north of New York City, not far from the western shore of the Hudson River, about a 40-minute drive southeast of Woodstock. Hubert had been visiting with Levon at the studio and the two of them decided to take a drive down to a bar called Cabaloosa on Main Street to check out a band called the Apple Picker's Union. Levon had recently gotten to know the members of the band—Brian Parillo, Andrew Shober, Julia Shober and Brendan McDonough among them—very well.

"It was just a bar band gig," Brendan, a New Jersey native who served as guitarist, vocalist and songwriter for the Apple Picker's Union, said of that performance at Cabaloosa. "Hubert came by The Barn that night, Levon knew we were playing and I guess Hubert wanted to do something.

They drove down to Cabaloosa and the two of them walk into the back of the room. I hadn't met Hubert yet. I was a huge Howlin' Wolf fan. They kind of just walked in the door while we were playing. Everyone said, 'We've got to do a Howlin' Wolf tune.' I don't remember what we did. We did something. I very poorly copped all of Hubert's licks. Afterward, I was in such awe of this guy and I apologized for copping all of his licks. He put his arm around me and he said, 'Son, you sounded like a freight train.' And that was one of the greatest compliments I'd ever gotten in my whole life. They hung out, listened to a little bit of music and then they bounced. It was pure joy."

The path that Brendan took to that magical night in New Paltz began a few years earlier. The Band and the dawn of the internet played very big roles.

Brendan would go on to become stage manager and sound engineer at the Midnight Ramble and a member of the Levon Helm Band road crew. He would also go on to work as a member of the road crew for Glen Hansard of The Swell Season; the Jonas Brothers; Rich Robinson of The Black Crowes; and Nine Inch Nails.

"When the internet first started, there were AOL chat rooms and there was a Band one that got created," Brendan said. "If a certain number of people didn't post in it, it would get deleted. Brian was avidly posting in it to keep it up and going."

Also from New Jersey, Brian Parillo when he was 14 inherited from family members a box of records. *Stage Fright* by The Band was by far his favorite and, from there, he got his hands on all their other releases.

Several years later, as he remained active on the AOL's Band chat room, Brian found himself at Woodstock '94, the festival held in Saugerties, New York, to mark the 25th anniversary of the 1969 Woodstock Music and Art Fair. The Band played Woodstock in 1969, and the second incarnation of The Band played Woodstock '94. Brian randomly walked past a guy in a Band shirt emblazoned with "The Next Waltz" and they struck up a conversation. The guy was J.R. Cunningham and he told Brian how he lived in Ulster County, members of The Band lived in the area and their road manager was Butch Dener.

Brian returned home to New Jersey, found Butch by calling information and told him about the AOL message board. Brian mentioned that it was hard to find tour dates for The Band and Butch gave him the okay to call him on occasion for their schedule.

Brian and J.R. met up for a Band show in 1995 and Brian later got a bootleg video cassette of The Band, in Japan, to Butch. It turned out that The Band entourage had never seen the video, and Butch mailed the tape back to Brian with an all-access backstage pass.

"Anytime I showed up to a Band show, I'd slide in—The Stone Pony, The Chance, a barbecue festival in New Jersey, the Philadelphia Folk Festival, Beacon Theatre," said Brian. "I saw 25 shows standing behind Levon."

Brendan and Brian met while attending Rutgers College, in a class called American Folk Songs and Ballads. They eventually formed a band called Real Family Values that played Grateful Dead, Allman Brothers Band, Dylan, The Band and Beatles music.

And the pair saw a lot of Band shows together.

"In college, with anyone who could drive to a Band show, it was, 'Let's go,'" Brian said.

Those adventures often included Brendan, and the pair developed a relationship with the members of the Band.

Referring to Brian, Brendan said, "We struck up a friendship. And I just started going to tons of Band shows and hanging out backstage and getting to know the guys."

Levon's cancer diagnosis put a halt to The Band's touring. And following the passing of Rick Danko in December 1999, Brian, Brendan and the gang headed up to Woodstock for Rick's memorial service at the Bearsville Theater. They caught word of Levon playing with the Barn Burners at the Joyous Lake that night and headed over for the gig.

They returned to Woodstock often for the Wednesday night residency. Brian reconnected with Levon. And Brendan and Brian's band, now called the Apple Picker's Union, received an offer from Levon they couldn't refuse, even though everyone lived in New Jersey.

"We would drive up two hours one way, catch the show and drive back," Brendan said. "We got to know Levon even better at that point in time. He really couldn't talk much at all, really, above the slight whisper. But he was determined to be the best blues drummer in the word. That was his new vision—'If I can't sing, I'm going to make myself the best blues drummer that ever was.'

"Amy was on the stage with them and you could see her really coming into her own, with the real master blues band, and she really killed it. Amy and I struck up a great friendship after that. At some point after that, Levon was like, 'You boys are always driving up here. Why don't you just move up here and bring your band up and you can be the opening act at the show?'"

Brendan, Brian, Andrew, Julia and the gang relocated to upstate New York and grew extremely close to Levon.

"Whenever we were playing down in New Jersey, Brendan McDonough and a couple of the guys would always say hi after a show," Levon said. "They had a band, so we would always talk band talk. And they were smokers. That was a match made in heaven there. Then they moved up to Woodstock and away we went. And it turned out that they got a better band. They're tighter. They've got some stuff they recorded; they're going to record some more.

"They had been here for maybe a year or so, playing around and stuff, using the studio to record. All of a sudden, it looked like it was going to go on the auction blocks. So we started thinking we better cut everything we want to and throw a couple of parties before it's too late; and the damn parties turned into rent parties."

Those "rent parties" turned into the Midnight Ramble.

Brendan, Brian and the gang headed northwest from Woodstock and found a place to live in Chichester, in the middle of the woods, about a half hour from Woodstock.

"I just wanted to be around him," Brendan said. "Even without speaking, he was full of so much wisdom. We kind of started caretaking Levon Helm Studios."

Levon Helm Studios at the time, Brendan said, was in disarray.

"It wasn't a studio, even. It was a barn that was in disarray. It was in bad need of cleaning and love. We were hanging out with Levon at the lake, rehearsing a bit; Levon would come out and sit in with us and teach us some stuff. He would be like, 'You're playing that wrong,' and kick the drummer off the drum set, jump behind the drum kit and show us stuff. He'd teach me things about guitar playing. He was just a mentor to us. He would show up to gigs."

Brian said the group's first visit to Levon Helm Studios was eye-opening.

Referring to the Band's 1998 and final album release, he said, "When we showed up there, it seemed like no one had been in the studio since they recorded *Jubilation*. There were empty bottles. It seemed like nothing had happened since they last recorded."

As the Apple Picker's Union spent more and more time at Levon Helm Studios, Levon would call Brian on occasion. During one call, Levon told Brian there was a strange car in the studio parking lot, and asked him to check it out. Another time, a large RV serving as a mobile television studio had parked at the studio and plugged into an outdoor electrical socket.

But things began to look up for Levon as time passed and his recovery began to take hold.

"Levon was struggling with the cancer and he couldn't talk and he was playing those weekly gigs at the Joyous Lake and, little by little, the voice started coming back, in a little bit more than a whisper, and a little bit more than a whisper," Brendan said.

"One day, we were sitting up in the very top of the studio, in the cupola, just hanging out. I had my acoustic guitar up there and there were old stumps of logs that we used as seats. We were hanging out and he wandered up. This one particular day, I had dragged my acoustic up there and he said, 'Let me see if I can make that acoustic work.' He started playing 'Havana Moon' by Chuck Berry and this whisper of a crack of a voice came out. And he sang the entire song and I was nearly in tears by the end of it and I was like, 'Goddamn it, he's going to get his voice back.' And sure enough, little by little, he started getting his voice back. They got offered some gig somewhere. He wanted to do it and he kind of had a second thought and said, 'Let's just do a gig here.'"

The road to the Midnight Ramble wound its way through, of all places, Schenectady, New York.

"Before we got things going here at the studio, we tried to play for a guy up in Schenectady who owned a club up there," Levon said. "I wanted to do this at his place, but I finally said, 'The hell to that.' I asked this guy about being a house band, more or less, you know, and putting a band together and trying to get my voice back and stuff. We never could get together on anything. He had a nice club up there, in one of those beautiful old houses up there. It was a big house they had turned into a venue. I can't remember the name of it now—a pretty nice place.

"I talked to him about doing a weekly thing, you know. He wanted to talk about once a month. I didn't want to drive all the damn way to Schenectady, anyway. I was glad he turned me down. I wasn't thinking right. I should have thought about the studio first. He was so damn unagreeable about it. I'm kind of glad we didn't do it. It kind of forced me to go ahead and do it here at home. And shit, I wouldn't want to drive up to Schenectady very much. Then when we got the Rambles going, he used to call all the time. I never called him back."

Levon had something of a similar experience at the Bearsville Theater in Woodstock.

"I was going to try and play the Bearsville Theater in Woodstock, back when Sally Grossman had it," he said.

Sally Grossman was married to the late Albert Grossman, who managed Peter, Paul and Mary, Bob Dylan, Janis Joplin, Paul Butterfield—and The Band.

Albert Grossman was the driving force behind the Bearsville Theater, which sits in the Woodstock hamlet of Bearsville, not far down Route 212 from the Village Green. The Bearsville Theater complex back then included The Bear Café; The Little Bear, a Chinese restaurant; and a building that would house Todd Rundgren's Utopia Studios and, later, Radio Woodstock, an FM station also known as WDST—100.1 on your FM dial. Grossman died of a heart attack, in January 1986, on a flight to Europe.

"I told the folks over at the Bearsville Theater that I wanted the joint one night per week," Levon said. "Whatever night they don't want, I'll take it. But when I tried to get something going at the theater, it was all closed up. I'd call over there—'I'd like to have one night a week, every week.' Shit—you thought I was asking for a half-million-dollar loan or something. You'd call out there. You'd talk about it. You'd think things must have been progressing. But you'd get, 'Sally ain't here. Sally's gone to Mexico.' You never could track her down. You never could get nobody to agree to nothing. I said, 'How about Sunday night? I want to have a blues night.' I just didn't want to do the old Band tunes. I didn't get well to do that shit. I've done that. I just didn't want to hear it for a long time."

Not long after Brendan, Brian and the gang had moved to the Woodstock area, the *Daily Freeman* newspaper, based in nearby Kingston, published a story saying that foreclosure on Levon Helm Studios was imminent.

"I had never seen Levon so upset," Brian said. "He had felt abandoned. He was at his lowest point in terms of his health and financial stability. He thought he'd get more support."

But Brian said Levon maintained a stiff upper-lip.

"That moment was the only moment of vulnerability," he said.

And then, the studio began to buzz with activity again.

Brian began spending more and more time there. He set up a desk and a computer in the basement and plans were put in motion for the first recording project in ages—Uncle Remus and the Whole Show featuring Levon, Amy Helm, Sean Costello, Andrew Shober, John Smith and Johnnie Johnson, Chuck Berry's piano player and the "Johnny" of the Chuck Berry song, "Johnny B. Goode."

As the end of 2003 approached, Levon kicked around plans for a New Year's Eve show at the studio, but that never materialized. He did, however, begin to lay the groundwork for the Midnight Ramble with a free show on January 10, 2004. News of the gig—the Midnight Ramble name had yet to emerge—spread by word of mouth.

The show marked the first time Levon had played in some time—and emotions ran high at The Barn.

"People were crying and cheering," Brian said. "It went great."

Brian after the show approached Amy, Andy and Sean about their availability for another show in two weeks. They said yes, and the next morning Levon agreed that they should strike up the band again in a fortnight. The admission, he said, would be $100 a ticket, a price unheard of at the time for an evening of music.

Four days later, Levon approached Brian to confirm that Johnnie Johnson and John Smith would be on the gig. Brian didn't know their availability, but Levon was determined to have them return. Brian said Levon's attitude was, "If we can't get Johnnie Johnson and John Smith, the show would be canceled."

Said Brian, "Levon was just intent that Johnnie had to be in the band, and we were going to treat Johnnie good."

The gig was in about a week-and-a-half and nobody knew what Johnnie and John's availability were. Working together, Brian and Paulie Schmitz, a musician involved with the launch of the Rambles, got ahold of both musicians and paid for their plane tickets and hotel rooms with revenue from the 10 tickets they had sold.

But then, Brian recalled, "Levon says, 'We have a grand piano for Johnnie, right?' I told him no, but we'll try to get one."

Renting a grand piano cost $3,000, but Levon told Brian there was no way around it. They had to have a grand piano for Johnnie Johnson. Norman Clancy, who worked closely with Levon during the years preceding the Ramble era and during the launch of the Ramble, stepped in and covered the cost and, Brian said, "The whole thing came together."

A second show, Levon's "rent party" as he described it, was held January 24. That was the very first Midnight Ramble. And Dr. John showed up unannounced. He sang "Livin' On Borrowed Time" and played guitar because Johnnie was on piano.

When the very first Midnight Ramble was held, Brendan said, "The wolves were at the door at that point. We were ready to have our last stand at The Barn. Levon was ready to stand there with a gun at the door, I'm pretty sure. We called in some favors and a bunch of hands came and a bunch of other people with some vision for it came. And little by little, person by person, we added a brick, added a brick. And we had a show."

According to Paul Shultis, the studio portion of The Barn at the time of the first Ramble included screened-in porches with retractable walls that were opened for the Ramble, to accommodate an audience. But along with the room for additional seating came that cold Catskill Mountain winter air, so Paul wrapped the porches in plastic to keep out the elements as best it could. The evening was still a chilly one, despite the portable heaters.

"They didn't do any Band songs," Brendan said. "They wouldn't touch them. The place still had screen porches. It wasn't insulated. It was cold. It was some ridiculous Catskill Mountain night with two feet of snow on the ground. Everybody was freezing. We had heaters surrounding Johnnie Johnson, around the piano, little radiant heaters. We had a tiny, little PA. It was barebones. The first one was such a success, two weeks later we did another one. And Dr. John was there. We advertised it on the internet. We sold tickets."

Speaking of Dr. John playing that second Ramble, Levon said, "He came over that night. He knew that I was having a Ramble and I was trying to get something started. He heard about it and showed up. I didn't have to call him and say, 'I wish you'd do me a favor,' you know? He showed up. That's Dr. John."

As bleak as Levon's financial picture was when the first Ramble was held, Brian said, "It's not something we were talking about a lot. It wasn't like we were walking around fretting. It was always a specter in the corner. Nobody knew what the future held and it didn't look optimistic."

Little Sammy Davis joined in, and by way of Sammy, guitarist Fred Scribner signed on. The three musicians jammed at the studio, which at the time was being used by California musician Chris Rondinella. Chris had reached out to Levon about using the space, then hauled his gear to

Woodstock. The summer days of 2004 at Levon Helm Studios were filled with Levon jamming with Little Sammy and Fred, with Chris engineering.

The momentum picked up dramatically with Barbara O'Brien stepping into the role she would maintain for more than a decade. Levon Helm Studios was incorporated in October 2003 and, Brian said, "It just grew from there."

When Levon Helm Studios was built, Brendan said, Levon "had this vision of it being a film studio and a recording studio. He always had the vision; this wasn't something that was created out of nowhere. This is something that had been in his mind for 30-40 years—the name, the 'Midnight Ramble,' the whole thing."

Operating on something of a parallel track with Brendan and the guys from the Apple Picker's Union, as far as the evolution of the Midnight Ramble was concerned, was guitarist, vocalist and songwriter Paulie Schmitz of Long Island. Paulie met Levon in early 2001 at a gig Levon played in Manhattan's Tribeca neighborhood. Pedal steel guitar player Buddy Cage, who had performed in Schmitz's band, The Last Hombres, gave Levon a heads-up that Paulie would be at the show. So with something of an advance introduction from Buddy, Paulie approached Levon and asked if he would play on the new Last Hombres record.

"I figured I had nothing to lose," Paulie recalled. "We shook hands that night, said hello, he gave me his phone number and said, 'Give me a call.' I called him the next day and he said, 'When are we cutting?'"

A Long Island resident, Schmitz had been playing music since age 12, mostly for fun. As an adult, he formed The Last Hombres, who toured around the Northeast—Long Island, Boston, Philadelphia. In 1996, the band's bass player had walked up to Buddy at one of his gigs and helped him load his gear. Cage and the guys in The Last Hombres hit it off and he played on the band's first record.

And then Paulie met Levon.

"When we met Levon, it kind of changed everything," he said.

When Paulie met Levon, he could only speak in a whisper. But that didn't dampen his spirit.

"He was always joking and telling stories, in his whisper. Nothing stopped him. I never saw him feel sorry for himself."

During the summer of 2001, Levon, Paulie and The Last Hombres recorded 17 songs over two days, with no more than two takes needed for each song. Once finished, Paulie, at Levon's request, sent him CDs with the songs.

"He called up me on Sept. 2, 2001, and said, 'I'm in the band.' I said I know you are.'"

Paulie thought Levon was referring to The Band.

"He said, 'No, no, I'm in your band.' I was shocked. We were just planning on doing the record and putting it out—and that was it. We didn't think he'd want to play with us. It took all of us by surprise—and then we started playing together, not a ton of shows, but we played some good shows. We did some traveling. We went to Boston, to Philly, New York City. Joe Lore was Levon's driver. They'd pull in and Levon would be driving."

The Last Hombres began rehearsing at Levon Helm Studios. And as the gigs continued with Levon, his voice began to return.

"We'd be playing a show and all of a sudden, I'd hear a harmony," Paulie said. "I'm the front guy and I'd turn around. It was him and he was singing our songs. I'd say, 'Do you want a microphone?' He'd say, 'I'll tell you when I want a microphone.'"

The Hombres eventually disbanded. But around the end of September 2003, Levon told Paulie to come up to Woodstock "and we'll start a rockabilly thing."

That never materialized—but Levon did pitch Paulie on the Midnight Ramble.

"He basically said, 'This is what I want to do. I built this place for a music venue. I want to have a TV show. I want to have it every Saturday night.' He said, 'There's nothing on TV Saturday night.'"

This discussion prompted Paulie to bring up the internet to Levon, who was for the most part unfamiliar with cyberspace. He had heard of the internet but wasn't exactly sure how it all worked. Paulie bought him a computer. Levon googled himself and he was amazed to find so much had been written about him online.

"As he was getting more excited about it, he kept adding to it," Paulie said. "We just piled stuff in and started plugging things in."

The equipment, purchased and borrowed by Paulie, was installed. He brought in two sound engineers and two weeks later the studio was wired and ready to go.

"After he pitched me on the Rambles, I felt like I was standing at the crossroads of history," Paulie said. "This was going to be a big thing. This was going to be a big thing for music and a big thing for the country. It had ramifications for altering the course of where music was going at that point. You could go to big, big shows and all the stuff in between. There was a lot of stuff in between, and you had your dive bars. At the time, house concerts were new, but they weren't done on this level."

After the first Ramble, Paulie headed out to Los Angeles for the National Association of Music Merchants—NAMM—show, hoping to drum up some financial support for the Rambles. But he had no luck. He returned for the second Ramble with Dr. John, but was also working to open a recording studio in New York City, which was consuming his time. Seeing that the seeds for the Midnight Ramble were taking root, Paulie moved on. He returned the equipment that had been borrowed to its owners, and he reclaimed the equipment he owned.

"At that point, other people had been coming in," he said of the early stages of the Ramble. "My thing was, okay, it's going. This is how it works. Just press continue and you'll be fine. It was an infant when I left. The structure was there, the idea, the whole thing was there. There was nothing much else I was going to be able to do. I am a fire-starter. I light fuses. I get projects going, then when my time is done, I move on to the next one."

According to Paul Shultis, his grandfather Ralph and Levon first started discussing the construction of Levon Helm Studios while Ralph was overseeing the construction of Albert Grossman's Bearsville Studios.

"Ralph Shultis, the old-timer, the stonemason, pretty much just went by the book and built a three-bay barn with the big room and then the two smaller barns on each end, for the apartment and the control room," Levon said. "I would draw boxes and tell Ralph they were 30-feet wide. That was before you had to have an architect—you could have all the fun yourself. I would get those Eric Sloane books, *American Barns and Covered Bridges*—a good gift for kids, too. And he does all those hand drawings—Pennsylvania Dutch barns, Tennessee corncrib barns, Kentucky tobacco barns. We had books and stuff and Ralph had been building all his life, so we kept everything pretty much simplified.

"We built that one big barn, then we built this little barn, then the other little one on the other end. This one is big enough to live in, and the other one is big enough for the control room.

"In the beginning, the only thing that I knew for sure was to make it big enough that we could do a commercial production and have room left over, so that you could have an audience—100 people, 50-to-100 people that, on camera, can look like a thousand. Now that it's set, since the Rambles started, it's turned into more of a concert thing. It's as much of that as it is a studio."

"We've got the best water in the world here—wait till you taste of it. It's our own well and it's 240-something feet deep, 60 gallon-a-minute. It is delicious. Garth dowsed it for us. How about that? He called it. He said, 'It's gonna be deep, but there is gonna be a lot of it.' He was doing it two ways: He had a couple of clothes hangers all bent a certain way, and then he had a twig, a green twig that he cut. He walked off a little thread there, then he would walk over there, where they were building The Barn, and he would walk north and south and east and west.

"I told him we wanted to get as close to the house as we could, if we could. He did it for about two days, three days, and he finally said, 'That's the spot, right there.' And it's right there, just before you come under the portico, just before you drive up under there. It's in a spot where we could make a little wishing-well thing if we ever wanted to. I've toyed with that idea in my head. If I can get someone throwing quarters in there, it might be worth it—sell 'em the coins to toss: 'Buy these lucky coins and toss them in the wishing well.'

"When we first built it, before we got the electricity, I used to brush my teeth down at the creek. We had the bare minimum. The control room had screens on the windows. I used to sleep there on an air mattress. Everybody was saying, 'It's a bad idea, it's a white elephant.' My dad, he said, 'You're trying to cut too big a hole with too little a knife.'

"I had always wanted us to have our own shop. Shit—we were good enough to have our own spot. That was the idea behind Bearsville Studios. That's what I thought it was. But part of Grossman's con was that we were all going to be partners, and then of course that didn't happen. All of a sudden there wasn't a damn partnership to it. I basically got mad and built that Barn on my own. That just pissed me off. I got visions of me with my own key and setting my drums up and never having to take them down and them always being there and being tweaked and ready to go. Every time you tear them down and pack them up, you've got to start over. It's a pain in the ass. Building The Barn was a response to Bearsville. We'd be up there at Bearsville trying to record something and someone would say, 'Guess who's coming in to record next week?' Who gives a fuck?

"Albert Grossman was the biggest goddamn crook to ever hit town. He screwed us. He screwed Butterfield. He screwed Janis. You name it. When you've got a greedy son-of-a-bitch like that, they're never satisfied. They want more and more and more. He was interested in one thing only. Then all of a sudden, he didn't want to have no partners. It became, 'You boys are pretty good, but you're not that good.' That's how it hit me. And taking all that abuse with Dylan and all that other shit, none of that counted. And I'm saying the same thing—'You're all right, but you're not that fucking hot, you old bastard. You're not that fucking knowledgeable or smart. You've just been lucky as hell. That's all you've been—and lazy and a goddamn crook on top of everything. He ain't never done anything but leech and mooch."

In 1991, Levon Helm Studios was destroyed by fire.

"What had happened, not long before that, Stan Szelest had died," Levon said. "Carolyn Szelest, Stan's wife, had come down to Woodstock for the first time since Stan had passed and was sleeping in the room where Stan used to sleep. Carolyn is just the best. You feel like you're kin to her.

"Damned if that wasn't the night the fire started, damn cook stove. They pulled it out and did something to have it repaired and pushed it back and the cord got bent.

"The studio was known as the biggest white elephant in Ulster County. Some people would look at it that way, which didn't bother me. I didn't give a damn. It was perfect for what I wanted. I always spent everything I could make on it and didn't have it turn into an immediate moneymaker, which goes against some people. When it burned, you wouldn't believe how many people told me, in all seriousness, that the smart thing to do would be to get that money, that insurance money, build something small and stick whatever was left in my pocket and be happy. I don't care about sticking nothing in my pocket. I wanted to fix it like it was. I need this place. I don't need nothing in my pocket.

"Most Americans think that if you ain't rich, you ought to be trying to get rich, you know. And if you're not just working night and day and just being as goddamn tight and stingy as you can, you're not no kind of a businessman at all. Good. Now that we know what the difference is, we never will be one."

Just like Tinker Street, the Village Green, Overlook Mountain and Cooper Lake, the Shultis family offers plenty of insight into the rich legacy of Woodstock the town, as opposed to Woodstock the festival.

The Shultis family's Hudson Valley legacy dates back to the early 1700s, when members of the family emigrated from Germany's Rhine Valley. They settled in the area known now as Clermont in Columbia County, on the east side of the Hudson River, across from Ulster. Paul

Shultis's great-great-grandfather had eight siblings and three of his brothers eventually headed west and settled in Woodstock.

They were farmers, Paul said, in an era when you grew what you needed to feed your family and bartered the rest, for things like a doctor's care. And the family left an enduring imprint on Woodstock's community fabric. Paul is a descendant of Henry Shultis, who served as town supervisor from 1827-1829. Paul's great-grandfather, Wallace Shultis, was the Town of Woodstock Justice of the Peace.

Born in 1904, Ralph Shultis, Paul's grandfather, served during the early part of the 20th century as foreman of the Overlook Mountain House, on top of Overlook Mountain, which towers above Woodstock. Back then, horseback was how folks got from Overlook into town.

Ralph also built the roof for the Colony Café in town, which decades later would operate as the Colony Woodstock, a music venue and restaurant that on Nov. 6, 2020, hosted a musical performance by Maya Hawke. Millions of television viewers know Hawke as Robin Buckley from Netflix's "Stranger Things." Millions more are familiar with Hawke's mother, actress Uma Thurman; and her father, actor Ethan Hawke. Uma, by the way, along with actor Charlie Heaton, who played Jonathan on "Stranger Things," were both in the audience for that performance by Maya.

Roughly a century earlier, Ralph Shultis ended up working on the Colony Café roof—the owner of the Overlook House also owned the Colony—because the New York City engineers enlisted for the job couldn't figure out how to top off the building. Paul's grandfather and grandmother eventually moved off of Overlook Mountain and into town when Paul's uncle turned 7-years-old and started school. Decades later, Ralph Shultis would build Bearsville Studios for Albert Grossman.

Known with great respect and affection as The Barn, Levon Helm Studios encompasses 5,500 square-feet without the basement—4,000 in the studio and 1,500 in the house. The basement, excluding the garage, accounts for another 1,200 square-feet. That garage, by the way, long before it housed the potluck table and merch counter on Ramble nights, was where Paul played pickup basketball games with Levon, Jim Weider and Levon's Arkansas pal, C.W. Gatlin.

Much of the pine and hemlock used to build the original Levon Helm Studios came from Levon's land and was cut at a sawmill. Likewise, stone for The Barn was taken from the property. In the original building, the fireplace that now stands opposite the stage in the studio featured the only stone found in the building.

But that changed following the April 1991 blaze that consumed The Barn, leaving only the fireplace standing and scattered charred beams.

On the morning of April 18, 1991, Paul Shultis was gassing up his truck at Cumberland Farms on Mill Hill Road in Woodstock when he learned about the fire at Levon's, the night before, from an Ulster County Sheriff's Deputy.

"I finished pumping gas and drove over as fast as I could," Paul said.

He found Joe Forno Jr., the local pharmacist who was managing The Band at the time, removing reel-to-reel tapes that had survived the blaze thanks to an encased vault in the basement. Paul left and returned that afternoon to find Levon on site.

"He said, 'Well, you ready to start rebuilding? We can't let it sit there like this,'" recalled Paul, who on occasion in his late teens would help his father and grandfather work on The Barn, usually when Levon was on the road. "I was like, 'Really?' I was 30-years-old. I was in construction, but nothing of this magnitude. But that's how we started the whole process of rebuilding."

Paul served as general contractor and Levon insisted that a massive, double-faced stone wall be put in place between the house and the studio.

"He said, 'Hell, Paul, I won't lose the studio if it starts in the house and if it starts in the studio, I'll always have somewhere to live,'" Shultis recalled. "That was his idea. He had to have that."

Under Paul's direction as general contractor, rebuilding began with the demolition of the ruins. Work proceeded from the ground up. What Paul described as a super-sub structure timber frame was pre-cut in a factory and assembled on site—fastened together with wood pegs, but no nails. That was wrapped with pine, which is what you see on the inside of The Barn. Insulated panels were applied to the exterior, then wood siding. The only sheetrock in the building is in the bathrooms, which also feature cypress. Levon also mandated that every electrical wire be placed inside a piece of conduit or firmly embedded in a masonry wall. Industrial fire hoses—the kind that a fire department would use to battle a blaze—were installed inside The Barn and connected to a standpipe outside.

As he planned for the potential of another fire with the massive stone walls and the hoses and the standpipe, as well as a second driveway for expanded access to his property, Levon also turned to a marsh on his property for expanded fire prevention measures. The marsh was fed by a stream and Levon turned it all into a pond so he would never be wanting for a water source if another fire should occur. And although it became a pond, Levon always called it "the creek."

Should another fire occur, the Woodstock Fire Department's pumper could draw water from the pond and feed the standpipe, which would in turn engage the hoses inside. Adjacent to the pond is a field that Levon had cleared at the time of the rebuilding, Paul said, for softball games, but could certainly be used for a staging area by first responders. Midnight Ramble attendees would eventually park their cars in what Levon called "the ball field."

Along with the trauma of the studio burning down, Levon and Sandy ended up on the receiving end of some good old Woodstock community spirit.

"A lot of times, you've just got to count your blessings," he said. "Vince Christofora—he owned Woodstock Meats in town and he's one of the best damn guys in Woodstock, right there. You betcha. Oh, man, when The Barn burned, he was the first call the next day. He called me at the hotel. He said, 'Have Sandy stop by the store.' Sandy went by the store and he gave her, I think, two grand—cash. He told her to call him later and let him know what was going on, what we needed.

"And I would go down. You know how the insurance companies are. Once we got to rebuilding, I'd have carpenters, stonemasons, everybody there, ready to get paid on a Friday and shit, there ain't no insurance check to have you covered. I would call Vince and go down to the store and he would have eight, ten, twelve grand, fifteen grand in a grocery sack; fives, tens, twenties, and he'd hand me that grocery sack and tell me how much was in there and he'd write it down. At the end of it, after I got the place rebuilt, I owed Vince probably between sixty and a hundred grand. I finally paid him off, everything I owed him, in 2009. I got him down to where anytime I'd get a check, I'd just take it in there and he'd cash it and we'd split it. That's who Vince is. Oh, what a guy."

As for resurrecting the spirit of The Barn, Levon said, "I learned that if I wasn't going to rebuild it, it would have, forever, it would have killed me. The only way around it was to build it bigger and better. The major changes involved making the cupola a little bit bigger. Then, on the apartment end, instead of having porches, I just went ahead and took the whole thing in. We closed in the big porch. I think that helped the sound. The place sounds a lot better. Just to get back in there, the dream was still alive, you know? When I first put it up, it was mainly just for us to record and to hang with friends. I never thought about trying to go into the studio business. I just wanted a place where we would always have the key and we would call for a truck and rent some equipment and have it our way. That was the reason for doing it.

"If it was just for the sound, I wouldn't have built it that big. I would have made it smaller. But I always believed that records were going to have pictures on them, eventually. It just makes sense. There are so many ways to show the songs. I knew you had to have enough room to have a film crew, which would take up that middle bay of The Barn. And in the balcony and by the fireplace there was enough room for 100 people. It was just big enough to have the camera crew and an audience.

"The studio was never big enough in my head to have a crowd of people. But all of a sudden, the times changed and there is so much phony bullshit in the world that if you'll bring people right up close and get musicians like Johnnie Johnson, for them to get right up next to, to hear, that's a pretty good ticket. So all of a sudden, two hundred people—that's a lot of money if you sell all those tickets.

"I never really thought of the studio for doing concerts, but I always thought it could be a place for doing film. The idea was to have it big enough to do videos. That was the big argument back in the old days: 'Oh they'll never put pictures on records.' At the time, I couldn't understand why Capitol Records wasn't excited that one of their artists would be wanting to go in for something like that, to build a studio where maybe we could do some filming. They don't want you building no studios—that's their business; they're not interested in that. It's like a song or a record, you know? If they don't own it, it's no good.

"The studio was the hang. It was the hangout. And when we would get something to do, a recording thing, we'd call in a truck and rent the equipment for a week or a month or something like that. But we really didn't get things started until Justin Guip got here. We had some equipment, but not really anything. That's been Justin's whole contribution. Without Justin, The Black Crowes wouldn't have been here and all this other good stuff wouldn't have happened."

Speaking of the sound crew, Justin Guip, Brendan McDonough, Andrew Shober and Chris Edwards, Levon said, "They live for the music."

Across decades, Levon's vision for the Midnight Ramble had gotten kicked around plenty. But it began to take shape thanks to a group of unlikely cohorts.

"We were green, we were kids," Brendan said. "It was a house party. Then it kind of became a rent party because times were tough. Levon said, 'If nothing else, we're going to have a big party, invite a bunch of friends, and play some music.' And he started being able to sing a bit. You'd hear 'Mary Ann' by Ray Charles and some of these gems—'School Days' by Chuck Berry. And we got Johnnie Johnson, Chuck Berry's piano player, at the last minute, and they put a show on."

Brendan said the early Ramble team was empowered and emboldened by their success.

"We were like, 'We can do this now,'" he said. "The first one was just a party. The second one, we had created a blueprint for what the Ramble would be. We figured out how we could do this.

"And then, little by little, more people came in. It was like Sisyphus pushing the boulder up the hill. You would get up the hill and it would roll back down on you. And you'd get up the hill and it would roll back down on you. Every time, you'd get a little further up the hill and build it a little more."

CHAPTER THREE

Jimmy Vivino and an All-Star Baseball Team Playing Football

Levon Helm and Jimmy Vivino were the closest of friends.

"Levon always said, when he was sick, no one came around, no one called, he was basically alone," Tony LoBue said. "Jimmy, at that time, had a house up in Woodstock and Jimmy was the only one who came around. Jimmy and Levon went down to the lake. Jimmy would sing. They'd have a great time, talking and laughing. He loved Levon. And Jimmy was the guy who was always there. And Levon never forgot that. Levon told me that so many times."

Jimmy V, as Levon called him, is a guitarist, vocalist and keyboard player who is perhaps best known for performing in and serving as music director for Conan O'Brien's late night television talk show. Vivino, whose history with Conan dates back to the first episode of *Late Night with Conan O'Brien* on NBC, is a founding member of The Fab Faux, a frequent collaborator with Woodstock resident John Sebastian of Lovin' Spoonful fame and he has sat in on occasion with the band Gov't Mule.

Jimmy V was among Levon's most trusted friends and most cherished musical companions. And the man from Turkey Scratch often said the Midnight Ramble would never have emerged without him.

"On most Ramble nights, it would just be another night to have fun," Tony said. "When Levon realized that Jimmy was coming, he'd be up and down the stairs three or four times—'Is Jimmy here yet? When's Jimmy getting here? I wonder what he's going to do. You know Jimmy, he'll do this.' He got excited when Jimmy was coming. He loved it when Jimmy was coming. He worshipped Jimmy."

Levon met Jimmy as the two crossed paths while playing gigs at venues that included the Stanhope House and The Stone Pony in New Jersey, and The Lone Star Cafe in Manhattan. And Vivino left a big impact at Levon Helm Studios, one that continues to resonate today.

"Jimmy is the guy that brought Hubert Sumlin and Johnnie Johnson, he brought them all in and recorded them and got them all in to meet us and stuff," Levon said. "With Jimmy, when I was recovering from those radiation treatments, I'd get short of cash—I'd hock one of my mandolins to him, you know, get a grand off him, have a little spending money, then I'd buy it back. Joe Lore, another friend of mine, he did that a few times for me, too. Hell, at one time, Joe had two or three of my guitars, maybe a mandolin. Joe's the best.

"Jimmy V would show up in the afternoons when he could and pull his guitar out and we'd set down by the creek. And at the end of the day, he'd have a song written and swear that I'd helped him with it. Jimmy V's presence was just the best. To back all that lip service up, Jimmy V brought Johnnie Johnson to town and we recorded Johnnie right here and I got to play on three or four of the songs. Then he did the same thing with Hubert, brought Hubert Sumlin in; cut him here, produced him and hired me and a bunch of us. And James Wormworth, his drummer, was gracious enough to kind of make room for me to come in. It wasn't like they needed more drums. James is one of the best—God what a drummer. Then, Jimmy started helping with these Rambles and really pulled that one together. Having Jimmy around back then, it kept your foot on base. You were still in the game. Things looked rough, but you were still in the ball game."

The relationship between Levon and Jimmy V, and the mutual respect they held for each other, personally and professionally, can be traced to The Band's tour bus, years earlier, as it made its way from a hotel in the Windy City to the Chicago Blues Festival. Jimmy was in the Prairie State to perform at the Chicago Blues Festival with Johnnie Johnson. At his hotel, Jimmy had missed his ride to the festival and, while figuring out his next move, ran into Hubert Sumlin, who was also scheduled to perform at the festival.

"Hubert was standing outside the hotel, all dressed for the evening, ready to go for the show," Jimmy said. "He didn't know who was supposed to get him where. I said, 'Excuse me, aren't you Hubert Sumlin?' I knew what he looked like, of course, from being a blues stalker all my life. These guys, when you would meet them, looked exactly like the pictures you saw. You never saw them in jeans and a t-shirt. When they were out of the house, they were dressed up."

At that point, Jimmy sees the tour bus for The Band. And Vivino knew road manager Butch Dener.

"The Band was playing over at the festival, so we got on their bus," Jimmy said. "Levon steps up and he introduces himself—'Mark Lavon Helm.' Mark—he used his first name. I don't know why he was so formal with me. It wasn't Levon—it was 'Mark Lavon Helm.'"

And then it was off to the Chicago Blues Festival on The Band's bus.

"I think that's when Johnnie Johnson and Levon met up and that whole thing," Jimmy said. "Then we had Levon on the show with the band when his book was out."

That would have been *Late Night with Conan O'Brien.*

"We got to be instant friends. Some people you meet and you feel like you've known them all your life; the door is open right away. It's all out there; there is no disguise, no mystery at all."

Sometime later, Jimmy became a part-time Woodstock resident. He came to town to play music with longtime Woodstock resident John Sebastian, who, like Levon and The Band, had performed at the Woodstock Music and Art Fair, in Bethel, N.Y., in August 1969.

"I had a house—you could throw a rock through the woods from Levon's and hit it—off of Glasco Turnpike, on Raybrook," Jimmy said. "Levon would say, 'You can walk through the woods and come over.' I met him through the years many different times. But I got to know him when I lived there. When I came up here and I hadn't been over to the house—I think John Sebastian took me over for the first time—we were knocking, trying to get in; we didn't even get in that day. We came to find out he was sick. I didn't know anything about the cancer."

Happy Traum, one of Levon's oldest friends, is the founder of the Homespun Tapes instructional video series for musicians. Happy, who sat in often at the Rambles, had asked Jimmy if he wanted to make an instructional tape with Johnnie Johnson. Jimmy and Sebastian had previously made an instructional tape for Happy featuring guitar and harmonica. So, Happy got Johnnie up to Woodstock and he stayed at Jimmy's house on Raybrook Drive.

At Happy's studio for the taping were Jimmy; Mike Merritt, bass player for the *Conan* band and long-time member of the Levon Helm Band before Conan took his show to Los Angeles; drummer James Wormworth, percussionist for the *Conan* band before taking over for Max Weinberg on drums; and Johnnie. They were at Happy's studio and Levon came over.

"His neck is ruby red," Jimmy said. "It's got aloe dripping from it; it's burning. There's heat coming off it. But he was going to be down there. And he could hardly speak, but he came to see Johnnie Johnson. He said to me in that gruff voice, he could barely speak, but he said, 'Jimmy V, we ought to have Johnnie over to The Barn and record him while he's here.' He saw the opportunity."

So Jimmy called Chris Andersen at Nevessa recording studio, not far from Levon's, and Chris brought the truck with recording equipment over to Levon Helm Studios. Rick Danko came over. Jim Weider was there. Sebastian, Garth Hudson and Richard Bell, who played keyboards in the re-formed Band, also showed up.

"It was sort of a receiving line of musicians," Jimmy said.

And after that recording session Johnnie Johnson played at one of the very first Midnight Rambles.

At the time, Jimmy worked in Manhattan on the *Conan* show during the week but spent his weekends in Woodstock and paid regular visits to Levon.

"I would just go down and he seemed to be getting a little better now and then," Jimmy said. "He would run a smoke fire down by the creek on his property to keep the mosquitoes away. It was a real Southern thing. I think it was a daily baptism for him to go down to that creek and get that smoke fire going. I thought the smoke was sort of a voodoo thing going on. And we wrote a couple of songs on the bank of the creek and it was almost some kind of process of healing. I would sing, and he would say, 'You're sure singing good.' And he would change a line here or there. We were writing songs together.

"I could see he was going crazy from not playing. Here's a guy that, when Robbie Robertson decided there's no more Band, he said, 'What?' His whole life had been on the road, working. I think he took that pill for about five minutes. I finally said, 'I know you can't sing yet, but I sure could use a good drummer. We should put a band together up here and just start playing. Let's do a gig. Let's call it the Barn Burners.'"

Mike Dugan played bass, Weider played guitar, Jimmy played piano and guitar and Levon played drums. That's the original Barn Burners. Jimmy's schedule didn't allow him the flexibility to perform in the band on a regular basis. But devotees of Levon's, who would ultimately perform with him, began to emerge.

"That's when the kids came to see us—Pat O'Shea, Chris O'Leary—the Irish blues kids," Jimmy said. "I couldn't do it all the time. Levon said, 'You don't mind if I take the name?' They started doing it. Then they got Sammy."

That would be Little Sammy Davis, a Mississippi native who Larry Campbell would describe during Levon Helm Band gigs as "one of the original bluesmen."

"Sammy's from Winona, Mississippi, and hitchhiked out of town when he was about 10-11 years old, on a damn chicken truck, and had to ride in the back with the chickens," Levon said. "He can make it funny, but it was like that day we were out there shooting film for *Dirt Farmer*, down at John Gill's farm in Hurley, and we were talking about this and talking about that and Sammy said, 'Well, I raised myself.' He said, 'I didn't have no mommy or no daddy.'

"Then I heard him talk about living with his grandmother and I think she was pretty stout on him. He would go to town and play on the street corner and he'd get dimes and quarters and she was afraid he was stealing and stuff.

"Sammy sings that Sam Cooke stuff, that Ray Charles stuff. Sammy's one of the few blues guys who can make that transition—Mississippi, Arkansas, Louisiana, Tennessee, that little nook there, Southern Missouri, there. There is something about the way the music sounds down there, way in there on the bottom, right down on the bottom. You hit something down there and it vibrates.

"I remember playing shows with Sammy and his band. And then Chris O'Leary, our harmonica player in the Barn Burners, got sick; had those polyps come on this throat. And it knocked him out of action for years. And he called Sammy in to fill in so we wouldn't lose the gig. And we've been hooked up ever since.

"Sammy's just the best and that harmonica—isn't that a wonderful, amazing instrument? And it always fits. It's always been there. It's the horn for country blues. That's the horn line. Instead of a violin or a horn, you got the harmonica and back in those days, when Sammy was a kid, back then I guess, they were 50 cents apiece. But 50 cents back then was half a dollar. That was a lot of money. Now I think those damn harps are $40-$50 a piece. They're like an accordion; an accordion does the same kind of thing. It can play an organ part or it can play a saxophone part. And traditionally, the harmonica is easy to travel with."

Regarding Levon's approach to making music, Jimmy V said, "Levon had this process of slowly building things, of not rehearsing."

Jimmy continued, "He'd turn to me with that sign."

That sign would be Levon holding his thumb and index finger about a half-inch apart.

"He'd say, 'We're that close. We're that close to getting it,'" Jimmy said. "Nobody was leading the band. It organically happened. Nobody is giving it to you. There was some great music. Levon had some things that bugged him about the way people were playing the blues, as opposed to how he heard Sonny Boy Williamson on a flatbed or Elvis riding through town. Everyone heard these stories. He grew up looking over the fence at these guys. And I grew up looking over the fence at him and John Sebastian."

Speaking of the Barn Burners, Jimmy said, "Every time I got a chance, I'd find out where they were playing—little dump clubs in Kingston, the basement of a place. We were always looking for some place to play."

Times had changed in Woodstock.

Years earlier, when Paul Butterfield and The Band lived in town, you might walk into Deanie's at the intersection of Routes 212 and 375 and find Richard Manuel of The Band playing the piano. Gone was the Sled Hill Cafe, where Richard would play the piano late at night, and the Joyous Lake on Mill Hill Road in Woodstock. And gone was the Tinker Street Café on Tinker Street, which had previously been the Café Espresso, where Dylan rented an upstairs room when he lived in town many years earlier.

"In the old days," Jimmy said, "You could walk over to the Lake, or walk down to Tinker Street, when there was stuff happening. We're looking—'Hey Weider is playing over in Kingston.' We went down and if Lee was around, he'd go if it was close enough or if he felt like it. I'd play piano or guitar or whatever. I didn't care, I just wanted to play."

Then came the 2001 birthday show for Hubert Sumlin at B.B. King's Blues Club in Times Square—"Howlin' for Hubert." Levon was still recovering from cancer and had not been singing.

"I had this idea once to put something together with me and Levon and Mike Merritt and David Johansen and Brian Mitchell," Jimmy said. "This is all pre-Ramble stuff. We'd back Hubert up. I said, 'Let's put the right thing together for him and play at B.B. King's and do a party for Hubert.' Levon says to me that night, 'Jimmy V, I think I'll try to sing one tonight.' Right now, I just get tingled all over thinking about it. I'm going through it right now, again."

Jimmy asked him what he wanted to sing. Levon's response was, "I think I'll try 'Main Street,' Muddy Waters, 'Going Down To Main Street.'"

According to Jimmy, "It comes out, he starts singing again, and it's all there. It's changed—we all change when we get older—but it's all there. It was the voice I believed every time I heard it, whatever he was singing about. The world was a Mathew Brady photograph when this guy sang. I could smell the dirt on the boots. And he's back there and we're doing 'Main Street' and then it starts, little by little, getting better."

As Levon continued with his recovery, the Barn Burners began to pick up steam.

"When we were playing out at clubs with the Barn Burners, some people, at first, when they started coming, they had no idea how serious it was," Jimmy said of Levon's cancer. "They had no idea. They wanted Levon singing. We kind of kept ignoring that 500-pound gorilla in the room. We're pushing through. And we all know, as we get older, people don't expect us to change. They expect us to rekindle all the memories they had. They want us to look the same. They want us to sound the same. After a while, that went away and people just really wanted to see him."

The Barn Burners underwent some changes, including the addition of Amy Helm to the lineup.

"Levon brought Amy into the Barn Burners because he was always looking to be more than just a blues band," Jimmy said. "With Levon, music didn't have labels. Everything should be coming from everywhere. Amy was just getting her confidence as a front person, as a lead singer. And she was getting better and better with every gig we did."

Jimmy had known Amy for quite some time when she started performing with the Barn Burners.

"I met Amy as a kid," he said of the performer who would go on to play in the band Ollabelle. "She was shy. She wasn't singing. She was a kid in school. When this thing happened to Levon, she was taking control of a lot of stuff, getting him to his therapy. Then she started singing with the Barn Burners and I started to realize that there was this thing that was there with her. Then Ollabelle happened—and the fusion of what that band brought out in her."

And then the Rambles got under way.

"I was playing a lot of piano, because we didn't have anybody yet," Jimmy said. "There was a Hammond B-3 organ. Levon insisted on getting a real piano. He wanted the upright bass and a real piano—the two things he loved about the rhythm section. I remember, I was playing bass—we did a Ramble in Arkansas and I had to play bass that night—he turns to me, he says, 'Don't play like Ricky.'

"Early on, I would play piano, or bass, or whatever. Mike Merritt hadn't come in yet. Lee says, 'Let's bring Mike Merritt in.' Then, I think, I brought Brian Mitchell over. Brian was the obvious choice. Levon remembered him from the Hubert Sumlin gig—'That guy, Brian.' Right away, it was him building this thing, getting the players. Then he had Erik Lawrence on saxophone and Steven Bernstein on trumpet, the two horns. Then it got bigger, it got to five. Everything got to where he wanted it—slowly. He didn't want to rebuild The Band. That was the last thing he wanted to do, 'Let's not do that again. Play like you and the songs will hold up with new arrangements.' And he organically made these arrangements.

"I remember bringing a horn chart once and he said, 'That's like the record, right? Why don't we do this—why don't we have them play big chords?' He appreciated our reverence for those Band records, but at the same time, it was 'Okay, This is us now.'"

Regarding Levon Helm the musician, Jimmy said, "There is a sound that comes out of that man that is him."

As a band leader, Levon gave his musicians freedom.

But, Jimmy said, "At the same time, he could pull the reins in when things were wrong. I still see that he's in charge, even though he likes one of us to lead the band, and he always did—somebody has to count the songs off. I think The Band was very democratic like that. Whoever sounded best on the song, or made you believe, that's who did the lead singing. And in The Band, they deferred to Richard Manuel as lead singer a lot, I think. That's just my thought. I just think there is never a better singer for me. I could listen to Ray Charles, but I always say, Richard is my Ray Charles."

———⬩———

Jimmy knew Larry Campbell from playing around New York City. Andy Murray, brother of comedian and actor Bill Murray, had a band, and Jimmy and Larry played together in that ensemble.

"Larry was from the Upper East Side," Jimmy said, "You would think he is from Tennessee. He figured out pretty early that no one in New York would play the shit he was going to play."

Jimmy's first impressions of Larry were, "My God. First it starts out, two alpha dogs onstage. Then this guy was so cool about it. We just got along great. And since then I hadn't seen him for a long time until the Rambles. I'd see him with Bob, or at a session."

One night, Jimmy and Brian Mitchell were playing together at the Parkside Lounge on Houston Street in Manhattan. Shawn Pelton from the *Saturday Night Live* band played drums. Andy Hess, of Black Crowes and Gov't Mule fame, was playing bass.

"This guy comes in with a trombone case and a giant tuba case," Jimmy recalled. "I said to myself, 'One horn and it's a trombone?' He sits up in front of the band on a stool and I was mesmerized all night by this guy. I said, 'How come I don't know you?' He told me he came from Seattle. I was like, this guy's from New Orleans."

That was Clark Gayton.

"So Clark, Quincy Jones and Jimi Hendrix are all from Seattle," Jimmy said. "I put Clark up there with those guys, I really do. He's a great arranger. Having Clark around, there is always a twinkle in his eye, like everything is cool. He plays better than anybody I know. After it was just the two horns, Levon wanted to get more horns. The first guy we had was Bones. Tom Malone goes back to *The Last Waltz* days and when you're in Levon's book, you're in Levon's book. Bones wasn't really available so much. Me and Mitch had been playing with Clark. Bernstein is a wildcard—what he does with his Sex Mob. Outside of this band, there is all the other stuff.

It's so different from what the Ramble is, or you listen to Erik Lawrence's records. Amy brought in Jay Collins on tenor saxophone and I got to meet a really great musician I wasn't aware of and we had another arranger and front man on our hands. Everybody, it seemed, was a leader in their own right. Everybody who came into that band had led bands before. It was a band full of leaders with a guy who didn't want anyone to be leading it. So a band of leaders becomes a band of followers, of each other. Everybody's respect got elevated even more. With Levon, nobody told anybody anything. We played and played and played and played until it was right."

How would Jimmy V describe the Levon Helm Band?

"It's like an all-star baseball team playing football," he said. "We're not playing our game, but we know something about sports, so we can put a team together. That puts the ball down the field. But we're not playing our game. We're playing this other thing. So if it works, you won't always say, 'He's not an R&B guy,' or 'He's not a country guy.' Everybody at some point is playing out of his or her field, out of their limits, but bringing something new to it. Nobody tried to shove their thing into the Ramble band. Everybody became a member of the band. It's funny how everything fit together, when it should not have fit together.

"When Little Sammy was up there, it turned into this other thing; Sammy was a guy who was enthralled with Little Walter. Then Howard Johnson started coming around and, whoa, if Howard's interested, there is something to it. Levon said to somebody at some point, 'What we've got to do is we got to get Howard here.' And when that happened, I was like, 'Wow.' To have Howard Johnson there—this is only the best guy in the world, of the known universe of human beings. There is nobody that does what he does, playing tuba and baritone sax. He was in that four-tuba thing with Taj.

"And Levon was always like, 'First class—let's go first class, even if we spend every dime we're making.' The Band had five horns; that was what he was used to hearing. If it's four, it doesn't sound right to him. He has that saying, 'I don't know what it is, but that ain't it. I'll know it when I hear it.'"

And then Band songs found their way into the repertoire.

"It started out as almost an unspoken word," Jimmy said. "I'll take full blame for sneaking things in. I would ask him, 'Do you think we can we do this if I try it?' Usually, it was 'Yeah.' Sometimes he would say, 'I don't know. Maybe next week.' Then I knew it was a 'No.' Then, three weeks later, he'd say, 'What about what you asked me about? How come we're not doing that?' It wouldn't leave his head. I think part of it was, no matter what, that is Levon's legacy of work, that he is very proud of. He always wants to make sure that he's up to wanting to do it, because it's a lot on him. If you want to do 'Life is a Carnival,' that's a lot of work on the drummer. That's an incredibly intricate thing. We started to learn the difference between stuff that we could pull out and try and stuff that needed a lot of work, because those guys worked hard on those things. What happens on some of those records didn't just happen."

CHAPTER FOUR

Barbara O'Brien

In March 2004, Levon Helm placed a very important phone call to a woman he barely knew. Her name was Barbara O'Brien.

Levon and Barbara had met more than once over the course of years. They had even worked together, presenting live music. And she had attended the first two Midnight Rambles ever held.

Neither knew much about the other. But the friendship they forged would ultimately navigate treacherous cliffs, scale valleys and conquer peaks. Above all, it endured.

Barbara was an administrative assistant at the Ulster County Sheriff's Office. Levon was a rock star whose triumphs had come and gone years earlier.

On the day he phoned Barbara, Levon was recovering from cancer of the vocal cords, speaking in a labored whisper. On top of this, he was buried in bankruptcy and struggling to save his home from foreclosure.

But Levon hadn't exhausted all of his firepower. He hadn't stopped kicking up dust. He hadn't abandoned faith in himself or neglected his ability to stir it up in others. Levon wanted to roll the dice one last time. And he wanted Barbara to join him at the craps table. Levon was ready to set sail. And under his vision for the future, he would be the commodore of the navy and Barbara would be the captain, steering the ship.

The sails were shredded. The seas were rough. The stakes were high. But neither could pass on the gamble of a lifetime.

"Out of the blue one time, he invited me over to the house," Barbara recalled of that 2004 phone call. "He took me on a tour of the studio and he had this vision."

That vision included Barbara working at Levon Helm Studios, with her own office downstairs.

"He was saying, 'We can put a desk over there. And a phone over there.' I think it was his way of offering me a job."

Despite the tough times, Barbara said, Levon remained optimistic.

"At that point, I didn't know all of the history, all of the details, other than being a Band fan. And I wasn't quite sure what he wanted me to do."

As Levon showed Barbara around the studio after that initial phone call, she grew a bit confused. Did he want her to quit her job? At the time, she had been with the Ulster County Sheriff's Office for 21 years.

"Levon would never, ever come out to anybody and say, 'I need your help.' After talking to him a couple of times, I sensed that's what was being asked, without being asked."

"My interpretation was, he wanted me to do a fundraiser. I knew the place was kind of in trouble. He was walking back and forth, rubbing his chin. I thought he was thinking that a fundraiser was a good idea.

"But he said to me, 'You know what, baby, I can't go to anybody with my hat in my hand.' That was the first lump in my throat. That's when I thought, 'Wow, it's going to be tougher than I thought. How do we raise the money?'

"I just started going over there on a regular basis. And before you know it, we're doing a Ramble."

"Barbara O'Brien is the MVP of the team," Levon said. "That ain't no lie. Barbara for sure is the one who turned the Ramble into a moneymaker. It was just going to be a big party with us. When we first started the Rambles, Barbara and I had kind of talked a little bit, but she hadn't really come over and took over yet. When we got the Ramble going, then, all of a sudden, there was something to look after. She got that going and that led off into everything else.

"She used to do the Armed Forces Appreciation Day in Kingston. And she finally started calling me to handle the band, and I'd put a band together. She called me. She didn't have to call nobody else. And I'd get it wound up. Then we got a lot of people trying to be a part of it. Somebody, I forget who it was, wanted to be paid for his sound system. I can't remember who it was. I got rid of him right off the jump. I told Barbara I'd get somebody else and not to worry about him. The bastard wanted to get paid. Everybody else was doing it for nothing.

"That was it. So we did that for two or three years, then she came over and started running the Ramble. Barbara and I hit it off—right from the front end."

Four years after receiving that 2004 phone call from Levon, Barbara said with a laugh, "I'm still unclear about what my role is."

Turning serious, she said, "I just know that I can't quit."

On visiting Levon Helm Studios in early 2004, Barbara said, "It was so heartbreaking to be there, to know that The Band had been what it was, that this man lived in five-star hotels and had been treated like royalty, and to know that the industry let him down like that."

On one visit to see Levon at the studio, Barbara met Bill and Jean Speight. Bill was a retired Yonkers firefighter and they lived in Putnam County with their children. Bill first saw The Band in the summer of 1970. He later worked security at the Midnight Rambles and he and his family grew quite close to Levon. But that night, Bill was making his second visit ever to Levon Helm Studios, after bumping into Levon on the sidewalk in Woodstock outside of the Joyous Lake, before a Wednesday night Barn Burners show.

On the night they met Barbara, Bill and Jean recalled with a laugh, Levon told them about a molasses concoction he had left out for the bears that visited his property, to eat. And Barbara, Bill and Jean got a personal tour of Levon Helm Studios, courtesy of the man from Turkey Scratch.

"We started out in Levon's house and he brought out all these spiral notebooks with lyrics he had written," Barbara said.

Then, Levon took Barbara and the Speights around the studio, the part of Levon Helm Studios where the Midnight Ramble was held and where *Dirt Farmer* and *Electric Dirt* would later be recorded.

"We walked out into the studio and what you see now isn't what it was back then. There was no piano. There was no heat. It was freezing cold. And then he took us up into the sound room."

The sound room is the part of Levon Helm Studios that sits elevated behind the performance space. It later became home to the equipment used to record each Ramble and the records. Though it was not separated from the performance space by a wall or window, it was equivalent to the control booth in a traditional recording studio.

"It was just furniture all over the place," Barbara said of the sound room. "I remember things covered in sheets. And he was explaining to us who recorded there and what they did, and it was at that moment I had the second lump in my throat, the size of a golf ball, because I could not imagine that he had gone from where he was and it turned out that way."

A few moments later, Barbara was sitting in the studio with Bill and Jean.

"It was just the three of us," Barbara said. "Levon had gone into the house for something. They were asking me, 'What are you going to do?' And I said, 'I have no idea.'"

But, Barbara told them, "I guarantee you, this can't continue."

She ended up becoming Levon's manager and guiding Levon's career through the success of the Midnight Ramble; live performances at Radio City Music Hall, the Beacon Theatre and Bonnaroo; and the three Grammy wins. When Barbara first became involved at the studio, she was working full-time for the Sheriff's Office, she had her own transcription business and she was the bookkeeper for a nearby condominium complex. But, in typical Barbara O'Brien fashion, she focused on committing to Levon, rather than the obstacles—they were many and they were daunting—in her way.

To begin with, she conceded, "I'm not from that world."

But, Barbara said, "I had to help this man, just because of Levon. He deserved help. The industry he made so much money for had left him. They abandoned him. I think that's a sin. I was willing to do whatever I had to, to help him."

To generate interest in the Ramble and gauge the response, Barbara began sending out mass e-mails to just about everyone she knew.

The first Ramble held with her involvement took place in April 2004.

"We weren't charging people. I needed to see that people were willing to come to Woodstock, to Plochmann Lane, to listen to music."

The next Ramble took place in September and drew a crowd of four hundred. Ulster County Sheriff Richie Bockelmann was cooking hamburgers outside on a grill and his wife was helping as well. A friend of Barbara's was selling t-shirts.

"It was any friend I could find, to come and help," Barbara said. "And it was a success."

Barbara and her mother, at the time, were cleaning the studio. The O'Brien women went grocery shopping and set up a banquet table in the studio, near the big windows, with chips and dips. That culinary offering evolved into the Midnight Ramble potluck table down in the garage.

"Once I saw that people were showing up, I thought, 'God, maybe this will work,'" said Barbara, who emphasized she was part of a team that supported Levon. "All I did was organize it, which is what, I think, was all he needed. All of those years, since the Band disbanded, all Levon needed was an organizer.

"All this needed was some structure, someone to go in there and kick some ass—which I asked Levon if I could do. And he said yes. Get rid of the dead weight. Everybody kind of learned that, if you're going to be there, you're more than welcome to be there—but you've got to pull your weight. Just like I'm pulling my weight. Just like my mother is pulling her weight. That's how it evolved."

If you ever attended a Midnight Ramble at Levon Helm Studios, the chances are pretty good that you crossed paths with Barbara O'Brien. She may have been pleasant; she may have been stern. She was, in all likelihood, on her way somewhere on the grounds, moving quickly but making time to chat with you, putting out fires along the way.

"Barbara willed herself, by God, to make shit happen and she did," said Levon Helm Band bass player and vocalist Byron Isaacs, who now performs with The Lumineers.

"Levon had a long string of managers who were percentage-ers, as he called them—15 percenters or 10 percenters. He hated the idea of a person taking a percentage. I don't know why. I think that's a pretty great idea.

"He just had too many experiences with all kinds of S.O.Bs that really turned him off from that. I think he needed a mother, quite honestly—not a mother for himself, but someone who was a mother. He understood what that was about.

"I think he had been around dudes for a long time and it was pretty disruptive. He needed someone in there who was nurturing in a certain way.

"Barbara didn't know a lick about the music industry and she made up everything that she did as she went along. Of course, every one of us around knew more than she did and we all had our opinions about what she was doing.

"She was bullheaded, because Levon had said, 'I don't give a fuck, you're the one I want doing this.' She took it very seriously, that he wanted her to do this and so she made herself do it and she figured out how to make it work. It's amazing what she did—amazing.

"If Levon was going to go the non-traditional route, he found the best person. At times, it seems, to a fault, he was resolved to going the non-traditional route. There was pride in doing it that way.

"And Barbara made amazing shit happen. Barbara assembled a great team. She saw, right away, that what he needed, mostly in the beginning, was to have someone scrape off all the parasites. There were a lot of parasites around. He had barnacles. She figured out a way to scrape off the barnacles and keep them away.

"Barbara said this, and I think this is right, Levon could be generous to a fault. He would definitely give you the shirt off his back, when he had no other shirt for himself. She felt it was her job to protect him from his own generosity. So what she was doing a lot of the time was, Levon would give somebody something and she would go take it back. Instantly, she was making a lot of enemies. That's a hard role for Barbara.

"I can't imagine anybody else having done as much as she did and lasting as long as she did. It wasn't easy building all that. It was really fucking hard. A lot of those hangers-on had to be let go. There certainly are a lot of people who feel very betrayed. The fact is, Levon wanted to cut them loose, too.

"Barbara was willing to be the villain. She felt he was getting bogged down by these parasitic characters and, if she was going to save his life, she had to drop them. She took the heat for that and she was willing to take the heat for that and that's remarkable. There aren't many people who are willing to be the villain—and she was. Who but a mother is willing to do that? That's my take on it."

Her goal was simple—help Levon get out of debt, let him keep his house and let him live his life with dignity while continuing to make music.

"Levon never wanted somebody to do the job that they were supposed to do, meaning, if he wanted an agent, he wasn't going to get someone who worked as an agent," Larry Campbell said. "If he wanted a manager, he wasn't going to get someone who worked as a manager.

"He always needed people around him that he felt he could trust and he let them do the stuff that these other professionals, in his mind, have screwed up his whole life. And that didn't work too well until Barbara.

"She had a tenacity. Some of the people Levon had around him before this would just do whatever Levon wanted, and it was not necessarily for his benefit. It was for the camaraderie. They didn't know what they were doing. Barbara had a way of doing what Levon wanted—and still making smart decisions."

As Levon thrilled the crowds by performing, Barbara established the Ramble framework, creating something of a county fair atmosphere inside the studio and outside on the grounds. Through it all, she meant business and didn't take any crap from anybody.

One night, a couple pulled up in a pickup truck about halfway through a performance. The man driving said he was a big supporter of live music in Woodstock and that he often worked as a sound engineer for musicians performing in town. He said he was glad to pay for a ticket. But was he trying to grease the wheels in hopes of getting in for free? Barbara's radar was dialed in.

Barbara, who surely had 27 other places she had to be at the moment, but just happened to be standing near the ticket booth when this guy pulled up, looked at him, said, "You support live music?" She then began clapping her hands slowly, as if to say, sarcastically, "Well, let's give this guy a big round of applause—he supports live music."

She smiled. He smiled. She let him know with a look that he wasn't getting in for free simply because he held a job that involved music. And then she told him she would go inside and check the set list to see how many songs were left, because he shouldn't pay full price for at ticket with the show underway. That happened in 2016, more than four years after Levon died, as performances continued to generate the revenue that kept the doors to Levon Helm Studios open. Barbara's loyalty to Levon remained firm, while he was alive and long after he had died.

Barbara first met Levon when he played The Getaway on Route 212 in Saugerties, not far from downtown Woodstock. The building that would later house New World Home Cooking was where the seeds for the reincarnated Band would take root. Barbara was a partner in The Getaway and a waitress.

The place had a dirt floor basement where the bands played. Dressing rooms were delineated by white sheets. And Barbara's interaction with Levon back then taught her a lot about working with celebrities.

"I've always felt a little stupid being starstruck," she said. "Even if I felt I kept my composure."

Barbara took what she learned at The Getaway and applied it when she settled in at Levon Helm Studios when the crowds started turning out, first for the Rambles and later for the road shows.

"I have to remind myself that people would cut off limbs to be in the position that we're in," Barbara said in 2008.

"And that's why I feel bad for him when people treat him like an object. Even though I know that's what's done in the industry—'Can I touch you?' 'Can I have my picture taken with you?' 'Can I have your autograph?' Then, he's no longer a human being. He's an object.

"I don't think he minds it all that much. But after years and years of people pawing at you and wanting you to sign something, I would start thinking, 'Do you like my music or do you want my signature?'

"So that's why we kind of protect him from that. He's not an object.

"If you love him, then just love him. You love his music? Buy a ticket. You love the CD? Is the music going to sound any better with his signature across the front of it? Everything he gives is raw, natural, love and respect. That's what he gives and that's what he deserves back."

Barbara said the only time she ever saw Levon grow angry was, "when we talked about the past, where he legitimately feels like he's been screwed. And even when he's pissed off about that, it's not about him entirely. It's about Richard, it's about Rick."

Barbara said she and Levon rarely disagreed.

"He's not afraid to tell me his opinion and he always encourages me to give mine. The bottom line is he calls the shots. Yeah, I've walked away a couple of times saying, 'Damn, that would have been good, but I understand why he said no.' A couple of times, I asked him to rethink a decision he made.

"Levon's favorite saying is 'Let's sleep on it.' He'll say that when it's something he doesn't want to do. I'll ask him one more time. But I'm not going to keep pushing."

Levon's needs, she said, were simple.

"He doesn't ask anybody for anything. He loves playing music. He loves acting. He wants to get paid for it. He's not looking to be a millionaire. He just wants to be able to pay his bills and have some money in his pocket. That's one thing he said to me one time—'It would be nice to reach into your damn pocket and buy someone a cup of coffee.' I made a promise to him and a promise to myself that no one ever again would take advantage of him.

"At least I know that no one can come along, like people have come along in the past, for self-serving reasons, and get a piece of him. He deserves to have it all himself. Then, if he wants to give it away, he gives it away, but it's not somebody getting a piece of it before he even gets it."

Regarding those in Levon's past, Barbara said, "I don't know why they didn't succeed. Maybe it was Levon, maybe it was them. Maybe it was timing. Maybe it just wasn't meant to be. But they didn't succeed. They succeeded to a point.

"Some people have asked me, 'Where did you get the stamina, the stick-to-itiveness?' I just think it's this stubborn Irish thing and the fact that the timing was right. Levon was ready for his life to be different, for his career to take a different path."

CHAPTER FIVE

Tony LoBue: 'He Was Who I Thought He Was'

Sometime in 2007, Levon Helm Studios Webmaster Tony LoBue received an e-mail from a Levon Helm fan who lived in Iowa.

This guy had purchased a ticket to the Midnight Ramble and was driving from Iowa to Woodstock, by himself, to see Levon perform. And like Levon, he was a cancer survivor. He lived in fear of the disease returning but found inspiration in Levon, and a sense that everything would turn out okay. He explained all of this in his e-mail to Tony and, like thousands of other people who had attended Levon's Rambles and road shows, asked if he could meet Levon.

Tony wrote back and said, "I really can't do that. We have three hundred people and everyone wants to meet Levon. I can't make you any promises. I just can't. I'm sorry."

The guy arrived at the studio after driving more than 1,100 miles. He found Tony, introduced himself and asked again if he could meet Levon.

"I said, 'I'm really sorry—Look at all these people. They all want to meet Levon. They all want to shake his hand,'" Tony recalled.

At a typical Ramble, upon the conclusion of the final song, which was usually "The Weight," Levon would rise from his drum stool and walk around to the back edge of the stage. As he made his way from the drums to the piano, he would hold up each band member's arm. Similar to the manner in which a boxing referee lifts the arm of a prize-fight winner, Levon would see to it himself that each of his band members received an individual acknowledgment from the crowd. This was how Levon ended each Ramble. The last arm he raised was typically that of Brian Mitchell at the piano. From the piano, escorted by security, Levon would head into the house.

That routine occurred hundreds of times over the eight years that Levon staged the Rambles. But on the night of the Ramble attended by the guy from Iowa, that routine had to wait a few moments.

"On that night, Levon stood up; the show was over," Tony said. "He walked along the front row, he reached back and shook this guy's hand, out of the blue," Tony said. "He knew nothing. I was like, 'What the fuck? How did that happen?' There was no contact—nothing at all. Even if the guy had waved his hand and called Levon, Levon would not have gone over. He would have waved to the guy. Levon was just drawn to him like a magnet. He reached back through two rows of people and shook his hand and I don't know how the hell that happened. That was scary."

Tony LoBue first met Levon Helm in 1994 at the Stephen Talkhouse, a music venue in Amagansett, N.Y. that sits on the eastern tip of Long Island, near Tony's home. Tony and his wife, Dawn, would see The Band whenever they played the Stephen Talkhouse, but it wasn't until a Levon Helm & the Crowmatix show that they met Levon.

"At the end of the show, Dawn grabs him and gives him a big kiss," Tony said. "And that's how he got to know us."

Added Dawn, "I went up to him and said, 'We love you, Levon.' He turned to me and said, 'Well, bless your heart.'"

From then on, Levon always recognized Tony and Dawn at shows and on occasion, during performances, would wave and point his drumstick at them.

Tony and Dawn would also see Rick Danko perform solo shows at the Stephen Talkhouse. Rick once invited Dawn up onstage to sing with him on a tune. And Tony had gotten to know George Lembesis, who worked with Rick. One night, Dawn left Tony at their table and headed to the restroom. She returned and Tony was gone. She found him running the merch table.

"George was jammed up and he asked me if I would do the merch," Tony recalled with a laugh. "I was selling shirts."

Like many, Tony's relationship with the music of The Band dated back to the release of their 1968 album, *Music From Big Pink*. But unlike a lot of people, Tony, who has played classical piano since he was a kid, was drawn to the music of The Band because of the classical influences he heard.

"When *Big Pink* first came out, they played the hell out of 'The Weight' on the radio," Tony said. "I used to hear 'The Weight' all the time. But I didn't know who it was. I don't think they knew who it was—there was no name of a band. So I finally went out and bought the album. When I listened to the whole thing, I loved, for some reason, the chord progression of 'This Wheel's On Fire.' The sound of that was very classical to me and I was into classical music. It just builds and builds and builds. And so did 'The Genetic Method.' That was classical also—and that got me. And then 'Chest Fever' after that was amazing. That caught me and I played the hell out of that album. And then I couldn't wait for the next album and the next album.

"Not many people knew of them. I would tell people, that's The Band. They wouldn't know who it was. But if I said it was the guys who used to back Bob Dylan, they would know what I was talking about. They had radio play of all their albums constantly. *Stage Fright* was always on. All the songs were always on.

"I saw them in Madison Square Garden in '74 with Dylan. I got tickets for me and my sister and her friend. As it turned out, they got sick and couldn't go. I went by myself. I scalped the two tickets and I went in. The Band came out first. I listened to 10 songs and they were done. Dylan came out and I went home. I wasn't interested. I saw what I went to see. I went to see The Band."

Three decades later, Tony was in charge of www.levonhelm.com and was managing the Rambles under the eye of Barbara O'Brien. Along with Barbara, Tony had become one of Levon's closest confidantes—and friends.

"It was like, 'Holy shit, that's the guy,'" Tony said. "That's the guy who's in those movies. That's the guy who was in *The Last Waltz*. That's the guy I was listening to when I was 16 years old. I'll never forget when he called me by name the first time. It was the biggest thing in the world to hear him say your name. And then to hear him introduce you to people: 'This is my friend Tony. This is one of my managers.' I was hoping he was who I thought he was. I wanted to like him. I wanted to respect him and I wanted him to stand up to my idea of him—and he did. He was who I thought he was."

The Midnight Ramble era, Tony said, was the happiest time of Levon's life.

"He said that right up until the time he died. He loved it. He loved having all of us around there, whether he came out to hang with you or not. It was the idea—he knew you were hanging out in that studio having fun. He'd come down to the basement and hang out with us for a while. He would hear us laughing. He'd come down for whatever reason. That clubhouse nonsense that they always talked about—that was the real deal. This was Levon's clubhouse and he wanted that. He wanted everyone to be there all the time, just hanging out and having fun."

If you were going to enter Levon Helm's world during the Midnight Ramble era, there were two ways it could be accessed.

You could drive to Woodstock and head for the ticket booth at the end of the driveway off Plochmann Lane. Or you could log onto www.levonhelm.com to buy tickets to a Ramble or road show, check Levon's performance schedule, read about the staff, peruse past set lists or look into booking recording time in the studio. And the man who conceived, created, maintained, upgraded and oversaw www.levonhelm.com, through which a lot of the revenue earned by Levon between 2004 and 2012 passed, was Tony LoBue of eastern Long Island.

In 1999, Congress passed the Anticybersquatting Consumer Protection Act, which, among other things, made it illegal to purchase the internet domain name of anyone, famous or otherwise, with the objective of holding it ransom and selling it back to that person. About two years prior, Tony had purchased and registered www.levonhelm.com to protect it for Levon.

"I secured it so no one else could, and I'd have it for a website devoted to him, or if he ever wanted it: 'Hey. I've got it—and no problem.'"

Around 2001, Tony received a call from Norman Clancy. Norman had tracked Tony down through the internet domain registry.

"He wanted to know what I was doing with it, if they could have it," Tony said of the domain name. "He said that they were thinking about doing a website, but it wasn't up to him, it was up to Levon's manager, Butch Dener. I told him, 'So many people have been calling me about this.' I didn't trust anybody. Everybody said they were connected. People wanted to buy it and I wouldn't sell it. I just thought it was another guy calling. He said, 'We're playing a show in Brooklyn. Come on down and we'll hook you all up.'"

Tony couldn't make that show. But a couple of weeks later, he got another phone call from Norman.

"Norman called me again and wanted to know what we could work out with the domain. I said I'd like to do a website. He said, 'You've got to call the manager.' I called Butch. He said, 'Come on up. I'll hook you up. You'll meet everybody.'"

So Tony and Dawn LoBue embarked on their first trip to Woodstock.

"Butch knew who we were right away. Levon recognized us immediately and we had a great time."

Levon was performing that night with the Barn Burners at the Joyous Lake in Woodstock. After the Barn Burners show, Levon invited Tony and Dawn back to the house.

"We were up until 5:00 in the morning," Tony said. "We had so much fun hanging out in Levon's house with Levon. And that basically was the end of it. We never did anything with the website."

But Levon did invite the LoBues back to his home the next morning.

"We were on cloud nine," Dawn said. "Tony and I were like, 'Should we go? Not go? We should go back and say goodbye.'"

When Tony and Dawn told Levon they had to head back home, Dawn recalled, he said, "Why do you have to leave? Stay."

But Tony and Dawn had to get back home for work. "He said, 'Damn baby, that's a shame,'" Dawn said. Levon gave Tony and Dawn his personal phone number and they went back home.

The LoBues later saw Levon perform on a blues boat that departed from Manhattan's South Street Seaport.

But years passed before Tony heard again from anyone at Levon Helm Studios. Tony still owned the domain name, as he kept re-registering it on an annual basis. Then he got a call from Nick Mancuso, whose young son, Myles, a musician, was sitting in on occasion with Levon. Like Norman Clancy, Nick Mancuso had tracked Tony down through the internet domain registry. At the time, the early incarnations of the Midnight Ramble were evolving.

"I said, 'All right, I've done this. Give me the name of who's running everything. Who's in charge?' Nick gave me Barbara O'Brien's name and her phone number at work. I waited a week or so and I called her up and introduced myself. I told her, 'I have the domain name. I'd like to do a website, if that's what you want to do. Whatever you want to do.' She invited me up there. So I took a ride up."

It was August 2004 and Levon was performing with Little Sammy Davis in the studio for the public, under the name Little Sammy Davis and the Levon Helm Blues Band. Tony met Barbara that night and saw Norman again. And, of course, he saw Levon.

"I spoke with Levon a little bit. He said, 'Where's your wife?' Those were the first words out of his mouth. I hadn't seen the guy in years. He said, 'How are you guys doing? Where's your wife?'"

Before Tony headed back to Long Island, he and Barbara made a deal.

"Someone wanted to do the website for $2,500 a month and everyone was trying to get on the bandwagon. I told Barbara, 'Look, you're trying to get the guy on his feet. You can't be paying someone $2,500 a month for a website.' I said, 'I'll do it. I'll do it for nothing.' So she started giving me some stuff. We started taking PayPal. I started doing the site, which was very limited. I started adding things to it, like the next show."

Tony came back for a Ramble on the Saturday of Thanksgiving weekend in 2004. Levon left Woodstock the next day to film scenes for the Tommy Lee Jones film, *The Three Burials of Melquiades Estrada*.

At that Ramble, Tony said, "My head was spinning. I was thinking, 'If I'm going to do the website, where am I going to get the information for this? Who's going to give me the information? Is it the right stuff? What do I put on the website? What don't I put on?' And I'm looking around—what do I take pictures of? All of these things are running through my head. And then I'm saying, 'Holy shit—this is really going to happen. I'm going to do a website for Levon.'"

Tony was in. As he worked on the website, the studio was gearing up to release *The Midnight Ramble Sessions: Volume One* on CD and DVD.

"That was the big thing. I had the cover, I had the picture, I had the set list. I put it on the website—'Coming soon.' I'll never forget it. We're going to start taking internet orders for the CD—now this is for a CD we don't even have. All we have is the cover. It hasn't been mastered. It hasn't been pressed. It hasn't been anything. We need the money to do it. And in those days, anything went. I'll never forget, Norman said to me, 'All the money's going through your website, so keep in touch with me.'"

To promote *The Midnight Ramble Sessions*, Levon and the band appeared on the Don Imus show on the day it went on sale. The night before, Norman called Tony.

"He called me about eleven o'clock. I had to take the day off of work the next day because I was so afraid the website would screw up. Norman says, 'Remember one thing—this is all up to you; if anything goes wrong, it's your fault.' He was dead serious. He laid that on me the night before Imus."

The next day arrived and a couple thousand copies were sold through the website.

"Norman kept calling me every five minutes—'How many did you sell? How many did you sell?' My head was ready to explode. The stress was like being a flight-control operator. I was so afraid that if the website went down, Levon Helm's going to be pissed off at me. These were the things running through my head. It was very frightening. But it was a lot of fun. As it turned out, they did the album, got all the CDs out and that was that."

In 2005, Levon Helm Studios hosted a pay-per-view webcast of a live performance. And once again, Tony was in the middle of everything.

"I can't tell you the amount of hours it took to get that to work, with this company in California," he said. "The signal would go from my computer to this company in Michigan; they would take it and send it to a repeater in California; and then from there, it would come to your computer. We hardly sold any tickets. We had monitors set up. It was raining in the studio. The roof was leaking."

Rain leaking through the roof of Levon Helm Studios, in the early days of the Midnight Ramble, was not an isolated event.

"For years, he was playing the drums and behind him, he had a garbage can with the water dripping in," Tony said. "We couldn't afford to put a roof on at that time. There was no heat."

At the time Tony became involved, Levon's finances teetered precariously on a cliff.

"This was a last chance—and it had to happen," he said. "And I always remember saying that this has got to happen, because I don't want to be one of those guys on VH1, telling the story of how we put him out of business. The drive was always there and of course the ringleader of the drive was always Barbara—always pushing and pushing. You had on your head that, 'Yeah, I love this guy, but now we have to make it happen for him.' That's why he wants us there. And we told him we can do this. So now he's relying on us.

"The pressure was enormous. Are we going to get the mortgage? Are we not going to get the mortgage? Are we going to sell tickets for a show? Are we going to make money on the show? All these things—it was a constant pressure, in the beginning, of the money. Every time you thought you were ahead and you were starting to get towards something, an IRS bill showed up; or somebody showed up and said, 'He owes me $50,000.' It never stopped. It never ended. And finally, they got the mortgage. Frank Flynn, Levon's accountant, managed to get him a refinanced mortgage, with much better terms. Mike Pinsky, Levon's attorney, handled the closing. The weight was lifted. There were a few times he came close to losing the place. We were using money from the Ramble before we even had the show. The money was gone toward bills and getting the shows together, making payments. There were car payments, there were mortgage payments, and everything was months and years behind. It was just a tremendous amount of pressure to get this thing to happen. And the next thing you know, it started happening. We started selling tickets and things were going good."

Incidentally, Levon's new mortgage was approved on September 12, 2008. That was the Friday before the Monday of September 15, 2008, the day upon which Lehman Brothers filed for bankruptcy. Frank Flynn said Levon took special pride in the fact that the mortgage was not pulled in the midst of that dire, global, financial turmoil.

"What made this bankruptcy different," the U.S. Treasury Department said of Lehman Brothers, "is how extremely disorderly and destructive it was, sending shockwaves around the world's financial markets, driving other financial firms to within inches of collapse, and plunging the economy into the Great Recession, which hurt millions of people and businesses."

On Dec. 3, 2005, Emmylou Harris came to Woodstock to join Levon at the Midnight Ramble.

Emmylou appeared in *The Last Waltz*, performing a duet with Levon on the song "Evangeline." And she arrived at Levon Helm Studios at the invitation of Larry Campbell, who mentioned the Rambles to her when the two musicians were playing duo shows in New York City. Emmylou as luck would have it was headed to nearby Kingston to record, so performing at Levon's worked out perfectly.

"The explosion of blues had yet to start ricocheting off the walls of Levon Helm's Woodstock recording studio," read the review in the *Poughkeepsie Journal* of that night Emmylou came to Woodstock. "The Persian rugs on the floor and the attention of hundreds belonged for now to the woman who talked like the Alabama girl she was, but who emanated an air of royalty as though a monarch from some far-off land. She wore no tiara, but stood nonetheless in sparkling light, as the Saturday night spotlights of rock 'n' roll danced on her beaded guitar strap.

"If Elvis Presley is the king, then Emmylou Harris is the queen. Harris did not simply thrill those who turned out to see her Saturday at Helm's Ramble. She left them stunned…She was so quiet and still during her song 'Red Dirt Girl,' that the audience seemed to have stopped breathing, fearful they might miss one note of singing."

That night that Emmylou Harris played the Ramble, well, you just had to be there is all anyone could probably ever say about it. Everything changed for the Midnight Ramble that night, Tony said.

"Larry got Emmylou Harris to come up. That did it. Without a doubt, that's when the ticket sales started to just flip. At that time, we would put up a show, the tickets would be gone in a day. Most people didn't know about the Ramble. Afterward, people were saying, 'Wow, Levon Helm, he's got this thing going on in his house.' That was another mysterious thing that people couldn't figure out: 'What do you mean—it's his house?' Nobody knew. We were doing one every month or two. Before Emmylou came up, Levon said, 'I think we ought to do one a month.' And I'm saying, 'Jeez, I'll have to come up once a month; that's not too bad.' Then that started selling out. He said, 'I think we ought to do them every other week.' I said, 'Jeez. I have to come up here twice a month? All right, we'll figure something out.' Then that went along. We started selling them out. The next thing we know, Levon says, 'You know, we gotta do this every goddamn Saturday night.' He said, 'This is going to be a regular thing on Saturday nights.'

"Norman, at that point, came to me and he said, 'Let's get the calendar and just mark off every other weekend; we'll put up a show.' I said, 'How do we know people are available?' He said, 'It doesn't matter. We'll get people. Levon knows everybody.' I listed 24 shows and they all sold out. We had a band, but we didn't know their availability—and Norman didn't care. He said, 'We gotta do this. Between Larry Campbell and Jimmy Vivino, they'll get people to fill in. They'll fill in for each other.' The next thing you know, okay, June is all sold; okay, July is all sold. August is sold. Next thing you know, the whole entire year is sold out. Within three months of Emmylou being there, the show was sold out for an entire year.

"Then more and more people started coming up. Jimmy got his friends to start going to shows. Elvis Costello was very close after that. Larry started bringing people he knew in the business up there. And the next thing you know, it was a hell of a show. And it went on like that. It went on like that from, I would say, '06 to the time he died in 2012. If they weren't doing a show on the road, they were doing a show at the studio. It was every single Saturday night. That was it—done."

The night that Emmylou performed at the Midnight Ramble was big. So was the first night the Levon Helm Band performed at the Beacon Theatre in New York City. That show took place on March 16, 2007, in the midst of a colossal snowstorm.

"To me, if you make a movie of his life story, you end the movie with the Beacon," Tony said. "That said it all. When Jim Glancy of The Bowery Presents got to Barbara and said he wanted to do a show at the Beacon, Levon said, 'There's no way we can sell those kind of tickets.' He said, 'You're going to need other people. There's no way I can do that.' Plus, he hadn't been playing at big places yet since his voice came back. We told him, 'Glancy is good. This guy did his homework.' Glancy knew just what he was doing. He did his homework and he knew Levon could sell those tickets.

"Levon was not sure and he would not give an answer, he just would not. I remember one night, it had to be four or five o'clock in the morning after a Ramble. Me, him and Barbara were sitting at the kitchen table and she's trying to get a 'yes' out of him so she can tell Glancy, and he just wouldn't commit. Finally, Barbara says, 'Levon, do you think you're not going to be able to sell tickets?' He just put his head down and he nodded. Barbara said, 'No. This is going to sell. We're going to sell this out. It's going to be okay. You've got to trust us, and you've got to trust Glancy, and you've got to trust the whole thing. It's going to work.' And I said, 'Glancy—this is his business. He's not going to invest his money unless he knows this is going to work. He's comfortable with this. If he is, you should be too.'

"Barbara asked him for a firm commitment and he said okay. She popped up. I don't know where she went. Levon and I were just talking. I don't remember about what. She came back and said, 'Good night. I'm tired. We've got to go.' She had run right downstairs and at four o'clock sent Jim Glancy an email saying, 'We're doing it.' That's it—now there's no backing out. You're signed. You're committed—that's it."

And then came the day that the tickets went on sale.

"They went on sale at nine o'clock in the morning," Tony said. "I'm home that day. This was his first big show. And to me, this was like, 'Oh my God. This is the big time, working on something like this—the Beacon.' Then I get an e-mail from someone: 'I can't buy tickets. The website isn't working.'"

Tony thinks for sure the Ticketmaster website is down. And then he receives a phone call from Levon Helm Studios office manager Geanine Kane.

"Geanine calls me—'People are screaming. They can't get tickets.' So I'm thinking, this is great—this guy's first big show and Ticketmaster isn't working. I called Ticketmaster, I finally get ahold of somebody. I identify myself. I tell him who I am and I'm off the wall with this guy. I tell him I can't believe the website doesn't work. The guy says, 'You don't understand. It sold out. It sold out in 15 minutes.' I say, 'Okay, thank you.' I call Geanine—Geanine's screaming. She runs up to tell Levon the show sold out in 15 minutes. Imus is telling everybody the show sold out in 15 minutes. Imus didn't stop. He pumped the hell out of it, constantly, every morning. He was our only outside source. We couldn't afford advertising. All we could do was advertise through our website.

"Then I got an email—Jim Glancy couldn't get ahold of Barbara. She was flying back from Florida. Glancy copies me on the e-mail. He wants to know if Levon will do another show on the night before, on the Friday night. I call Levon. He says, 'Hell, yeah!' He was all excited. I said, 'All right. I don't want to e-mail Glancy. Let's wait an hour. Barbara will be back from Florida. She can make the deal with Glancy.' Now, I'm e-mailing Barbara. By the time I got to her, she had already gotten back to Glancy.

"The second show sold out in about a day and a half. That's six thousand seats he filled, for the first time, out of the gate, since he was with The Band."

CHAPTER SIX

Justin Guip

A Pennsylvania native and recording engineer who relocated from Manhattan to the Hudson Valley after the Sept. 11 terrorist attacks, Justin Guip one day in 2004 found himself at Bearsville Studios in Woodstock. He was touring the historic sound facility with an eye toward launching his own recording studio there.

While looking the site over and plotting his next move, Justin ran into videographer Chase Pierson, who was editing footage he had shot across town at Levon Helm Studios. Chase told Justin that Levon was looking for a new recording engineer.

"I called Geanine, I sent over a resume, got a call back immediately and was asked to come over," said Justin, who in addition to being a sound engineer is a drummer. "I took one look at the place and said, 'Wow.' I really admired the architecture and immediately recognized the sonics."

Justin knew Levon had been ill, but, he said, "I didn't know the extent of everything that was going on and the situation at The Barn. I was picking that up when I got there. Brendan filled me in. I was excited to meet Levon because I was a Band fan growing up, and a fan of his drumming."

Justin got the gig as chief engineer at Levon Helm Studios and would go on to win three Grammys. The guy who never received any formal training in a recording studio also ran the sound during the Midnight Rambles and road shows. And he sat in regularly on drums at both, when Levon played mandolin.

"Being a drummer, I learned a lot from him," Justin said. "Just learning how to play for the song, playing for the pocket with minimal drum fills. That was validating and a very big inspiration."

Levon was still getting back on his feet when Justin first arrived for his new job on Plochmann Lane. At the time, the studio as a recording facility lacked organization and needed work.

"I really wanted to make the place look nice and look like a home and look inviting," he said. "I brought in lighting, I brought in carpets. I brought in chairs. I was hanging art. I brought in all of my acoustic treatments and recording equipment. I started organizing, cataloging the instruments. I started going into the vaults and seeing what was there and what had not been released. It was my goal to put that place on the map as a recording studio proper, as Levon had intended. There was always the goal of thinking ahead and making it bigger and better.

"During the week, I would come in and test stuff with Brendan. As we'd get a little money, we'd buy new speakers and microphones, constantly try to build it up and move forward. I remember thinking, 'Wow, this is going to be really cool.' I was not only excited for putting on the shows and being able to record all the shows, but also being able to make records there, open it up to the world for anybody to come and make a record in that room, because that room is special and it just sounded amazing."

At the same time, the operation as a whole was pushing ahead. A new roof had been put on the building and a massive beam inside the studio was moved to improve sight lines.

And Levon Helm Studios is where Justin met a certain multi-instrumentalist whose impact on this whole scene would be a game-changer.

"Meeting Larry was really special," Justin said.

Justin Guip and Larry Campbell would go on to form a musical team that triggered a major pivot at Levon Helm Studios. With Larry producing, Justin engineering and, of course, everything revolving around Levon, those three Grammy Awards would be handed out for *Dirt Farmer*, with Amy Helm co-producing; *Electric Dirt*; and *Ramble At The Ryman*.

Justin and Larry would also bring other bands into the studio for recording projects, most notably Jorma Kaukonen, of Jefferson Airplane and

Hot Tuna fame, for his 2009 album, *River of Time*; and Hot Tuna for their 2011 album, *Steady As She Goes*.

———•———

Justin Guip grew up in Sewickly, Pennsylvania, which sits on the Ohio River, about 15 miles northwest of Pittsburgh.

He played in bands as a teenager and, "I grew up listening to Levon," he said. Set list staples back then included Band songs like "The Weight" and "Up On Cripple Creek." After graduating from high school, Justin studied music at the University of Maine for a year while playing in a band with a repertoire of original songs.

While at the University of Maine, he met an agent from Burlington, Vermont, who was putting together a cover band to tour the East Coast. Justin moved to Burlington and joined up with that band to earn cash while gaining as much experience playing live music as possible.

He also immersed himself in the local music scene. It was the late 1980s and this city on Lake Champlain was the stomping ground for a band that would achieve great fame. Justin recalled seeing Phish play on their home turf of Nectar's, a bar on Main Street in Burlington, long before this ensemble played places like Madison Square Garden, Fenway Park and Wrigley Field.

While in Burlington, Justin joined another band, that was playing originals. That ensemble ended up moving to Boston to make a record with a producer, in hopes of securing a record deal. Justin was then off to New York City, where he played in a band called 700 miles that landed a record deal with RCA. 700 Miles later folded and while continuing to nurture his love for drumming and live performance, Justin expanded his musical focus to include sound engineering.

"Growing up, I was always fascinated with the process of making records," he said. "When I was in bands and in the studio, I was fascinated with being in the studio; being in recording sessions, watching and learning the trade. Then I purchased my own recording equipment and set it up in our rehearsal space to teach myself the process."

Justin took a job at Sterling Sound, the New York City mastering studio. He also worked nights, doing live sound at Brownie's, a club in the East Village. Touring gigs as a front of house sound engineer also came along and Justin was eventually hired as director of operations at Sterling.

He moved north to Dutchess County and was commuting into New York City for his job at Sterling Sound. Then 9/11 came, he was laid off and he settled in the Hudson Valley permanently. Once settled in at Levon's, Justin starting ramping things up.

He thought at the time, "With the combination of my equipment and what they had and a lot of elbow grease, I could make great records there."

And along with becoming chief engineer at Levon Helm Studios, Justin ran the production and technical side of the Rambles.

"Nobody was really doing that at the time, having a big house party," he said. "It was so intimate. You could come see a band and sit in the band's lap and see the count-offs and the false starts and the fuck-ups. You could see how everybody interacted with each other. You could almost be a part of the performance. You were there."

Among Justin's favorite Rambles was the night in February 2006 when Elvis Costello and Allen Toussaint joined in.

"I just remember everything really clicking right," he said.

There was the Black Crowes residency in February 2009, the "Cabin Fever" run of shows performed in front of an audience and recorded for the band's album, "Before the Frost...After the Freeze." And Billy Bob Thornton rolling into town always generated something special, Justin said.

"Whenever Steve Earle would show up was just always amazing," Justin said of the singer-songwriter whose song, "The Mountain," was featured on *Dirt Farmer*. Steve's Ramble and road show performances of his song, "This City," with a horn riff that Levon particularly enjoyed, was also a favorite.

"There were so many—Ricky Skaggs, Los Lobos, having Mumford & Sons there, when we started getting all of these big openers, that was really special," Justin said. "It started getting so popular, we got all these A-listers for the openers and the collaborations would happen. It was pretty insane. This is what Levon always wanted and intended.'"

———

But with all the achievements and accomplishments, the A-listers and openers, the recording of *Dirt Farmer* will always stand out when anyone looks back at Levon's Midnight Ramble era.

"Lee's voice was really strong," Justin said. "He was on top of his game. His health was back. His voice was back and it was just brutally honest. It was Levon. It was a comeback for him. It was just really raw and honest and that's why I think it hit so many people."

But, he admitted, "It was a challenge for me. How do you make Levon Helm's comeback record sound? You can make records sound so many different ways with production. But we wanted to keep it as natural as possible and that hit a home run because it translated. You could hear Levon's feel."

Speaking of Levon, Amy Helm and Levon Helm Band member Teresa Williams, who is married to Larry Campbell, Justin said, "You could hear his voice in such detail and the way Larry had arranged the layering of the instruments—pump organs, mandolins, Teresa and Amy on the harmonies, the piano—it was just brutally honest and real."

After passing his audition to mix the sound for *Dirt Farmer,* and beating out other engineers considered for the slot, Justin got to work.

Justin said his work on *Dirt Farmer* revolved around him, "Always thinking ahead. It was being Levon's right-hand man, where he didn't have to think about the drums, all he had to do was think about playing them. From having a great headphone mix always ready to having a fire going to the wood being stacked, just being there and present and being an assistant to everybody as well as being the recording engineer; and just making sure everything was being captured as good as it could be and as clean and pure as possible. That was the goal—trying to present something really honest and true. Larry knew what he wanted to hear. We assembled the right team. This was around the time people started making records in their homes and we were proud this was made at Levon's. We had the luxury of just turning the lights on and the power on and setting up to record. I always made it that we were ready to go and it was comfortable and shit worked."

Beyond the recording and the Rambles and the mechanics of operating a studio and playing in a band, there was plenty in play between Justin Guip and Levon Helm, on the personal side.

"One of his greatest pieces of advice was, 'Kill them with kindness,'" Justin said. "'When in doubt, you can't go wrong if you kill them with kindness.' I will always cherish that."

Very often, Justin would stack firewood inside the house each morning, and set the fire in place so it would be waiting for Levon when he emerged for the day, and all he had to do was light a match to ignite the blaze.

"After he stoked the coals, that's when we would sit and talk in front of the fire, inside the house," Justin said. "I'd tell him what was happening during the week. I could fill him in with what was going on with the Rambles, recording sessions, my family. I could open up to him. He became family. He was so good with my kids.

"He was a huge influence musically, but also being there soulfully for me and being there as a brother, that's what was really special. I have all those times we were looking at books on architecture, talking dogs, making ham sandwiches and walking around the property, pulling weeds down by the pond and talking about the outdoor shows we wanted to throw at the studio, just always talking about what we wanted to do next and how I was able to tell him, 'This is what I'm thinking of doing, what do you think if we do this and that?' There were all those special moments that I got to share besides sharing the stage with him and recording him and being involved in the production. There was the whole outside element of that, of just having a really good friend."

Asked about that which made Levon tick, Justin replied, "Playing music—he loved when it came easily; in the studio, when the playback was sounding good, we were getting good takes, he was on his game, we were on our game. We were building something. He liked building. He always liked doing renovations to The Barn. He liked when we were being successful and he liked helping other people and making other people successful; when the music was flowing, we were accumulating tracks, a record was happening. The minute a stick got in the spokes, things got complicated. But when the wheel's rolling, man, he was happy.

"He loved it when there was wood in the fireplace. He loved the fact that there were bands next door in his studio, that he built, making music, because that's what he wanted. He loved the fact that he had everyone coming to his house, hosting all his friends at the kitchen table after the Rambles. That's what made him tick, the fact that all his old musical friends were coming up to his house to perform at the Rambles, and it was paying the bills."

CHAPTER SEVEN

Larry Campbell

The first time Larry Campbell saw The Band play was in 1968, when they backed Bob Dylan at a Woody Guthrie tribute concert at Carnegie Hall.

He went with one of his friends, Bob Thiele Jr. Bob was the son of Bob Thiele, the record producer who co-wrote "What A Wonderful World," the song made famous by Louis Armstrong.

"I didn't know anything about the guy," Larry said of Bob Thiele Sr. "His son played drums. I played guitar. His father, I came to find out, was a well-respected producer, especially in the blues and jazz worlds. Bob's father used to get us into all these great musical things. We used to go to The Fillmore all the time."

One of those great musical things was the 1968 Woody Guthrie tribute concert. According to the Woody Guthrie Archives, that 1968 Carnegie Hall concert was the first time Dylan had performed after his infamous motorcycle accident in 1966.

"Tom Paxton and Arlo and all these great folk singers, they all came out and did their thing," Larry continued. "Each one's playing solo and it was just great, it was just fabulous.

"Then Bob comes out and he's got this band behind him and he just blew the roof off the place. They did 'Grand Coulee Dam' and 'I Ain't Got No Home.' I didn't know who they were, what they were called, they were just the guys backing up Bob. And soon after that, I go over to Bobby Thiele's house and he's got this record, *Music From Big Pink,* and he said, 'These are the guys who were backing up Dylan.' We completely absorbed that record."

And Larry's reaction to the album?

"I thought it was weird," he laughed. "I thought it was completely weird. It was just odd. Everything I was listening to at the time was groups like Moby Grape and Jefferson Airplane and the Grateful Dead and these easily-identifiable rock and roll bands. These arrangements and these songs on that *Big Pink* record were something I had never heard before. But it was completely compelling, even though I didn't know what to make of it. There was some sort of subliminal honesty about what I was hearing. I couldn't stop listening to it. I didn't know that I liked it, but I knew it was moving me—and, to me, that makes a good record. If it moves you, then it's great music. But it was so unique and original at the time, I didn't know how to absorb it — and I didn't become a real fan of those guys until years later.

"The first thing for me was The Beatles, like everybody else, then the Rolling Stones, Bob Dylan and all these San Francisco bands and all this great late-sixties creative stuff that was going on. Right around the time I saw The Band, I was starting to become fascinated with the roots guys, the old blues guys, back to Hank Williams, Rev. Gary Davis—he changed my life—and all these American roots guys, back to Jimmie Rodgers and the blues guys, Blind Blake, Robert Johnson, and the country guys, Riley Puckett.

"When I was listening to The Band—and I felt this more when I was listening to *The Brown Album*—I was hearing this thing that these guys were doing that was really cool. But I was more interested in the roots of where it came from. That's more of what I was fascinated with. I initially felt that this record was the rest of them taking all these roots genres and styles and making this new thing out of it, which was something that really intrigued me. Through their whole career, you can't deny the honesty in that music — the way the songs were written and arranged and the way they were performed."

The next time Larry saw The Band was June 30, 1971, when they performed at Wollman Skating Rink in Central Park, as part of the Schaefer Music Festival. The opening act, interestingly enough, was Happy Traum and his brother, Artie, from Woodstock.

"I was completely enthralled," Larry said. "But I was almost afraid of these guys because they were making music that I felt I hadn't gotten to yet as a musician, and they made something out of the stuff that I was fascinated with, that was their own. I almost didn't want to be influenced by them. I wanted that opportunity to make something out of the stuff I was fascinated with that would be my own.

"When I felt I had broadened myself as a musician sufficiently, I'd go back and listen to this stuff and, even now, I'm more into these guys than I've ever been. At the time Levon and I hooked up, it was perfect timing for me to really appreciate what he had contributed to those guys and what those guys had contributed to music in general."

Levon left a very big impact.

"People have said he was the heart and soul of that group, which is not to diminish the contributions of anybody else, but Levon brought the dirt on the boots; the soil; he was the fertile soil that all this stuff grew out of," Larry said. "His drumming alone is completely unique. I don't know that I've ever played with anybody with a deeper pocket, a deeper groove, but in a carefree way. There are drummers that are just right in there and really tight and precise and that's its own thing, too. That wasn't Levon. But what he could make you feel when he was playing those drums is this kind of loose and grooving feeling that was completely unique to him. You can't overstate the value of Levon's drumming in The Band.

"And you listen to that voice—it embodies everything that comes out of that Delta region of this country. The history of America is in the sound of that voice. You hear the Civil War. You hear the Southern churches. You hear the docks of New Orleans. You hear the riverboats on the Mississippi and you hear the blues joints in Memphis. You hear all that in that voice. And though Richard was an incredible singer in his own right and Rick had his own way, Rick had a very unique voice, Levon's voice in that band—it was America."

Part of The Band's legacy is the bitterness with which Levon looked back on his relationship with Robertson, a bitterness driven by, according to Levon, the manner in which Robertson claimed songwriting credits and ended up with the royalties they generate.

"I only know Levon's side of the story about the composition of the songs in that band and I don't know Robbie," Larry said. "I've met him, but I don't know him, and I haven't heard his side of the story, so I can't weigh in on that. But I do know, when you listen to these songs, that Levon's influence—in whatever capacity—is undeniable. It's just undeniable. The characters in 'The Weight'—Anna Lee, Crazy Chester—these were people from Levon's past. Whether he sat there and fed Robbie ideas, I don't know. I know from my experience of writing with Levon, he wasn't gonna do much labor. If it comes to putting a pen to paper, it wasn't going to happen with him. But that song, 'The Growing Trade,' I had written the tune and brought it to him. I said, 'I want to improve this a little bit.' We sat there for a couple of hours and just talked about the subject matter."

"The Growing Trade" appeared on Levon's 2010 CD, *Electric Dirt*.

"I had known in Tennessee, where Teresa is from, there are these old farmers who couldn't be farmers anymore and were about to lose their land because the corporations were only using the big farms. You couldn't keep a small farm and make a living and this farm that had been their responsibility, their family—the farm is as much a part of you as a family member—some of these old guys who were dyed-in-the-wool, fundamental Christians, right wing, America-Red-State guys were deciding to grow reefer, because on the amount of land they had, this was the only way they could make a profit. And they would rather do that than lose the farm, on a moral level.

"Levon and I talked about it, back and forth. I went back and rewrote the song. He may have given me one line. We were talking about the cotton fields. He said, 'You look at that in the spring and it's like a view from heaven's door.' His perspective on the whole thing, the guy who comes from that—I rewrote the song and it's a much better song now than what it was. My understanding of the subject matter was deeper from my kicking this around with him, so it's half his song as far as I'm concerned. The labor was all on me, but it wouldn't be the song it is if it hadn't been for that collaboration. So I have to assume that something similar transpired with those guys. You could hear and see and feel and almost smell his influence on that material from The Band. I feel like, if he hadn't shut things down, he could have found a way to resolve this bitterness. I wish he had done it, I really do. But that's a part of his life that I wasn't part of."

Twenty-nine years after seeing Bob Dylan perform for the first time, during that Woody Guthrie tribute concert at Carnegie Hall, Larry Campbell found himself performing with Dylan as a member of the legendary songwriter's band.

Larry joined Dylan's band in 1997. He landed the gig through his friend, Tony Garnier, Dylan's bass player, and parted ways with Dylan in 2004.

"I remember when I left Bob's band I was in a pretty dark place," Larry said. "That's a big ship to jump off of and I wasn't real sure where I would end up. My plan was to get more into producing. During my run with Bob, production opportunities would come up that I would try to schedule for off-times and then find out we were going back out on the road. I'm most comfortable in the studio, but still, I was looking for that elusive live experience that was just about the joy of making music and where I felt creatively involved. With Bob, we could make creative contributions, but understandably, we had to stay within the parameters that were set by the fact that these were his songs and ultimately, they should be presented the way he wanted them to be."

After leaving Dylan's band, Larry was invited to sit in with Levon and Jimmy Vivino at that B.B. King's Club show with Hubert Sumlin. And that gig represented yet another instance over the years when Larry and Levon crossed paths.

"I met Levon casually a couple of times in the mid-eighties," Larry said. "It was years until I saw him again."

The first time Larry met Levon, Rick, Richard and Garth was at the Lone Star Café in Manhattan.

"I played there regularly," he said. "I was there every week with somebody. Bands would come in from out of town, local bands would be the opening act. I played there with Buddy Miller; every Sunday with Kinky Friedman; or sometimes I'd be hired as a ringer to play with whoever was in town. That's how I hooked up with Doug Sahm. I think it was with Kinky, one of the Sundays, The Band had played on a Saturday night, they were hanging around. Kinky introduced me to Rick, Richard and Levon."

And Larry had been coming up to Ulster County since 1978.

"I was also spending time in Woodstock, playing in John Herald's band," he said. "That's how I met Happy and Artie. Every once in a while, some recording project at Levon's studio would come up. The next time we hooked up was when I was playing with Bob, after Levon lost his voice and was playing with the Barn Burners. Butch Dener was a friend of Tony Garnier's and came to see me with Bob. He asked me to sit in with Levon. I thought it was a great idea.

"Then this thing came up, while I was with Bob, doing the *Love and Theft* record. I get a call from this guy named Jerry Klause, who has a record company, Treasure Records. He wanted me to play on this musician's record, a woman named Patty Blee. We did this project. Soon after, he got this idea to do a record that I should produce—a record for the Dixie Hummingbirds 75th anniversary. He said, 'Wouldn't it be great to get Levon and Garth to play on this record?' I got in touch with Butch, who got in touch with Levon, and Levon said, 'yes.' That's where Levon and I really gelled musically, on this Dixie Hummingbird project. This was 2002. The record was released in 2003. We did that record and Levon loved that record."

Following Larry's departure from Dylan's band in 2004, he received a phone call from Levon.

"So I hear you're free," Larry recalled Levon saying. "Well, come on up to Woodstock. Let's make some music."

Larry played his first Ramble in early 2005.

"This first Ramble I did with Levon was crude in form, kind of embryonic for what it would become, but it was nothing but joy," he said. "It was just, 'Come on, man, let's play and have a good time.' I came up to that first Ramble. It was completely disorganized. The place was kind of a wreck. There were a lot of bare walls. It was cold in there."

But, Larry said, the music "was so much fun, from the first note until the end of the night, just playing music and having a good time. It was Sammy singing at the time. I don't even know that Levon sang at that first Ramble. It was Jimmy Vivino and Mike Merritt and me. Brian may have been there, and Erik and Steven.

"And they said, 'Can you come back next week and do it again?' They had a definite date. And I said, 'Yeah, I'll be there.' That first Ramble just completely energized me. I pretty quickly became a regular member of this thing and Levon wanted me there as bandleader with Jimmy because he knew Jimmy couldn't be there all the time.

"We did real well together, sort of splitting that role. And these Rambles, every week they grew. They became more diverse—'Well let's try this' and 'Let's try this' and Levon started singing. And then Amy brought Teresa in."

Around the time of that first Ramble, Amy called Larry and asked him about producing a record for Ollabelle, the "roots collective" as Amy describes it, the band of which she was a member. Ollabelle also included bass player Byron Isaacs, keyboard player Glenn Patscha, drummer Tony Leone and vocalist and guitarist Fiona McBain.

Larry took the gig and the result was *Riverside Battle Songs*, which was released on Verve Records in 2006.

"And that was a great experience," Larry said. "I got to know those guys and it was a great musical relationship. Those guys had this little bar on the Lower East Side where they would go and play, this tiny, little hole in the wall across from where Glenn lived on 5th Street. Glenn and Tony and Byron would go in there and just play for the fun of it. Toward the end of my run with Bob, Teresa and I started working on singing together, because we loved to do it. So Glenn or Byron asked me to come down and play. I brought Teresa. I said, 'Maybe we'll sing some songs.' That was where Amy and Teresa first met.

"And then we did this gig with Cindy Cashdollar—Amy, Teresa, me and Cindy. Amy and Teresa started working on songs together and there was this incredible thing going on between the two of them. Their voices, together, they're like two pieces of Velcro. They just sort of stick together like that. So Amy and Teresa developed this relationship together, personally and musically. We're still doing Rambles—this is before Teresa comes up—and Amy gets the idea that I should come up to Woodstock, sit around with Levon and her, and play some tunes and record them and see what happens. And the idea was to get at the roots of who Levon was. There was no real material agenda, except Amy and Levon had been singing these songs that he knew as a kid. Amy thought that was a good place to start. I came up. The first tune we did, I think, was 'Blind Child,' and it was just great. And then Amy said, 'Why don't you bring Teresa with you and we'll see if we can do some backgrounds together or sing with Levon.' So Teresa came up with me the next time we got together that way and it was magic. Amy would sort of complement the soul side of Levon and Teresa would complement the country side of Levon, and all together, it was this beautiful thing.

"After we did these initial recordings with Levon, Levon said to Teresa, 'You've got to come up and play the Ramble with us.' So Teresa quickly became a member of that.

"I kind of had to pinch myself. I'm playing with this guy who I have nothing but admiration for, playing music that completely stimulates me in every way, and every time we do it there is something new and exciting happening.

"It's nothing but joy and I've got my wife right next to me. All I wanted to do those last few years with Bob was spend more time with her. She was doing her thing, I was doing my thing, it was rare that we had an opportunity to be together, let alone perform together. Here is this situation where everything I wanted in life is starting to happen—and the whole family aspect of this whole thing was alluring to me. It felt like family. Here's Levon and his daughter, here's me and my wife; everyone around us, it felt like one big family. And we all have this center, which is this commonality of this thing we all love to do. I looked forward to every one of these Rambles. This was the first time I ever had a gig like this in my life.

"I couldn't wait to do the next show and when it was over, I felt like a million bucks—and that's every Ramble we ever did, every show we ever did. There was never a night in this thing where I felt like I wanted to be somewhere else. There was nowhere else I wanted to be."

And while these relationships were unfolding, the *Dirt Farmer* CD began to emerge.

"We took our time with *Dirt Farmer*," Larry said. "The beauty of it was, no one was paying studio time, no one was looking for money up front. We're just having a good time playing music—if something comes of it, great; if not, we're enjoying every moment of it. As this record was starting to gel, I was starting to think, 'There is something really heavy going on here.' It just all started adding up to me—Levon's rising from the ashes. And not only that, it's a rebirth. But it's a rebirth back to where he came from. And the stuff had that honesty element in there.

"*Dirt Farmer* was Levon's journey from this great thing he had with those four other guys to where it just got dark and uncentered and he sort of lost himself for a few years. There was a time when you'd say his name, and 'Oh yeah, Levon.' And now it was this point in his life where there was complete equilibrium inside him and all around him. He appreciated the fact that he was alive. He appreciated the fact that he had his daughter, Amy. He just loved the fact that they were making music together. People who really knew and respected him surrounded him. So all this stuff was gelling. We're about three-quarters through the *Dirt Farmer* record and I realized there was something magical going on here."

Sometime prior to all of this, Larry had performed on television a couple of times with Dolly Parton and he struck up a relationship with her road manager, Steve Buckingham, who went on to take a job with Vanguard Records.

"He called and asked if I was involved with anything interesting lately," Larry recalled. "I said, 'As a matter of fact, we're way down the road with this record with Levon.' And his ears perked up. He said, 'When you get it to a point where it's ready to listen to, let me know.'"

A meeting with Amy, Larry and Steve followed.

"We got him the roughs when we were at a point when we thought they could be heard and he was all over it. He flipped. So we cut a deal with Vanguard. I remember telling Amy, 'We're going to win a Grammy with this record.'"

In addition to playing with Levon, Larry performed with Phil Lesh of the Grateful Dead, as a member of Phil Lesh & Friends.

"Whenever I'd talk about the fact that I was working with Levon, I could sense the interest from Phil and others," Larry said. "It was kind of a perfect timing. He had been under the radar for so long. The fact that he was singing again, that he had this project going, had a lot of people interested."

And then *Dirt Farmer* was finished.

"I knew the value of it, but that doesn't mean it would count for anything out in the real world," Larry said. "My taste in music and what's great music doesn't always correspond with what sells."

Larry laughs.

"But there it was. We put it out. And you know, Levon never liked to let anything go. He kept saying, 'We've got to redo that song; we've got to remix this.' He drove Justin and me crazy. I don't know, but I surmise it was because once you let it out there, then you're subjecting it to opinions. As long as you have it in your little world, then it's yours to do whatever you want with."

But in the end, Larry said, "*Dirt Farmer* blew up. It just created all this buzz and interest and excitement. And then—we win a Grammy."

CHAPTER EIGHT

The Midnight Ramble

Each Midnight Ramble began with a few words of welcome and warning from Barbara.

"Welcome," she would say, "to Levon Helm Studios, home of the Midnight Ramble."

Barbara always drove home the point that everyone was in Levon's home. She asked everyone to give the space the respect it deserved, while enjoying themselves.

"There's a bathroom in that loft, there's a bathroom in that loft," she would say, pointing here and there, upstairs. "And please be careful—it's rocky and hilly outside. Remember, you're in Woodstock. We don't want to have to light this place up like it's Madison Square Garden."

Inside the house, that portion of The Barn where Levon and Sandy lived, the musicians were gearing up to perform.

"First thing on a Ramble night, Jimmy and Larry took off and they wrote down the tunes for the set list," Levon said. "That kept me from having to do it. The ideal thing of course was to have Jimmy and Larry there. Some nights we had one and not the other. If we couldn't have one of them, then we needed to reconfigure the organization.

"When Jimmy V and Mike went west with Mighty Max and Conan, we had young Byron Isaacs step in and play that stand-up bass. You just don't hear a big stand-up bass anymore. And my ears are just hungry for that sound. The electric bass is just too damn predictable and it's too domineering. It just takes up too much space. If we were a three-or four-or five-piece band, it would be not as bad—you've got that extra space. But with all those horns and everything, boy, you don't need that extra drone in there, rumbling and roaring. The stand-up bass is real full and there's a lot of air around it. It's just touchier. You've got to play better. You've got to come on when it's a stand-up, because there isn't that roar. It just makes the whole thing cleaner, right on the bottom. It makes you fix that bass drum and those tom-toms so that they're not so loose and floppy. You get them up so their pitch is correct."

Once the opening band at the Midnight Ramble finished, you had to be sure and pay close attention to what was going on, because there was no announcement, no big deal of any kind made when Levon walked out of his living room, into the recording studio, for the Midnight Ramble. He simply showed up. There he was, shaking hands, waving to the crowd, giving a peck on the cheek to a woman, being a rock star—all inside his home, as roughly two hundred people gazed in amazement.

From up in the loft, situated next to Levon Helm Studios Chief Engineer Justin Guip, Andrew Shober, the lighting director, catches Levon in a white spotlight and follows him across the stage. Now the crowd begins to buzz, and that buzz grows louder, as everyone notices that the man with the booming voice, usually wearing a dress shirt and black nylon running pants, is making his way through the room. He sits down at the drums. He puts down his drink—Coke or Boylan's grape soda in a red plastic Solo cup, with plenty of ice, placed inside another red plastic Solo cup—he places a black drumming glove on his left hand, and BOOM! The band, the room, the crowd and the evening—everything explodes.

Onstage is a 12-piece ensemble with a four, sometimes five-piece horn section—and who knows, maybe Donald Fagen from Steely Dan is sitting in tonight on piano and melodica, maybe Jon Fishman and Mike Gordon from Phish are watching from the standing room only section up behind the band, perhaps Jane Fonda is sitting up in the loft.

"You definitely felt like you were playing in someone's living room," Brian Mitchell said. "The audience was staring you right in the face, or they're looking down from the balcony; and the band, too, we're all kind of right around each other. The combination of that was unlike anything else. We felt it on stage."

The momentum built from song to song and Ramble to Ramble.

"Everyone fed off that," Brian said. "When Levon would throw stuff around—'You do a song,' 'You do a song,'—it wasn't competitive but everyone kept pushing everyone higher. You kept wanting to take it up another level and take it up another level. As performers and musicians up there, it was like we were in the audience too. There were times I just wanted to stand up and applaud."

Playing in the Levon Helm Band, said vocalist and guitarist Teresa Williams, "was like levitating. The way Levon played drums was its own unique, true-to-himself thing. He played uniquely—you ask anybody who tries to imitate him. Levon's drumming had his feel—and you can't duplicate that feel. I think Amy's got a pretty good vibe of it, I'm happy to say. But having that feel under you, and then those horns—incredible.

"Howard Johnson, the things he would do would just make a song go way over yonder. The things that horn section would do, it would make me go places in a song—if I could stay out of my own way—that the song didn't know it wanted to go, and I didn't know I could do. The way I do certain songs is still heavily influenced by singing with that horn section. They are great players, all of them, just some really, really innovative stuff that Levon surrounded himself with. He brilliantly left enough space in the room for that innovation to happen with that whole band.

"Levon expected you to just be creative, bring what you had and let's see what happens. It was wildly fun. Singing with Amy is really fun, because she doesn't adhere to restrictions. It's like surfing. She may not stick to the harmony line because she's just feeling the flow of what she's hearing, so you weave around each other. It can be really fun and exciting. You had to be ready to surf—surf the night, surf the music."

Speaking of the Ramble, Levon Helm Band bass player Mike Merritt said, "Everything would flow through that band effortlessly."

He continued, "There was never any energy that felt wrong, that was blocked. The energy moved regardless of what material we were playing, whether it was the New Orleans thing that Brian Mitchell was singing on; whether it was an instrumental thing that the horn section was doing; Howard Johnson doing another badass solo on 'Rag Mama Rag.'

"I felt the crossroads of American popular music flowing through this situation and the reason why was because of Levon. That's what he represented to me. He was respectful and allowed that music to flow on that bandstand through everyone. I've never been around hardly anybody that could just be a conduit for all of this energy, from all these great musicians in this band, all the cross-currents. Everything that made American music what it is was flowing through there. It was one of a kind."

Asked what comes to mind when he thinks about Levon Helm, Mike Merritt said, "His way as a person. His way of talking, his way of just being so gracious and his smile; and when something didn't go right on stage, bellowing, 'NO — THAT'S NOT IT.'

"Levon had that primal survival instinct—I'm playing like this because my life depends upon it kind of thing—without him even being conscious of it; this happens at all cost; no matter what happens, we're doing this; we're playing music and that's that and I'm bringing everything I've got, no matter what. That's what I got from Lee."

Levon and Mike shared mutual admiration for each other.

"Mike Merritt—what a great guy—and what a wonderful bass player," Levon said. "They don't come no better than him. I don't know anybody who can play any better than him on that goddamn bass. He never lets up."

Levon's Hudson Valley neighbor John Regan played bass for Peter Frampton from 1979 through 2010. He also played on the recording of "Dancing in the Streets" that Mick Jagger and David Bowie featured in a music video shown during Live Aid. John performed with Ace Frehley of Kiss and once auditioned for the Rolling Stones.

In March 2011, John found himself at Levon Helm Studios for a Midnight Ramble courtesy of a friend, Jon "JD" Dworkow, who was selling a bass to Byron.

"He said, 'Would you like to go to the Ramble,'" John recalled. "I said, 'Are you kidding me?'"

That Fender P bass Byron was buying, incidentally, had previously been loaned to Rolling Stones bass player Darryl Jones. And Byron since purchasing the instrument has played it on every album he's performed on, including "Cleopatra," "III" and "BRIGHTSIDE" by the Lumineers.

John at the time was marking five months of not touring after working as a professional musician for decades, since age 18. He was still adjusting to this change and that night at the Ramble went a long way to easing his transition.

"I saw the pure joy of Levon playing music," he said. "Every ounce of him went into that. It was so genuine and sincere. It really hit home. It turned me around that night. It was an amazing experience and it put me back on my feet. I said, 'Wow, this is why we started playing in the first place.' It really had a profound effect. I needed that night, more than I knew. It lit a spark and I've got Levon to thank for that."

John had previously met Levon in 1995, when The Band opened for Frampton in Boston.

"I remember sitting stage left, where Levon always set up, and watching that shoulder lean in," John said. "I could picture it like it was yesterday."

After The Band's set, Levon invited John and his fellow band mates on to The Band's tour bus.

"It was one of the most amazing moments," he said. "He held court. He's telling us stories about the movies he's in. I'm looking at this guy and I'm going, 'absolute legend,' but one of the most down-to-earth human beings I've met in my life. That experience, Warren Buffett's money can't buy that. It has to happen organically and when it happens like that, you're reminded how blessed you are to be in the position you're in. I'll never forget that night."

As Levon Helm did, Danny Louis maintained a passion for Ulster County that led him to call it home for decades. Danny was born in Ulster, graduated from Rondout Valley High School and parlayed the musical chops he honed as a young man into some very big gigs.

In addition to anchoring Gov't Mule as a multi-instrumentalist for decades, Danny recorded and performed with Joe Cocker, The Kinks, the Allman Brothers Band, Gregg Allman, Eric Clapton, UB40, Coheed and Cambria and Cheap Trick, among others.

In 1993, Danny was playing keyboards in the Warren Haynes Band when that ensemble opened those shows for The Band. Thanks to his old Ulster County friends Jimmy Weider and Randy Ciarlante, Danny on that tour found himself sitting in with The Band. In the new millennium, Danny was performing at the Midnight Ramble.

He said the physical setup of the Ramble stage—it was floor level with no physical barrier between the performers and an audience that sat at the edge of the stage—was unlike any other musical experience he has known.

"There was a compression, like a pressure cooker," Danny said. "The band could sense how the people were and the people could sense how the band was, and they could feel the communication among the band members or watch the smiles and the glances and all the interaction and how the band leader was running things. It was a much more involved experience for the people who were enjoying it."

Danny said the stage arrangement of the piano and the drums at the Midnight Ramble—just like Brian Mitchell, he looked directly across the stage at Levon for the entire show—gave him a special perspective on the man from Turkey Scratch.

"Unlike a lot of drummers, Levon seemed to hand-lay in each backbeat. It was like he was crocheting each snare hit, and you could see, even when he was singing, he would pay special attention to where he was putting the pocket of the groove. It didn't seem unconscious at all. A lot of drummers will play time in their sleep and it seemed like Levon was cognizant of every beat and laid it in, each one. You could see his shoulder drop. You could see him paying attention to it.

"I don't know if it was something he practiced. I would say, unlike any other drummer, he seemed to just hand paint every bar that he played, and yet it was a continuous stream. You could see him breathe this life into it, so there was nothing metronomic or robotic about his playing at all. Levon was so dynamically active in the most minute, little ways. It just helped breathe that stamp of his on everything. It was probably there in his mandolin playing, too.

"If you found yourself tapping your foot when Levon just played something simple, or you hear a Band song and you find yourself tapping your foot, even before you realize you're paying attention to the lyrics or to what Garth or Robbie did or who was doing what or who was singing harmony, Levon's pulse is in there and it's essential and it's absolutely unique, creatively, sonically, and the placement—incredible. You were affected by the danceability and the propulsion of his playing.

"How many people call up and say, 'Hello' and you know who they are just by the way they said hello. That's the way Levon played the drums. You knew it was him. The analysis of that would be a book."

What was Levon's take on Danny's playing?

"Playing with Danny Louis is nothing but fun," Levon said. "It's butter on the popcorn."

And how did Levon sum up the Midnight Ramble?

"The easiest thing I've ever done," he said. "The whole place turns into a temple for me. There is nothing else and time and everything else is kind of suspended. All I'm conscious of is the pitch, if the pitch is correct. There are no echoes or fancy sound devices. And about 50 percent of what you hear, even on a full electrical tune, is acoustic. And walking out of your living room and playing a show—it's the best. It's the best. Especially the way the room responds. All I have to do is go shave, take a shower and head out there. We usually stop when it feels like it's time to stop. When the show's over, I just walk next door and take my boots off. I believe this might be my payback for all the traveling and stuff. Musicians, their years are like dog years. All that traveling around and now, all of a sudden—I don't know how we got it to happen. They're coming here and we don't even have to crank a car. We leave everything set. And we've got all my best equipment; we can sound better here than we can anywhere.

"Each band plays at least an hour, and we probably play at least two hours. By the time we quit, which is between 11:30 and midnight, they've had four-to-five hours of music and that's just about enough in one day. You really can lose the outside world and all those aggravations. At the end of each tune, you can kind of feel that embracement, where you start to realize—music being medicine, you know?"

"There is no pressure around here. When you play, you can start pretty much and finish when you want to and play what you want to. We try to leave it that way, let it be what it wants to be."

Adding to the atmosphere was a rented popcorn maker and that undeniable, buttery aroma it generates.

Referring to accommodations for the audience and the local hardware store in Woodstock, Levon said, "We used to rent the chairs for the audience from Houst. As soon as we could afford it, we bought the chairs and we bought the popcorn maker. We started doing it with the Rambles just to give it that showtime feel—it smells like show time with that popcorn machine. People love it. Sammy usually got him a cup."

As for performing in The Barn, Levon said, "It just always sounds good and you don't have to worry about something going funny and you don't have to listen to some club owner—'Could you guys do a few more of the old ones?' That was one of the things I wanted to avoid.

"We try to play every Saturday night if we can. We'll take it on the road if we can get a good job. Our problem is there are so many of us that we've got to wait until that money is real good or, shit, we can't go. Hell, I'd rather stay home. I don't want to hitchhike to get there. I want us to have a good ride and feel like we're somebody. I'm not bragging, but it's just hard to beat this band. You play as many nights as you can. I used to think that if you could record about half the time and play shows the other half of the time, that might be a good medium. I'm not a big rehearsal guy. I'm more lazy than I am ambitious. Most of those tunes you kind of know anyway, so you're kind of taking the shine off them to work them to death. If you have to, you can modulate, or you'll change it tomorrow night. That makes a song that much more fun and you haven't taken any of the fun out of it and it's still fresh."

By virtue of the Midnight Ramble remaining at Levon Helm Studios, where it was born, where it evolved and where it triumphed, the impending calamity that it allowed Levon to narrowly avoid informed the spirit of each evening in a way that said, "Look how far this rent party has come."

"Those first Rambles, some of those nights had a hell of a spirit," Levon said. "Every now and then we'd have somebody come in. Anytime that would happen, we'd get somebody to bring in some equipment. We had some real wonderful players. But it was a brief operation. We didn't have Geanine Kane or Barbara O'Brien coming by, or anybody, really. We had to secure the place ourselves."

The Levon Helm Band might open the Midnight Ramble with a Band classic— "Ophelia" or "The Shape I'm In" or "This Wheel's On Fire"—or who knows what. It didn't matter. Audience members who could have literally stood up, leaned over and touched Levon while he played the drums were in awe. They wore rock-solid smiles for the next few hours as the Levon Helm Band tore through song after song of Band classics, gospel, R&B, rock 'n' roll, country, blues and who knows what else.

"When I came to the Ramble, he and I were the older ones and we had a history, so that was something that was in place," said tuba and trombone player Howard Johnson, who, like Levon was a cancer survivor.

"There wasn't anything either of us had to do about it. It was just there. I had a different sense of who he was. He was this tremendous musician, with all the great players in the band. This was his gig. He was the leader, not just by title or anything, he was taking the music somewhere."

During the Ramble, if the band was about to play "Got Me A Woman" or "A Train Robbery" from *Dirt Farmer,* Larry would mention a certain honor that distinguished Levon's comeback record from other albums by other recording artists.

"We recorded an album called the *Dirt Farmer*," Larry, beaming with pride, would tell the audience. "And on behalf of Levon and the band, I'm very proud to say that it won a Grammy."

The crowd would applaud, cheer, hoot and howl. Levon typically responded by saying into his microphone, "Even a blind chicken gets a piece of corn every now and then."

Larry continued, regarding *Dirt Farmer*, "And it just happens to be on sale downstairs." He was referring to the merchandise area—Levon called it "the company store"—in the garage.

At that point, Levon would chime in, regardless of whether it was November or July, saying, "And Christmas is right around the corner. You just might want to pick up two copies!"

One of the best things about the Midnight Ramble was the opening act, who in most cases could have easily headlined their own gig, at just about any other venue, large or small.

You could very often count on the Brooklyn-based Alexis P. Suter Band to be on hand. But there was also Joan Osborne. Billy Bob Thornton—who like Levon is an actor, drummer and vocalist from Arkansas—brought his band, The Boxmasters. The Hudson Valley's very own Felice Brothers—featuring Simone Felice, who later became producer for The Lumineers—might be opening the show. And the list goes on. Phil Lesh of the Grateful Dead performed with his sons, Grahame and Brian, joined by Larry, Teresa and Justin. Bob Weir of the Grateful Dead played a different Ramble and Bruce Hornsby joined in.

At an earlier Ramble, Hornsby sat in on the same night that drummer Jack DeJohnette, Levon's Woodstock neighbor and a veteran of performing with Miles Davis, played alongside Levon on what the man from Turkey Scratch called his "cocktail kit," a three-piece percussion set with cymbals.

Norah Jones was joined by Catherine Popper and Sasha Dobson for the Puss N Boots Ramble performance.

Another special Midnight Ramble moment took place on August 23, 2008. Upstairs in the loft, Chris Robinson of the Black Crowes was just hanging out, watching the show with everyone else. During the Ramble, Chris sat in on "Shake Your Moneymaker" with the Levon Helm Band, which you can hear for yourself on *It's Showtime: The Midnight Ramble Sessions Vol. 3*.

Ricky Skaggs showed up in the waning moments of the Aug. 25, 2007,

Ramble after headlining the Dutchess County Fair, across the Hudson River in Rhinebeck, earlier that evening. On another night, Glen Hansard, from the Swell Season, sat in with the Levon Helm Band and decided to walk everyone through the chords of a new song he hadn't quite finished yet, on stage, in front of two hundred people.

In October 2010, My Morning Jacket opened the Ramble and lead singer Jim James joined the Levon Helm Band during their set to sing The Band classic, "It Makes No Difference." Levon when the song was finished expressed his happiness with James by offering up a resounding, "JIM-BO!"

Mumford & Sons opened a Ramble in March 2012.

"We're going to try and do justice to this hallowed room," Marcus Mumford told the crowd in between songs of their set. "We're not sure we'll succeed, but we'll certainly try."

On Aug. 2, 2015, Graham Nash played a duo show at Levon Helm Studios with his guitarist, Shane Fontayne, and the Sunday night performance did not disappoint. Nash delivered a solid set that featured fan favorites from his deep catalog of songs, "Teach Your Children," "Wasted on the Way" and "Our House" among them. But it's safe to say a majority of those in attendance did not know that Nash donated his fee for the evening back to the studio.

Speaking in 2020, Nash said, "I encourage other people to do the same."

And then there were those things that simply did not come to pass.

Prior to the release of his 2011 solo album, "Man in Motion," Warren Haynes was planning to make a record with Levon, Leon Russell and T-Bone Wolk, at Levon Helm Studios.

"Everybody was fired up about doing it," Warren said.

The four musicians began to discuss the scheduling of the recording sessions and the possibility of starting to work on the project during the winter of 2009-10. Leon wanted to wait until the winter had passed, so the group delayed the first recording session a bit. But T-Bone sadly passed away in 2010. Levon passed in 2012. Leon died in 2016.

"Now they're all gone," Warren said. "It's a really bittersweet memory for me, to think about what kind of record we would have made, in that place, with that group of musicians. I'm getting sad just thinking about it."

One of the most outrageous Rambles had nothing to do with the lineup of musicians, but everything to do with a freak Halloween snowstorm and the power outage it caused. Embodying the spirit of "the show must go on," the Midnight Ramble on Oct. 31, 2011, proceeded without the benefit of electricity. On that night, the regional utility, Central Hudson Gas & Electric, along with much of the Hudson Valley, including 160 Plochmann Lane in Woodstock, had gotten clobbered by wet snow.

That night marked one of the Ramble's finest moments and underscored the fact that there was very little that could stand in the way of Levon Helm. Here was a guy who, by October 31, 2011, had overcome so much in life. Why should he let a little thing like the lack of electricity stand in the way of a night of live music powered by electricity?

Barbara, never one to let a catastrophe spoil anything, oversaw the whole thing, including the rigging of battery-powered lanterns on microphone stands so they looked like those mailbag poles you might see positioned next to railroad tracks in the Old West.

That night was a perfect example of how Barbara just kept moving forward, and forward, and forward. That night embodied in so many ways how her energy and determination and refusal to give in to defeat had unleashed so much momentum at Levon Helm Studios.

In addition to the lanterns on microphone stands, there were lanterns on the floor, and the light they projected upward onto the faces of the musicians created some serious atmosphere with a tinge of Halloween spookiness. Every now and then, against the backdrop of the lighting, someone dressed in costume as the Mad Hatter or Alice in Wonderland would walk by, and it was a little eerie, but in a fun Halloween way. The spirits themselves even seemed to chime in when, during "Ophelia," the lights flickered on for a moment.

There were many Midnight Ramble moments, both on and off stage. One unfolded shortly before a Ramble and involved a song that Howard Johnson sang, "Get a Little Lovin' Done," accompanied by Larry on guitar, Teresa on vocals and Levon on drums.

Larry was sitting at Levon's kitchen table, putting together the set list, and he called out to Howard, who was in the living room. "Hey Howard, how about 'A Little Lovin' tonight? Howard's response? 'I haven't even shaved yet.'"

And there was the first time that Levon sang "The Weight," by The Band, during a Midnight Ramble at The Barn.

For weeks, Jimmy Vivino had been putting "The Weight" on the Ramble set list, as the last song or encore, with hopes that Levon would thrill the house by singing this epic tune. Levon, according to Tony LoBue, would look over the set list each week and when he got to "The Weight,' would smile and shake his head, as only Levon could.

Then came the Ramble where Jimmy arrived a bit late and listed "Rock and Roll Shoes" as the last song. The time came for the tune and Levon shouted, "Wait." Jimmy replied with, "Wait for what?" And then it hit him, Tony said, it wasn't "wait," it was "Weight." Levon, at long last, wanted to perform "The Weight."

"Needless to say, the roof exploded," Tony recalled.

And with that performance of that song, a cascade of Band tunes found their way into the Ramble set list from then on.

For all of its unpredictability, there were certain aspects of the Midnight Ramble that you could count on, like "The Weight" closing out the evening. After "When I Go Away" or "Chest Fever," either of which was usually the second-to-last song of the night, and before the evening ended with "The Weight," Larry Campbell introduced the band, and started always with the horn section.

Clark Gayton

A tuba and trombone player who has recorded and performed with Bruce Springsteen, Clark Gayton grew up in Seattle. As a kid, Clark took up the piano but switched to trumpet in the third grade. Then his school band director needed a tuba player.

"It's funny looking back on it," he said. "He told me directly, 'You'll never be a good trumpet player, but you might have a chance on tuba.' I think I took it the right way. If he was around, or I knew where he was, I'd thank him for it."

Clark performed with the Seattle Little and Junior Symphonies, which were staging grounds for the Seattle Symphony.

But, he said, "I got sidetracked with my R&B stuff and my jazz. But I still stayed involved with orchestral music all through high school."

He began playing the trombone after hearing an Earth, Wind & Fire record.

"I wanted to figure out a way to be involved with the music. There wasn't much tuba action in Earth, Wind & Fire, but there was a lot of trombone."

Shaping it all were the musical influences in Clark's family—and New Orleans.

Clark's maternal grandmother hailed from New Orleans. She played organ and piano for silent movies in the local theater and she exposed him to the music of the Mardi Gras. Her uncle Manny Minneta was a piano professor in the city's Storyville neighborhood in the start of the twentieth century. Back in Seattle, Clark's uncle played organ and welcomed his nephew into his band on trombone when he was 15 or 16. The rest, as anyone who has seen Clark play with Levon Helm or Bruce Springsteen knows, is history.

Clark, who has also performed with Rihanna, Santana, Stevie Wonder and Sting, initially found himself playing in the Levon Helm Band as a substitute for trumpet player Steven Bernstein, who couldn't make a gig. That was when the horn section consisted of just two players—Bernstein on trumpet and Erik Lawrence on sax.

"Steven was in the habit of calling me in as his sub," said Clark. "He felt comfortable with me covering his part on trombone. Steven asked me to fill in and Levon dug it."

But as Clark geared up for that first trip to the Midnight Ramble from his New York City home, he wasn't sure what to expect. The extent of his exposure to Levon was limited to Band songs he had heard on KYAC, the local radio station he listened to while growing up in Seattle. A soul and R&B station, KYAC ended each day's programming at 11:30 p.m. with a hard left turn that featured such performers as Elton John, Boz Scaggs, Grand Funk Railroad, The Who—and The Band.

Speaking of the Ramble, Clark said, "I wasn't sure what to make of it. I didn't know if we would be playing in a venue. They said it was his house. We're playing in this front room. I had no idea. Everyone kept saying, 'You know the songs.' I kept saying, 'I don't know anything about The Band.' I had nothing.

"Then I got there and I saw the setup. It was very unusual. Levon is over by the windows. The horns were on the other side of the stage, which was unusual. But immediately I saw that the reason it was like this was so he could have eye contact with everybody. Everybody in the band could see him, which was important, and that was evident after the first song, that he had to be able to see everybody. And not just see them but be able to look at them, because even though Jimmy was leading the band, Levon was leading the band and he would give you these cues with his eyes. His eyes were very piercing and once you got that laser in on you, he could telephone it in with a look. You could tell when he wanted you to do a solo and you could also tell when he wanted you to stop and when it's not right to come in.

"Then there were bigger cues and that's what Jimmy did. But Levon never lost control of the band and that's important to point out."

As far as a band leader, Clark said that Levon, "would try to give people a chance. If they didn't know something, he would show them. Levon wasn't a disciplinarian. He wasn't going to give you private lessons. He'd let you know if something wasn't happening. If something was wrong with the horns, he'd put his sticks down and come over to the horn section and set us straight. That happened on a number of occasions. If the notes weren't right, he said something about it.

"I always felt as though we had a rapport. He kind of got me, even though, playing the trombone, I didn't have a particularly leading role.

But he seemed to like what I did and he seemed to know where I came from musically. There would be a lot of times when we would sit and talk about music and different situations. I really loved those times and, of course, we were on the road a lot. Every chance I got, I tried to pull him aside and see if I could see what his thoughts were about music. It's always great to experience another musician who has the same sort of values that you have, in terms of making sure the music feels good, making sure the people in the band feel good, everyone feels wanted and necessary. I just think of a certain warmth to the music when I think of Levon."

Once, Clark, Levon and Jimmy Vivino worked through a horn arrangement for The Band's "It Makes No Difference."

"I thought, let's sit in the kitchen and hammer it out," Clark said. "Me, Jimmy and Levon went to the kitchen and came up with an arrangement. Notes just came out of his mouth and I transcribed them. He gave me lead lines, where he thought the horns should come in and stop. I fleshed it out from there. That was an incredible experience."

And then there was Levon's style.

"Once I heard him play, I realized he's a funky player, a rhythm player. Then I realized what kind of boat I was in and that made things a lot easier, once I knew what direction he's going in. He wants to swing. It's feel-good music. It's funky. It swings. Every musician should want to be involved in something like that. It doesn't happen all the time. A lot of the situations you're in musically, they're not fun, they're not feel-good situations. It seems odd, but not everybody strives for that. Some people want music to be a very arduous experience. Some people just want to kick their feet up and have a good time and that was apparent—that's what Levon wanted to do. I wanted to be a part of that. He was good people. I loved the audience."

And all of this, following that first night, brought Clark back for more of the Midnight Ramble.

"The people around him were really cool. I felt at home. Everyone took me in immediately—'I'm glad your back. Thanks for coming up here, I know it's a long way'—that sort of thing."

Jay Collins

At 11:10 a.m. on April 20, 2012, the day after Levon died, Levon Helm Band sax and flute player Jay Collins posted the following story on Facebook:

"One more thing I forgot to say about Levon:

"He was a VERY generous man, almost to a fault. If he was down to his last dollar, and he was with you, he'd give you half of it. He was that kind of guy. Although he didn't have to, (because we would have all worked with him for next to nothing anyway), he paid his musicians better than anybody I ever worked with, and if you were sick or had to miss a gig because of a personal problem, he'd make sure you got paid anyway! There is very little of that kind of brotherhood in the music business, and I just felt the need to point that out.

"Just a personal story to illustrate his generosity: There was once a family member of mine who had recently lost his job that came to a Ramble at the barn. I happened to mention it in passing during a conversation with Levon. Unbeknownst to me, he went and got some money, and at the end of the night he handed me a roll of bills and told me to give it to the fellow. I tried to refuse, knowing my relative would turn it down and possibly be embarrassed. That's when Levon showed his even truer colors: He said, 'Tell him it's from you.'"

A native of Portland, Oregon, whose step-father plays guitar and owns an extensive collection of blues records, Jay Collins was a pillar of the heavy-hitting Levon Helm Band horn section.

Jay beginning in 2001 was a member of Gregg Allman & Friends, the Allman Brothers Band co-founder's side project. That gig continued until Allman's passing in 2017.

Jay has also performed with Little Feat; the Dukes of September (Donald Fagen, Michael McDonald and Boz Scaggs); the Allman Brothers

Band; James Hunter; Ray LaMontagne; jazz musicians Andrew Hill, Jacky Terrasson and LeRoy Vinnegar; and Afro-Cuban drummer Bobby Sanabria.

In fact, Jay launched his music career in Portland's jazz scene, where he began playing gigs at age 18.

"The scene in Portland was very, very good at the time," said Jay, who played in bands as a teenager while immersing himself in the esteemed music program at Woodrow Wilson High School, now called Ida B. Wells High School, in Portland. "There was a lot of room for a young person to get a lot of experience."

He later moved to New York City and established himself in Manhattan's East Village. During the 1990s, he assembled his own band, released three CDs and toured and recorded with other musicians.

Jay extended his reach by immersing himself in Latin music. He spent 1996-2004 leading the band Mambo Macoco, touring Cuba and the Caribbean, and playing with Bobby Sanabria's band. He studied Afro-Cuban rhythms and their links to American and New Orleans music. In 1999, Jay shifted from instrumental jazz to song-writing, and formed a new ensemble, Jay Collins and the Kings County Band. He worked at putting his poetry to original music, and the guy who would not sing publicly for the first time until he was 30-years-old took singing lessons.

Jay met his future wife, Amy Helm, while in the recording studio, working on the Jay Collins Band's first album. That collection of songs was released in 2004 and titled "Poem for Today."

For Jay, playing in the Levon Helm Band, "felt like you were on a train that was not slowing down and not speeding up—it was just really steady."

"I was always blown away by the simplicity with which Levon looked at music," said Jay, who received a music scholarship to Mt. Hood Community College in Gresham, Oregon, and attended for a year. "He had a very simple way of thinking about it."

Jay, who is no longer married to Amy Helm, continued, "A lot of musicians, they're not thinking about it as bedrock-simple as Levon thought about things. He would say, 'You play on one and three, don't play on two and four, those are my beats.' Or, he would say, 'Just keep sprinkling those seasonings in there on the guitar.' He had a very simple, direct way of looking at things. That was one of the things I really admired. It was such an art. It was almost like somebody painting a picture. He could take all the ornaments out of a song and just make it real cut-down-to-the-bone—real simple.

"It seems like it would be easy to do, but it's not and he would do it in his way. That's why he could do somebody else's song and his way of doing it would be really original-sounding—because of the way he approached music with this simple way of breaking it down."

"Levon could be very demanding about certain things," Jay said. "He had a very direct, simple way of playing the drums and he could really bear down on the time. He had very good time—never slowing up or down and being in the pocket all the time. He could play a shuffle, a very slow blues shuffle, which is a very hard thing to do for most drummers. He could play real slow and it still felt really good, like he wasn't going to let you fall and that's very rare. Most drummers can't play that slow and make it feel good.

"Sometimes, he did things on the drums that, on paper, you would think, 'Well that can't possibly work.' You would see him doing something that seemed so simple, and you would say, 'Well I could do that.' It looked like the kind of thing: 'Well all he's doing is playing that one thing on the snare drum.' He simplified it so much, he'd make it look like you could get up, go over there and do it. But you couldn't.

"He would play something that, if another drummer played the beat that way, for the whole song, you'd fire the guy. You're sitting there, thinking to yourself, 'How come this sounds and feels so good, when he's doing this really simple thing?' It was a magic that certain, great musicians have. Gregg Allman had it too. They can do a lot with a little."

Steven Bernstein

Trumpet player Steven Bernstein played with everyone from My Morning Jacket to U2. Bernstein was also well known for his work with the Lounge Lizards, the Millennial Territory Orchestra and Sex Mob, whose 2006 CD "Sexotica" received a Grammy nomination for Best Contemporary Jazz Album.

"He used to call me 'Steve-a-rino,' which is what my Dad called me, which is from *The Steve Allen Show*," Steven said of Levon. "He was so sweet and so real. My kids were raised around him. It was an amazing period for me. I had been a touring musician as a side guy with the Lounge Lizards. I was touring with my own band. I kind of put that stuff on hold for Levon. I still did a few tours every year, but that became my life and it was great. Instead of going away, I drove up to Woodstock. My kids were 11 and 9 when I started this. So there was that whole period of junior high, high school, when they were around, they were part of that family. My daughter played a Kid's Ramble. She had a band—Aqua Melon.

"Maybe the first summer or second summer, I was leading my own band somewhere in Europe and I was missing some Rambles. This is the weird thing, I knew I was living my dream. I'm leading my own band in Europe—but I kind of missed being up in Woodstock, playing a Ramble. It didn't make any sense. My friend, this bass player—he's played with a lot of people—he said, 'Yeah, you're being taken care of by Big Papa.' Levon was Big Papa. He was the biggest papa of all—not just his personality, but his drumming. It took care of you. It was nurturing."

When Bernstein signed on for the Rambles, he said, "We're all doing weddings to make a living. We all have young families. Erik said, 'If there's ever a Saturday when you don't have a wedding, you should come up to Levon's.' So I went up one night."

Bernstein was a big fan of The Band.

"The first non-jazz record I bought was *Rock of Ages*—not because I liked The Band, but because it had Howard and Snooky on it. My parents took me to see *The Last Waltz* when it came out and I liked that because it had a lot of horns."

Snooky was trumpet and flugelhorn player Snooky Young.

Bernstein owned *Rock of Ages* by The Band on vinyl, CD and cassette. And when the remastered version was released, "I bought that, too."

Of the *Rock of Ages* horn charts written by Allen Toussaint, Bernstein said, "I based my entire way of writing music on those horn charts. It's the only thing like it in the world."

Prior to that first Ramble Bernstein played, Midnight Ramble stage manager Brendan McDonough had burned a CD for Erik and Steven that included songs that Levon liked. Bernstein's first interaction with Levon was when he came onstage, to perform, at the Ramble. The two had never met previously.

"We played a set with Ollabelle," Bernstein said of the band that featured Levon's daughter, Amy. "Levon came out. We were set up next to the drums. Levon just looks at us, smiles and we start playing."

Erik Lawrence

Saxophone and flute player Erik Lawrence previously performed with Buddy Miles, Sonny Sharrock and Chico Hamilton.

Erik's father, Arnie Lawrence, founder of the School of Jazz and Contemporary Music at The New School in New York City, mentored the jambands Blues Traveler and the Spin Doctors. He played on *The Tonight Show*. He performed with Dizzy Gillespie and Clark Terry. And Arnie Lawrence played on that classic 1970s Saturday morning cartoon, *Schoolhouse Rock*.

Levon, Erik said, "could take a really good band like we had and make them sound like the best band in the world, just like he did with a bunch of Canadians. And he could take some superstar who wanted to sit in with us, like Elvis Costello or Chris Robinson or Sheryl Crow, and as soon as he kicks in on the drums on a tune, I can't tell you—from where I stood on the back of the stage—how many times I saw a superstar's knees buckle as soon as he kicked in. Literally, their knees would buckle. They would have to take a pause the first moment, like they never felt music feel like that before.

"Talk about addiction, that was an addiction for guys like me and Steven to show up and play there. We couldn't wait. We had our ritual. We'd drive up from Nyack every week and we couldn't wait to get there. As soon as we got on Route 28, we got excited. As soon as we got on Route 212, we got excited."

The original edition of *This Wheel's On Fire* ended with the re-formed Band performing at the 1993 presidential inauguration of Bill Clinton, the former governor of Arkansas who grew up in Hope, more than two hundred miles from Turkey Scratch. The Band played the Blue Jeans Bash, one of many inauguration parties. And that presidential inauguration served as something of an inauguration for Erik Lawrence, who played his first gig with Levon and The Band at that show.

Erik's neighbor in Rockland County, New York, where he lived at the time, about 85 miles from Woodstock, was John Simon, who produced The Band's legendary albums, *Music From Big Pink* and *The Band*. Simon alerted Erik to the inauguration gig and the fact that The Band was in need of a baritone sax player.

"John was a neighbor, he knew my Dad," Erik said. "We had done musical things in Nyack."

John Simon told Erik that multiple special guests were scheduled to perform with The Band.

"He listed all these people who were going to play—Dr. John, Bob Dylan, Vassar Clements, Dickey Betts, Steve Cropper, Duck Dunn. John said, 'When you get on the bus'—I met the bus at the Sloatsburg rest stop on the New York State Thruway—'say hi to Rick and Garth, Jimmy Weider and Randy Ciarlante, and Richard Bell and Butch Dener. Tell them you're a friend of mine and everything will be cool,'" Erik said. "I wasn't a huge Band fan. And I had grown up in a musician's house. My Dad was a jazz musician. I knew Clark Terry and Dizzy Gillespie. So I wasn't starstruck when I got on the bus. I looked at Garth and I said, 'What kind of music do you listen to?'"

Garth's reply?

"'Well, I'm really into polka,'" Erik said. "I told him I was into Ben Webster. He reaches into his briefcase and pulls out a piece of music, an exact, literal transcription—he transcribed, in beautiful manuscript—of Ben Webster's most famous solo, 'Cotton Tail,' with the Duke Ellington Orchestra from 1941. We instantly connected. Rick Danko was on the bus. Levon had gone down earlier. We drive down. We had a good time talking. I had been playing with David Tronzo. I played Tronzo for Jim Weider. We get down to D.C. and there's Levon, the first time I ever met him. He met the bus, classic Southern gentleman that he was. He was down there—'Hey guys. Great to see you, thanks for coming down.' It was all because of the Arkansas connection. We were playing for the Arkansas travelers, people from the Arkansas contingent.

"Dylan showed up. It was a beautiful, amazing party. All those people showed up and played—Stephen Stills; Don Johnson and Melanie Griffith were there; the Cate Brothers were there; Ronnie Hawkins and his band. It was Levon's call. Everybody Levon called showed up. We had a seven-hour rehearsal on Saturday. We're six hours into the rehearsal, 1:00 or 2:00 in the morning, and all of a sudden, this guy comes in from the back, he kind of slithers in. He's got two hoodies on. He's completely covered up. He really moves like he's slithering. I said, 'That must be Dylan.' He had a different presence than anybody I've ever come across in my life.

"All the band members and guests are onstage. Dylan picks up a guitar, goes to the mic and starts playing. Everyone tries to follow him, which is impossible because there are 40 people onstage. He starts mumbling some song. We're trying to figure out the chord changes. The song goes on for 25 minutes. As soon as he's done, he turns and he walks up to Levon. The horns are lined up behind Levon. He looks Levon in the eye and it was this moment where you're like, all right, these guys are brothers. He gives Levon this puckish, mischievous look, and he just starts playing the whole thing over again and we just go back into playing it for 15 minutes.

"Somehow, they tried to extract what it was Dylan played and what tunes they were and they wrote horn charts for them. And then, of course, when he got on the stage the next day, I didn't know if he was playing the same tunes or different keys. He did whatever he felt like playing and everyone followed him. It was the one solo I got that entire gig. As soon as he finished singing, John Simon, who was onstage, he points to me and I start taking a solo. The only solo I got the whole gig was with Dylan."

That was the first time Erik Lawrence had seen or performed with The Band. Years later, Erik got a call from Butch Dener, alerting him to the Rambles shortly after they had gotten underway. He played his first Ramble and was paid with a copy of Levon's autobiography, *This Wheel's On Fire*.

In advance of Erik's second Ramble, Levon called him up and asked if he knew a bass player who could join in for the gig. Erik dialed up guitarist Tony Scherr, who like Levon and Garth had played on recording sessions for *Feels Like Home* by Norah Jones. Erik told Levon that Tony was also a great bass player.

"I knew Tony was a natural player and he loved Levon," Erik said.

So the two musicians set out for Woodstock and, Erik said, "We slept over that time. There were lots of people living there and sleeping there. Levon took us around after the show. He borrowed a pillow from somebody. He said, 'We'll pull out a pallet for you.' He borrowed a mattress from one guy. He told him, 'You don't need it tonight.' It was like a big house party. It was much looser and soon after that, Levon started talking about wanting to bring in another horn. I was the only horn player at the time. Steven was the natural guy to bring in."

Howard Johnson

After introducing Erik Lawrence, Larry would say, "And look-ie here, everybody, it's the in-im-it-a-ble Howard Johnson."

Born in Montgomery, Alabama, Howard Johnson taught himself to play the baritone sax and tuba; was welcomed by Charles Mingus into his workshop; and performed with Gil Evans.

Howard played with Buddy Rich, Pharoah Sanders and Larry Coryell. And his list of associations and recordings encompasses John Scofield,

Freddie Hubbard, McCoy Tyner, Marvin Gaye, Miles Davis, Quincy Jones and John Lennon. In the motion picture industry, he can be heard on Spike Lee's *School Daze, Mo' Better Blues, Malcolm X* and *Clockers*. Howard's stage presence, the way in which his musicianship could light a room on fire, his personality off-the-stage, his celebrity, his lack of pretension, Howard's life and career are simply too overwhelming to capture anywhere in simple text.

But this story that Howard shared about Muddy Waters and The Last Waltz offers great insight into who Howard Johnson was.

"I used to have breakfast with Muddy every day," Howard Johnson said of the days leading up to The Last Waltz performance. "Other people weren't up at that time. He'd always be in the hotel restaurant about 7:30-8. I'd wander in and sit down next to him. We'd talk about stuff."

And then there was that beer commercial.

You may remember Howard from one of those infamous Miller Lite beer commercials from the 1970s.

Howard spoke in this sort of jazz lingo, and a bartender translated. For starters, the graphics describe "Hojo," as Levon called him, as "Howard Johnson, Famous Jazz Musician."

> Howard: "Us syncopators of progressive riffs have a unique style of jawing."
> Bartender: "Howard said, 'Jazz musicians talk funny.'"
> Howard proceeded to talk about Miller Lite beer: "It's super cool and a breeze on the calories, you dig?"
> Bartender: "Lite is less filing, with a third less calories than their regular beer."
> Bartender: "And the taste, Howard?"
> Howard: "Oh man. Its oh bop sh'bam. It's lay down, break down, birdie on the hot side of town."
> Bartender: "He likes it."

Watching Howard Johnson play tuba really was a sight. His solo during "The Weight" was a staple of the Midnight Rambles and the Rambles on the Road. At times, he stepped off the horn section riser and headed out in front of the entire band during "Rag Mama Rag."

The horn section could get a rise out of the audience like nothing else. Take, for instance, the Mardi Gras parade during Brian Mitchell's rendition of the Dr. John song, "Mardi Gras Day."

At the Rambles, the house lights would go up and the horn section would do a loop through the audience and the place would explode. It never failed, every Mardi Gras parade. And like a period at the end of a very long, very colorful sentence, when "Mardi Gras Day" was finished, Brian would say, "How 'bout them horns?" And once again, the crowd would explode.

Mike Merritt

Sometime in the mid-1990s or so, The Band appeared on *Late Night with Conan O'Brien*. They were gearing up to perform "Life is a Carnival" but wanted the show's house band, The Max Weinberg 7, to join in with them. That would mean two drummers, two horn sections and more, with Max Weinberg 7 bass player Mike Merritt sitting in on tambourine.

"Levon wanted everyone playing," Mike recalled.

That was when Mike first met Levon Helm. Levon was also on the *Conan* show a separate time, by himself. He sang and double-drummed with Weinberg on "Short-Fat Fannie," joined by Conan's band, including Mike on bass.

The two musicians crossed paths again at that recording session in Woodstock with Johnnie Johnson, Jimmy Vivino and the other musicians. That experience established a special bond between Mike and Levon.

"We spent all day recording all these tunes," Mike said. "I think that day we really locked. We had double drums. I had my electric upright bass. Danko's playing bass guitar. We're talking about who's going to go high, who's going to go low. We just had a ball. I think from that time on Lee and I really connected musically."

In 2004, Levon rang Mike on the phone.

"He calls me up and says, 'We're doing a show in downtown Woodstock, outdoors, can you make it?'" Mike said of the September 2004 performance on the Village Green in Woodstock. "The next day I drive up from my crib in New Jersey. We finish the gig and Levon said to everyone, not just me specifically, 'You know, that's the first time we've had an electric bass in the band for a long time.' I said to myself, 'Oh, I guess you want the doghouse bass there.' So I kept that in mind."

Not long after, Levon called Mike and asked him to perform with him at the Midnight Ramble. For the first couple of Rambles Mike played, he brought his electric upright bass.

"I'm figuring I could split the difference," he said.

But at Levon's request Mike eventually switched to the upright acoustic, also known as the "Doghouse" bass.

"Not only did Levon appreciate having the upright bass in the band, but it was his way of controlling the dynamics of the band," Mike said. "If people couldn't hear the upright bass, that means things are too loud. It was a little bit of a struggle. We would get to the acoustic parts of the set, that's fun. But with the electric guitars, the Hammond organ, the horn section, it was a little bit of a challenge pumping that doghouse through that band. But that's what Levon wanted. I was right next to him. He was directly to my left. We just created this groove. I had a lot of respect for his ability to know what was right for the band in terms of dynamics."

Born and raised in Philadelphia, Mike was heavily influenced by his father, bassist Jymie Merritt, who was classically trained but made a name for himself in the 1950s and 1960s while recording and gigging with B.B. King, Art Blakey, Sonny Rollins, Chet Baker and Dizzy Gillespie, among others. He also performed with John Coltrane and Max Roach and was one of the first jazz musicians to play a Fender electric bass.

Mike studied double bass and jazz and eventually left the City of Brotherly Love for New York, where he played in Texas blues player Johnny Clyde Copeland's band. He then became a freelance player on the New York City blues circuit and began playing with Jimmy Vivino and James Wormworth. The Black Italians ensemble emerged and the trio took up residence on Thursday nights at Downtime on W. 30th St.

Jimmy V would invite his brother Jerry, a horn player, to join in. And the list of guests grew to include Felix Cabrera, Catherine Russell, Danny Louis, Mick Fleetwood, Max Weinberg and Max's fellow E Street Band member Danny Federici. Max and Jimmy later called Mike when they were assembling the house band for *Late Night with Conan O'Brien*.

Mike and Jimmy would also anchor the Midnight Ramble.

Speaking of the early days of the Ramble, Mike said, "There was some uncertainty about it. We weren't sure where it was going to go. The Barn was not up to where it had become several years later. The lineup was uncertain, people would dart in and out because they had their other commitments."

But the entire experienced gained traction and never lost momentum.

"It was a very special experience," Mike said. "It was sort of like Mad Dogs and Englishmen. You had Muddy running around. You had kids running around. It was like a freight train, going down the tracks.

"I can look back now and say it was great. But I knew when we were doing those Rambles that it was special. I watched it evolve over the first couple of years. The band became this big juggernaut. The spirit that you felt in that Barn when that band kicked into high gear—you just felt these were special moments. I think it was the love that all of us had for Levon and his music and for him being so gracious and so open and so musical, as a drummer, as a singer, as a presence. We all had so much respect for that. I think that's what made it special for us.

"Sometimes, I'd look up at the rafters and I'd look at the people sitting upstairs, looking down. It would be a really quiet moment and a quiet song and I would say to myself, 'This is magical.' I'd sometimes just look at the people watching, and I'd look around at the other people I'm playing with and I'd just realize, this is the best spot in the world, for me to be here right now, to play and help move this train down the tracks by doing my little part to just lock in and make this groove happen on these songs, so that it elevates everybody else. This is once-in-a-lifetime stuff.

"I don't know what the spark was that set it off—something about the combination of being in that Barn and Levon being right there and the band members being who they were and the audience putting out this energy of sitting there and enjoying it. There was something about the combination of all those elements that created yet another element, that lifted all of us to another place. I haven't experienced a lot of that in my career. There's been bits and pieces and certain isolated events where I've had the chance to experience those sorts of things. But on a sustained level, it's hard."

Byron Isaacs

Bass player and vocalist Byron Isaacs was the only member of the Levon Helm Band to contribute an original song to each of Levon's two Grammy-winning studio solo albums—"Calvary" on *Dirt Farmer* and "Heaven's Pearls" on *Electric Dirt*.

Byron performed on the 2016 Lumineers CD, *Cleopatra* and their 2019 release, *III*, both of which were recorded near Woodstock at The Clubhouse recording studio in Rhinebeck. Byron also performed on the 2022 Lumineers album, *BRIGHTSIDE,* which was recorded near Woodstock at Sun Mountain Studios in Boiceville. Byron toured the world with the Lumineers, making stops along the way at Madison Square Garden and at MetLife Stadium, at the Meadowlands Sports Complex in New Jersey, where the Lumineers opened for U2.

A Texas native, Byron first met Levon in October 2002, when Byron and his bandmates in Ollabelle were recording their first album at the Magic Shop recording studio in New York City.

"Levon came in while we were tracking the basics, and the thing is, I vaguely knew who he was," Byron said. "The way my whole musical thing had come about, I happened to miss The Band up to that point. Right about the point I would have gotten to The Band, when I was 16 or so, I discovered Charlie Mingus and that shot me off in a completely different direction and I got deep into jazz. It was right when I was ready for that kind of epiphany. Here it is, it's 2002, and I'm 30-years-old and I'd never listened to The Band. The other folks in Ollabelle are freaking the fuck out when Levon showed up. I was looking at them like, 'What's the matter with you guys? Just chill out. He's Amy's dad. Clearly, he's a cool dude.' He was very nice, and he had, to me, a very familiar accent. He's from Arkansas and I'm from Texas. I kind of felt something of a kinship to him right away."

Levon at the time had yet to regain his voice following his battle with cancer.

"He was whispering, he was still rascally. In those days, he was still a little more ornery than he was later, as the Rambles really got going. He really chilled out a lot. But he was still full of a lot of piss and vinegar in those days. He was always really damn funny. He showed up and he had Butch Dener with him. He rolls in. We ended up getting him in to play on a couple of tunes. The other guys were losing their minds and acting very strange around him, which I wasn't. I think Levon liked that a lot."

Levon sat down at the drum kit and Ollabelle kicked into "Soul of a Man."

"He came up with this really weird beat. At first, I was like, 'What the hell is he playing?' Then, it's like, 'That's fucking cool.' It was weird. It was great. He came up with parts right away. If you listen to the tunes and check out what he's doing, he came up with identifiable parts that were sculpted in the song and came back around. He composed a drum part for that song on the spot. It was consistent and very unusual. It was a signature drum part. I couldn't believe how cool he was, and his feel was so great. I had never played with someone who had a feel like that—where his pocket sat was really special. I came to find out, the more I played with him, that where his pocket sat was naturally right where mine did, which is unusual."

The playback followed the recording, and everyone gathered around to listen.

"He leaned way over the console and his ass was sticking out, and he started doing a super groovy dance," Byron said. "His head was down. He was grooving along with the music, doing this funky-ass dance. I was like, 'Amy's dad is cool.' Then he came in and played one more tune with us and both of those are on that first record. On 'Ain't Nobody Can Do Me Like Jesus,' he just played super-killing funky. At the end of the session, Levon's taking off, he says goodbye to everybody. And Butch takes me aside. He says, 'Hey. You know any blues? You know any Willie Dixon songs? Get these records.' He writes out a list of records and says, 'The boss is going to call you for some gigs.' I'm like, 'Okay, great.'"

Byron said Amy told him years later that she spoke with her father and told him he couldn't take Ollabelle's bass player.

"I never did get the call," he said. "But we hit it off right away."

After Levon left, Byron thought to himself, "I have to see what this Band thing is all about."

So he asked Ollabelle drummer Tony Leone and keyboard player Glenn Patscha about the Band records he should check out to learn more.

"They look at me like I've got three eyes," he said. "They say, 'You've got to get the first two. You've got to get *Music From Big Pink* and *The Band*.'"

The music of Charles Mingus left a monster footprint on Byron's life when he heard it for the first time at age 16.

"That's when I knew I had to be a musician," he said. "I had been playing a little bit with friends, but that was a defining moment—what an epiphany. A friend burned Mingus on either side of a 90-minute cassette."

At the time, Byron confessed, "I was into terrible music."

But after listening to Mingus for the first time, he said, "My mom remembers me sitting at the stereo with my jaw on the floor saying, 'This is like Metallica, but better.' At the time, that's what I was into. I was also into The Beatles, Stevie Wonder—a lot of stuff that was great. The reason I probably said Metallica was because there was this power to their music, and Mingus, in a completely different way, harnessed even more power than anything Metallica ever did. It knocked me on my ass."

Byron thought hearing Charles Mingus for the first time was the epiphany that had changed his life. Then he found The Band.

"When I put on *The Brown Album*, by the time I got to 'Whispering Pines,' my mind was completely destroyed again, in a whole new way—an experience not like any other experience I ever had," he said. "That's the only one I had in my adult life. It was just, completely, a game changer. Everything changed after that. The Band just completely fucked me up. I had never heard anything like 'Whispering Pines.' This is more than watching a movie. This is reading a serial novel. This piece of music, all my synapses were just exploding. I couldn't believe it. Everything I'd ever wanted in music was right there. The next time I met Levon, I was starstruck and acting weird around him. Just like those dudes had."

And then the Midnight Rambles got underway.

"It was amazing to watch that whole thing happen," Byron said. "What was more amazing was to see someone come from relative obscurity to becoming a legend and having that transformation happen before my very eyes. If he hadn't started up those Rambles and subsequently made those records that won Grammys and all of that, he could have died in obscurity. What he did in that last act took him all the way from an aging rock star, languishing in obscurity, to being a legend. And I saw the whole thing. It was unbelievable. I'm sure I'll never see anything of the like the rest of my life. It's crazy. It's amazing. And to see him laughing his way through the whole thing; he couldn't take it seriously. He was just doing the same thing he always did—'What? Now you all love me?' But he never got bitter about it. He really enjoyed it, very much."

Byron described the Midnight Rambles in the early days as "very loose."

Hubert Sumlin was around. If a tune was called and Byron didn't know it, Andrew Shober from the Apple Picker's Union would take over on bass.

"It was more like a jam session," he said. "It was like throwing songs around. Everyone was just sitting in chairs. There was a very little, minimal PA they found in the basement, an ancient PA. It was a very informal, jam-at-my-house concert type of thing. It was not the big production that it became."

Byron took over the Levon Helm Band bass slot permanently in 2009, when bass player Mike Merritt went to California with Jimmy Vivino and the rest of the Max Weinberg 7, to perform on *The Tonight Show with Conan O'Brien*. And as Byron played more and more with the Levon Helm Band, he learned more and more about Levon Helm.

"He was great at whipping things into shape," Byron said. "For anything like a horn solo that got too weird, he'd say, 'No, no, no. None of them funny notes. Stick to the blues. Play the melody, goddammit. Play the goddamn melody. Play some long notes. Slow it down. Play some nice, long notes.' Or, for someone singing, he'd say, 'Sing the melody.' He'd have some great things to say about singing. He said, about singing, 'Be sure to end your phrases right. The way you end your phrase is the most important.' I started thinking about that and I realized it's true. In a very few words, he could pinpoint the thing that would help you get your shit where it needed to be. When we were onstage, sometimes he would scream, 'NOOOOOOO!' Sometimes he'd catch your eye and whack his cowbell. Sometimes that was for humor—and sometimes it wasn't. You might fuck up a note. Sometimes he'd look at you with a funny look in his eye and he'd crack a smile and whack that cowbell and he'd start laughing, like, 'Yeah, yeah, you got me.' Sometimes he'd hit that thing and it's like, 'Oh fuck. I'm in trouble.' He was listening to everything. Nobody was off the hook.

"Sometimes he'd have his eyes closed and his head turned. That was because he was listening so hard. Even when he was singing, he managed to listen. He had incredible ears. He caught everything. Sometimes, for the bass lines, I'd be playing and he'd look at me; he'd keep the beat with one hand and he'd punch his fist to show where he wanted me to lay the beat. He really knew what he wanted and he knew how to communicate it. I found him to be great to work with—until I pissed him off. As a mentor, I can say the thing I got the most out of Levon was seeing how dedicated he was to every second of playing—and I mean focused.

"The most turned-on musicians that you know, Jimi Hendrix and the people we call gods, clearly are just so absorbed in the moment that there is no mind-wandering going on. There is something else happening. Their mind can't be wandering when they're on fire like that. Most musicians aren't on like that, to that level, at every moment. But Levon was the first guy I played with who was bearing down on every single millisecond of every song. And if he missed—I would see him, every now and then, he would miss a backbeat or something—he would have this moment of fury with himself and then he would just grit his teeth and bear down that much harder. No one was putting out as much energy as he was. He was so dialed in to every millisecond. He is one of those guys. That's why he blew everybody's mind. Standing next to him, I really got to see what that was. The energy coming off of him was crazy. He was like a ball of fire. The energy he was radiating was intense and he was completely soaked through with sweat every time. He was burning. I'd look over at him sometimes and his entire body would be covered in goose bumps. It was because he was fucking turned on. He was burning up. It was intense. It freaked me out. There were times I would look at him and he was just digging in, just bearing down. And he would be singing his ass off.

"I decided, at a certain point, that I was going to try to match him, energy-wise. I was going to step up and dig in the way he was digging in and focus the way he was focusing. I came close but I never could match it. And there wasn't a person on that stage who could match it. He was burning way harder than anyone. And that was a burning band. Everyone in that band was a bad ass. But nobody was burning like him. Not one person was burning as hard as he was, and every one of them would tell you that. Everyone knew it. It was fucking frightening to be next to sometimes. It was so intense. I saw firsthand that there was another level to get to and that I could either choose to see that as just the mark of a one-of-a-kind or I could take it as a mandate to up my game, and try to get somewhere else with it, push it farther, see how far I could get and not take anything but the very most that I could pour out with every pore of my being.

"Anything less than that was just not going to cut it. That was my mandate. It's like, I have to put it all on the line every time, or what the fuck am I doing? The world doesn't need another pretty good musician. Fuck that. The world needs more Levon Helm—that's what it needs."

Next up in the introductions was Jimmy Weider, a monster on that Fender Telecaster guitar who is discussed in a later chapter of this book. And then, as Larry put it, "the lovely Miss Amy Helm" and "the luminous Miss Teresa Williams."

Amy sang and played mandolin and sometimes the drums. Teresa sang and played guitar.

Teresa Williams

Teresa received a Bachelor of Arts and a Master of Fine Arts, both in theater, from the University of Tennessee at Knoxville. She headed to New York City with $11 in her pocket to pursue acting, and harbored a secret dream of seeing what she could accomplish in the music industry. Teresa launched her career by auditioning while working a temp job at a small publishing house.

Her theatrical path had already led her to auditions for the Royal Academy of Dramatic Art in London, and the London Academy of Music & Dramatic Art.

"I was on a legit theater path," she said. "I wanted the deep stuff, the serious stuff. I had auditioned for RADA and LAMDA before grad school, and even tried to study in Ireland close to the Abbey Theatre, but never made it there. But I could sing, and there wasn't much work for straight plays."

About three months after arriving in New York City, an old classmate of Teresa's set up an audition for a six-month singing gig on a cruise ship that traveled between Manhattan and Bermuda. A strong, loud voice in Teresa's head advised against it.

"I was not going to do it," she said. "It would take me off my serious acting path."

But on the other hand, she thought, "You're in your early 20s, you have a chance to see the world. Get on the ship."

So off Teresa went, performing just two nights a week. With her newfound freedom, she began studying great jazz and blues female vocalists. Having grown up with country blues, gospel, bluegrass, and rock and roll, she now delved into the likes of Ella Fitzgerald, Sarah Vaughan and Billie Holiday. But in an interesting twist, the ship's onboard entertainment offered another artistic discipline, one that resonated loudly with Teresa.

The onboard cinema would screen *Coal Miner's Daughter*, the 1980 film starring Sissy Spacek as Loretta Lynn, Tommy Lee Jones as her husband and Levon Helm as Loretta's father. Teresa's regular 20 minute-breaks between sets, which allowed her to peer through a deck window into the screening room, happened to fall during Levon's poignant scenes early in the movie.

The film was set in Butcher Hollow, Kentucky. But Levon, who Teresa had never heard of, hailed from just across the Mississippi River from where she had grown up, in Henderson County, Tennessee.

"Being so far from home, Levon's 'just-walked-out-of-the-cotton-patch-self' spoke to my soul," she said. "I would stand there on that deck crying every time I saw those scenes—every single time. I still do.

"Levon Helm was a touchstone for me as an artist when I was first starting out in New York and even as a teen when I was still home. I knew his voice, but not his name. When I put together that the father in *Coal Miner's Daughter* was the same voice in 'The Night They Drove Old Dixie Down,' I thought my head would explode. It was crazy. I never dreamed I would meet, much less work with him. That's another one of those crazy things where you look up at the sky and think, 'Okay, now I'm getting scared.'

"Levon was so honest. He was so honest in his art—music and acting. It's so honest it's painful. It just cuts you—look at his cameo in *The Three Burials of Melquiades Estrada*—and he was like that in real life, too. Levon was 'True North,' musically. He just was 'True North' in the authenticity of his art."

Years later, Teresa asked Larry for his insight on why Levon's role in *Coal Miner's Daughter* left such an impression on her.

"He said, 'He's like your dad, he is your dad.' Culturally, the sound of his voice, the idioms, the dialect. All of that.

"*Coal Miner's Daughter* was about us—my people, my hillbilly-roots people. The accent's the same. The upbringing's the same. It just happened to be up in coal country instead of cotton country. But most of these people in the Delta came from up in the mountains, up in Appalachia. They came over in covered wagons. It's not for nothing Levon and I were cut from the same cloth, culturally, for sure."

Teresa said all of this underscored the strong bond that developed between her and Levon, when she met him in Woodstock decades after watching *Coal Miner's Daughter* on that cruise ship.

"The personal part of the relationship was huge for me because it was like having a piece of my family up there, up North, because we were so culturally akin."

Teresa in West Tennessee, like Levon in Arkansas, grew up on a cotton farm.

"Everybody around us were cotton farmers, small-time cotton farmers," she said. "That's how you made your living. You didn't go to town much. You raised everything. You could live off of what you raised and that's what people did. It was subsistence farming, except when you had a good cotton crop year."

The Williams family farm sat on the eastern edge of the Mississippi River Delta, halfway between Nashville and Memphis, an hour from the Mississippi state line. Teresa as an infant was in the cotton fields with her mother, who could pick 200 pounds in a day.

"She's a dynamo," Teresa said.

Teresa as a kid picked cotton while wearing an old-time sun bonnet, starting with a flour sack, then moving on to a tow sack, junior sack and then the adult size.

"I picked cotton up until the big machines came in," she said. "And even then, they would make us clean the rows after the big machines, and pick the ends of the rows."

Everybody had large families and everyone in the family picked cotton, as opposed to relying on hired hands. Some of the folks in town, doctors and lawyers in some cases, sent their kids out to pick cotton, Teresa said, "So they would learn how to work."

Teresa walked to school through a cotton patch and, she said, "One of the best memories of my life is of when they'd let us ride on top of the fluffy cotton on the way to the gin."

Teresa while growing up was known locally as "the girl who sang." She says that she took her good fortune, of being born into music, for granted. Her artistic passion early in life, however, drew her to the theater.

"I wanted to study acting, I needed to do that," she said. "I don't know why. For my culture, it was as if I dropped from a pod from Mars."

But interestingly enough, when Teresa was growing up, "There was no theater—period. I don't know how I came to love it. The Christmas play at church? I like telling a story and come from big storytellers. I like words. I like research. I like history and it was all encompassed in theater. I'm a big nerd."

Music, however, she said, "was the wallpaper. All of my grandparents sang. My mother's mother sang while she was working. There were hours of singing at church and yes, we sang in the field. My mother and father were teaching me guitar and piano and harmony at home. It was music, music, music."

And there was music at the church "revivals," still common today in the South, that Teresa attended with her family, "from the time when I was so little they'd have us on a pallet on the floor."

These "Missionary Baptist backwoods revivals," as Teresa described them, would often last until 2 a.m.

"Back then, there was none of that little, 'fold your hands in your lap, on your hymnal and sing in a timid voice,'" Teresa said. "Most of these people knew all of these songs by heart. They had hymnals, but they would throw their heads back and sing full throttle with abandon. They would call the 'mourners' to the altar, people who 'wanted to be saved from their sins.' The mourners would come to the 'mourner's bench' down front while elders prayed around them. Older men and women would kneel down with them and pray for hours, while everybody else is singing, on-and-on-and-on."

Teresa said you can get a sense of it all by listening to a Rev. Gary Davis sermon.

"The rhythms, the guttural punctuation between phrases in the sermon were exactly the same," she said.

The revivals that Teresa and her family attended were held in churches, tents and brush arbors. For brush arbor meetings, poles would be put up with a covering of brush.

"That was my 'clean' version of the Midnight Rambles that Levon went to," Teresa said. "My parents at the county fair wouldn't let me near the hootchie-coochie show, which was probably near to what Levon saw at his childhood Midnight Rambles. We heard about it. I wasn't even allowed to look at a beer joint when driving by. I missed that whole journeyman part of my career, 'cause the beer joints were where the honky-tonk, country and rock and roll music we were hearing on the radio was happening live, locally. I didn't get to sing in those places—verboten. But it all worked out—the rock and roll people, the Brits, the San Fran groups were coming towards the stuff I was getting at my parents' knees and in church."

Teresa's journeyman work unfolded after she arrived in New York City, on cruise gigs, and later when she sang in a band that served as the opening act and backup band for the Tennessee Plowboy, Eddy Arnold. Thanks to that gig, Teresa was doing some serious traveling and really seeing the world by ship—the Pyramids, India, Sri Lanka, Singapore, Amsterdam, South America.

"I couldn't believe it was really happening, that this hick from the cotton patch was going to these places," she said.

While on board, Teresa continued immersing herself in the great female jazz and blues singers. Taking yet another ship contract after breaking off an engagement to be married, she moved over to a jazz ensemble, working seven nights a week.

Upon returning to New York City, she got to know a clerk at Tower Records who was appalled that she was unfamiliar with Etta James, and he quickly brought her up to speed. She was at this point temping at a different publishing house and moonlighting as a jazz singer with steady, weekly gigs at Café Society.

She continued to pursue acting and graduated from a two-year intensive Meisner program, the approach to acting developed by actor and acting teacher Sanford Meisner, whose students included Robert Duvall and Grace Kelly.

"But I kept being cast as 'the mountain woman' in original Southern pieces, rather than in Shakespeare," Teresa said with a laugh. "It was fun. I enjoyed playing mountain women and, hey, I did like to eat. But all the while I had my foot in both worlds—acting and the music industry."

The sudden death of Teresa's brother and subsequent breaking off of another misguided engagement pulled Teresa back to the music of her childhood. With renewed determination, she recorded a country music demo in Nashville, and that demo landed her a gig at the Bottom Line in New York City.

"Then I had to have a country band," she said. "I didn't know any country players in New York City—I thought that was an oxymoron. A friend marched me down to the old Lone Star Café to try to find musicians for my band."

A friend from Teresa's acting class introduced her to musician Michael Simmons, who heard her tape and was inspired to assemble a band that included a musician named Larry Campbell. Larry played pedal steel on that 1986 gig at the Bottom Line—and the rest, as they say, is history.

After working as a singer and actor for years, Teresa found herself performing at Levon Helm Studios at the Midnight Ramble with her original artistic touchstone, Levon Helm.

Teresa's foray into the Rambles began when Amy Helm called her to fill in on nights she couldn't be there. There was also a new project at The Barn that seemingly drew from Teresa's own childhood—the *Dirt Farmer* record.

"Larry was delighted that, for the first time in years, we were working together, thanks to Amy," Teresa said. "And working with Levon was like being a kid in a sandbox—creative freedom. Working with Levon was music utopia."

As for the locomotive of a band she was a member of, Teresa said, "I was right in the middle of that freight train. I had Levon either on drums or mandolin, along with Byron on bass, Amy and Jimmy Weider to my left; Larry right with me; the five horns behind me; and then Brian Mitchell and keyboard world on my right. I'm spoiled for life. Ruined. 'Rurnt' as we'd say down South."

There was one Ramble in particular that sticks out in Teresa's mind. She was late getting up to Woodstock from a trip to Tennessee, and arrived while the opening act was playing.

It was summer, the sun had set, the doors and windows of The Barn were open and, "the light and music were spilling out," she said.

"There were people milling inside and out. It just struck me as being like those revivals I would go to when I was little, in the heat of the summer, where there was no air conditioning—you've got that sticky, summer-sultry thing going on and the gospel flowing from inside, in no uncertain terms, and the golden light and music spilling out. I wish I could have painted it. It was magical. It was heavy but light at the same time. There was something spiritual going on in a big way, and always, always healing."

And then there were the post-Ramble hangs, in the house, around Levon's kitchen table, with the man from Turkey Scratch holding court, chatting up his band members, the opening act, friends and who knows who else. This epic conclusion to everyone's epic Saturday night offered Teresa yet another means of staying close to her Tennessee roots, courtesy of the guy from Arkansas who, she said, "still sounded as if he just walked out of the cotton patch."

"I grew up with all the men sitting around, under the tree, outside, after a morning revival meeting, and a big dinner at somebody's house—all the old men, my grandfather and great-uncles, my uncles, topping each other's tales, like Levon would do in the kitchen."

And before Larry and Teresa bought their house in Woodstock, on Sunday nights, they would visit with Levon and Sandy.

"We would sit with Levon and Sandy in front of their fireplace, exactly like we did with my mother's parents," Teresa said. "The only thing missing was someone spitting snuff toward the fireplace, or tobacco. That was massive for me, because of the cultural thing. It was like I was with family again and this is outside the music part of it. When my parents came to Woodstock, Levon knew they were from his neck of the woods, and that was a big thing. He really went out of his way to show them around Woodstock. I was a fish out of water in the North and I felt this deep connection with him—but he made everybody feel that deep connection with him."

Brian Mitchell

Rounding out the introductions was Brian Mitchell.

When Brian was a little kid growing up in the Bronx, his mother took piano lessons to help her unwind from raising him and his three siblings. As his mother played, Brian would hop up on the piano stool, sit next to her and play right along with her. She decided to send him for piano lessons to add some culture to his life because some of her family members were involved in Italian-American social clubs and nightlife. She did not want Brian to end up hanging out all night in bars and night clubs with, he said, "nefarious characters. Little did she know that my involvement in music would eventually put me in some of those same night clubs, with some of those same characters, that she did not want me to be around."

Decades later, Brian went on to perform with B.B. King, Al Green, Dolly Parton and Rosanne Cash, among numerous other musical acts. His original music was featured in the Robert Altman film *Tanner on Tanner*. And Brian's accordion playing can be heard in an episode of *The Sopranos*, accompanying Bob Dylan as he performs "Return to Me," the song made famous by Dean Martin. Brian also played accordion as he accompanied actor Christopher Walken on the soundtrack for the film *Search and Destroy*. In addition to the Brian Mitchell Band, he performed in The Weight Band; and Fatboy Kanootch with Clark Gayton, and Tony Leone of Ollabelle, the Chris Robinson Brotherhood and Little Feat.

At the Midnight Ramble, Brian's love of New Orleans stoked his fiery piano playing and crafted his nuanced onslaught with the Hammond B-3. He kicked off many Midnight Rambles by leading the charge on "The Shape I'm In" by The Band. And his version of "Lonesome Suzie" was a heartbreaker.

Levon loved all his band members. But Brian was the only guy that Levon looked at directly across the stage during shows. Brian looked directly back at Levon, as the drums and piano faced each other. The drum and piano duet that Levon and Brian closed "Mardi Gras Day" with, at just about every Ramble, was a show-stopper. And it was just one of the many great moments spurred by a phone call Brian received from Jimmy Vivino.

"I had a dear friend who committed suicide and it affected me in a big way, so I stopped playing music for a period of time," Brian said. "I had some people call me to play and I just couldn't feel it at all. And then I got a call from Jimmy Vivino going, 'Hey man, do you want to come up to Woodstock and play with Levon Helm?' And this light burst through. If there's one gig I think I'll get out of bed for, it's that gig. So I got up and played and I was there for the next eight years.

"In the early days, it was really freewheeling. At the second gig I played with Levon the atmosphere was, 'Hey Brian, you do a song.' We would just play songs off the top of our heads. I did this old New Orleans tune and I looked over at Levon and he does not look happy and I'm getting paranoid. I didn't know him that well but he looked miserable and I'm bumming out. Bad call—I should have done another song.

"So I go home and I'm thinking, 'Well, that's it for that gig. It was fun while it lasted.' That was on a Saturday night. On Sunday night, I get a call and it's Levon. He says, 'Hey man, I just wanted to let you know, I'm so sorry I screwed up that song of yours. It's been bothering me all day. I'm going to work on it. We're going to do it again next Saturday.' Who does that?"

Along with the musical memories, Brian learned a lot about Levon.

"I live on the Lower East Side," he said. "This one time I was going to buy groceries and I got jumped by a gang, punched behind the head. They weren't there to rob me. It was some kind of initiation. I grabbed one guy and took him down with me. Then they all cowardly ran away and I left. I get in the car and I go to the Ramble to play and I'm a little jacked up. Five minutes before we go on, Levon says, 'Bro, what's wrong?' I said, 'I'm okay.' But I was all scuffed and torn. So I told him the story and he said, 'Pull the truck up. Let's go get those guys.' I say, 'It's cool. Let's go do the gig.'

"We play the gig and afterward he goes, 'You ready to go? I'll go right now.' When this happened, Levon was 70 years old, not in good health, and ready to get in a pickup truck and drive two hours down to the Lower East Side in Manhattan to kick some ass."

And then there was that time that Brian introduced Levon to his father.

"My mother and father never heard of The Band," he said. "My father came up one time to a Ramble, or it was a show on the road, and he met Levon. My dad returned to a Ramble and Levon comes up to him and says,

'George, how are you?' My dad is like, 'He remembered my name—that's a man. A man shakes your hand, looks you in the eye, and remembers your name.' After that, every once in a while, Levon would ask me, 'How's Bob doing?' I would say, 'His name is George.' Levon would say, 'Okay.' A month later, Levon asks me, 'How's Phil doing?' 'It's George.' 'O.K.' My dad shows up at the Ramble and I'm like, 'Oh my God, here we go.' Levon says, 'George, how are you?' I'm like, what? I didn't know if Levon was putting me on or whatever. It gave my dad something to talk about to this day."

After introducing Brian, Larry would turn to Levon and lean into the microphone before declaring, "And the greatest drummer in the whole wide world: LE-VON HELM."

Levon would follow that up by saying, "And now, say hello to our band leader, a native son of New York City, that's LAR-RY Campbell."

If you want to hear a funny story about Levon Helm, then talk to Mary Cavette, Levon's childhood and lifelong friend. Mary shared a gem of a tale related to Larry's on-stage introduction of the man from Turkey Scratch at a Levon Helm Band performance that she attended with her grand-nephew Nicholas.

"At some point, when Larry was introducing the members of the band, he said, 'You all know the greatest drummer in the world, Levon Helm,' and Nicholas just sat up, and he said, 'Grand Mary, you didn't tell me he was the greatest drummer in the world,'" Mary said. "He was so impressed.

"So we get backstage and Nicholas is dumbfounded. He can't even talk. Lavon said, 'Would you like to have my drumsticks?' and he says, 'Oh yes.' 'And the set list?' And he gets home and he said, 'Momma, I think we need to put this in the safe, because he is the greatest drummer in the whole world and Joshie might play with them.' And he tells his little brother, who is 6, he said, 'Joshie, you should have been there. He was the greatest drummer in the whole world—not just Arkansas, in the whole world.'"

CHAPTER NINE

Team Levon

Levon over the course of his career played some very big gigs. There was Carnegie Hall and Madison Square Garden with The Band and Bob Dylan, Wembley Stadium in London with The Band and while leading the Levon Helm Band in July 2010, Radio City Music Hall with Willie Nelson.

It's all but certain, however, that Mark Lavon Helm would tell you that one of his favorite shows was the annual concert the Levon Helm Band played at the Gill Farms farm stand on Route 209 in Hurley, New York, just a few miles from Plochmann Lane and Woodstock.

The Gill Farms show was special for a lot of reasons—the hayride, the corn chowder, and the pumpkin cannon that launched pumpkins for what seemed like a mile over the Gill family's fields, in the direction of Hurley Mountain Road. That swath of Ulster County reminded Levon of the Mississippi Delta cotton country, where he grew up.

There were typically thousands at these shows. But with everything going on—and there was a lot, including dogs and kids running everywhere—the most incredible sight was watching Levon when that pumpkin cannon got ready to fire. You could hear the mechanics of it kick in right before takeoff—and see his grin grow wide.

Those free concerts at Gill Farms typically took place in early October. We call that autumn, but Levon would refer to it as "harvest time." These gigs were probably the only concerts where Levon was driven to the stage in a John Deere Gator. The Gill Farms shows struck at the core of Levon's origins—performing live music for an audience and farming. And they usually took place on one of those stunning, crisp, sun-drenched autumn days that you can only find in the Hudson Valley.

About 18 hours earlier, the Midnight Ramble would have been in full swing on Plochmann Lane.

And while a lot of very famous people joined Levon for these shows, he would have been the first to tell you that a whole group of other people, whose names you may not know, played as pivotal a role in the success of the Midnight Ramble. They were the Levon Helm Studios volunteers, known affectionately as Team Levon.

"We've got folks like Bill Speight helping us out," Levon said. "Bill and I and his whole family, we've been friends for years. There is something about Bill. He is one of the most likable damn people you've ever met. I mean, you just can't beat him."

Bill worked security. Meanwhile, Dane Turner's official title had to do with hospitality, but he was involved in just about everything when it came to staging the Ramble and he was usually out on the road as well. The same could be said for Walter Turk.

"Anytime The Band or the Barn Burners would play in New York, Dane would always come and see us," Levon said. "He used to live down there and worked out of the New York local there—the steelworkers' local. And me and him would always talk, and he'd help me load up, stuff like that. He ended up getting himself a place up in the country, right here in Woodstock. We just became friends over the years. Walter Turk is a good guy, too. He's a good guy to have with you out on the road. I've been lucky like that all my life. I've met some of the best damn people.

"Tony and Dawn LoBue are like the Speights and Dane—folks who would show up to see us perform in their neighborhood. And before you knew it, they were helping us out with the Rambles. What Tony did for us, when the damn internet thing first came to be, Tony went ahead and grabbed www.levonhelm.com before anyone else could. He checked around, and I didn't know what a damn computer was, much less my own page, my own station, but that's what Tony did. He went ahead and grabbed it. And Dawn was telling him, you know, 'Go on and do it. And then some day, if he wants to do something about it, you can give it to him, just save it for him, hold it for him.' And by God, that's exactly what he did. Then he came in and ran the whole damn thing for us. And he's learned so much.

"None of us were really showbiz folks. But shit, showbiz, it's just like any other half-ass biz. There ain't no fuckin' rules. You're better off keeping your word and not fucking with anybody who won't keep theirs. There ain't no damn book or nothing you could read. Everybody had to put in all those years of Rambles and now, we don't make too many mistakes.

"We play Road Rambles, down to the Beacon Theatre in the city. Just the difference between our first year and our third year at the Beacon, it was just easier. Our team really came together. The first two years at the Beacon, that was when the work got done.

"There is an old saying: 'He's a pretty good old boy, but you couldn't send him for the ammunition. He might get lost, or drop it, or not make his way back. And now we're stuck.' So you want people in the foxhole with you, who, you know, you can send for the ammunition. That's what it's been for the past few years—anybody who wasn't in it for the long haul had to run for cover. Everybody is on the same level. We're not going to high-hat each other, or put somebody in that stupid-ass role to play, shit: 'I'm going to play the big star,' you know; what a dumb-ass predicament that would be."

As a Midnight Ramble attendee, your anticipation could easily accelerate from zero to 60 in just a few seconds as you turned off Plochmann Lane and into Levon's long, tree-lined driveway on your final descent into Levon Helm Studios. The first stop was the ticket booth, a small, enclosed, freestanding structure with a window and a door. Levon Helm Studios would be to your right, the ball field for parking was to your left.

Tom and Cathy Gagliardi were in charge of the ticket booth, with

Margaret Stewart and Jeff Stephenson typically on hand as well. You stopped to check in and were gently warned of the Ramble dos and don'ts: Turn off your cell phone, no pictures, no cameras, no bottles, no cans and no autographs.

Bob Brinkman, Mike Sheehan or John Peck were among those likely to assist in the mechanics of parking your car. After which, your first stop would be Levon's garage, which housed the potluck table and merchandise operation. Jeannie Douglas, Kathy Gillis or Deb Manfredonio would be selling the merch. After placing the potluck dish you had brought on the table, and noshing on some nibbles left by someone else, it was time to head upstairs for the Midnight Ramble magic.

If you failed to remember the do's and don'ts from the ticket booth, you might have to wrangle with "Helmland Security." You really had to be a big problem for Pat Cahill, Mike Manfredonio, Bill Speight, Steve Farrell, Perry Gallo, Fran Prendergast or retired Ulster County Sheriff Richie Bockelmann to give you a hard time. But if they caught you taking pictures with your cell phone, they would ask you nicely to delete the photos—and watch you delete them. Dolores Farrell, who is married to Steve, and actor John Scurti, who starred in the television series "Rescue Me" with Dennis Leary, and also appeared in "The Marvelous Mrs. Maisel," were also on the scene with Team Levon.

Watching it all from the corner of the room, right next to the popcorn machine, standing guard over the hallway that connected the studio to where Levon lived, was Chris Howe, Levon's long-time right-hand man, his driver, his confidante during long road trips.

Each Ramble volunteer played an oh-so-critical role in the launch, evolution and success of this singular initiative. Every one of them slugged it out in all kinds of weather—pounding downpours and below-zero winters and the Hudson Valley's 100-plus degree summers—for nothing more than the satisfaction of sharing in the magic of a Midnight Ramble and playing a role, no matter how large or small, in its success.

"The ones who stayed didn't have agendas and wanted to be there because they wanted to help Levon," said Tony LoBue. "That's a big accomplishment in your life; I'd be happy with that on my tombstone: 'I helped

Levon.' I don't care if anyone understands it or not—I do. Without the staff, it would have been absolute and total chaos. People would be coming all night long for free. Nobody would be paying. There would be disagreements in the audience. It would be overcrowded. There would be no order, no structure to the whole thing. And these people, the staff, the volunteers, myself included, we all learned along the way how to do this. And we learned from our mistakes. People were outside. They had little a potbelly stove going in the pouring rain. During the Black Crowes shows, there was six or eight inches of snow on the ground. It was freezing cold. There was total ice no matter where they stood. And those people—between glove warmers and fires and coming in and out—nobody ever, ever complained. Nobody came to me and said, 'This isn't fair. I don't like this.' A few did and they were gone because they didn't fit in. They were just there to say they were there or to see what they could get out of it."

Dane Turner

They were both from the South. Both of their jobs revolved around extensive travel. And they were both proud union men.

Atlanta native Dane Turner first crossed paths with Levon Helm in 1998, at a Barn Burners show in Fort Lauderdale, Florida. After the show, Dane spotted Levon behind a backstage door.

"I shouted his name," Dane recalled. "I saw him and shook his hand as he was closing the door. It was a spiritual experience for me. He's a hero. He always has been—just his presence."

In Fort Lauderdale that night, after shaking Levon's hand, Dane saw a shooting star.

"You kind of blow things like that off," he said. "But, you know, there might be something to it."

Dane saw Levon perform often and, when he could, he'd take a shot at saying hello. Sometimes he was successful.

"I never pushed it," he said. "You never know how to act around someone like that. He was a pretty impressive dude. What do you talk about?

You come to find out that you talk about tractors and picking cotton and football and politics."

Dane was a union ironworker. He worked on The Oculus transportation hub—which was built at Ground Zero in lower Manhattan after the Twin Towers were destroyed in the Sept. 11, 2001, terrorist attacks. And he scaled its evolving frame as part of his day job.

That colossal building, which means so much to so many people, was one more ironworking gig that kept Dane moving around the country, from town to town, city to city and job to job, his entire adult life.

"If I wasn't going, I was planning on leaving," he said of his life in general. "I always had a trip planned, a working trip. There was always a plan."

Dane once worked out of Morgan City, Louisiana, on a dredge that dug sites for oil rigs and channels for navigation. He'd go out for two weeks and come in for a week. He'd sleep in the back seat of his Ford Pinto during the week off and he'd listen to a cassette recording of *The Last Waltz*.

In either 1999 or 2000, Dane flew into New York to visit a friend who was living in Point Pleasant, New Jersey, on the Jersey Shore.

"Levon was doing a show in Manhattan at Chicago Blues with Jimmy V. We came up for the show."

During a break in the show, Dane said, "I approached Amy, asking to meet her dad. She said, 'Talk to Butch.' Butch took me downstairs. I told Levon the story of shaking his hand in Fort Lauderdale. His voice was a whisper. He said, 'Come on up to Woodstock' at that show.

"I told him I'd been traveling so long, I wanted to plant some roots. He said, 'Why don't you come up and plant some roots in Woodstock?' I went up to Woodstock and when I found the studio, I knocked on the door and left.

"He'd always say, 'Come on up to Woodstock. Come on up to see me.' I told him one time, wherever we were at, the Stone Pony, he said, 'Come on up to see me.' I said, 'I did. I came up a couple of times. No one answered the door.'

"He said, 'Be there tomorrow at three o'clock.' I came up and he greeted me and he gave me a blood orange. I'd never seen a blood orange. We went and walked around the lake and talked. He checked me out."

Dane visited Levon regularly and crashed in the studio. As the Rambles got underway, he moved to Woodstock full-time, got an apartment and helped with studio renovations. These included building the deck off the control room and taking in porches, which extended the space where the Rambles were held.

Dane became a pivotal piece of Team Levon, at the Midnight Rambles and on the road. His official title was "Hospitality Manager." But Dane was more of a platoon player, a Jack-of-All-Trades on the logistics end of Levon Helm Studios.

He met Barbara prior to her taking a formal position with Levon.

Asked about his first impression of the woman who helped Levon Helm craft the Midnight Ramble, Dane said, "She's a lady, for one thing. She was organized. She had all her ducks in line."

And Levon?

"He wasn't different than what I expected. Expectations are kind of a big word. He's an all-for-one and one-for-all kind of guy. He's a union man. He was proud that he had his card out of the same union as Johnny Cash. He was a gentleman—and he expected you to be a gentleman, too."

Dane said Levon was human just like the rest of us.

"He was one of those guys, when he was down, he just withdrew," Dane said. "He stayed upstairs, whatever. He might disappear and you might not see him for a couple of days."

Dane said Levon's fame created a compelling contrast.

"There was Levon the hero and then it was Levon—just Lee. Sometimes it was kind of weird to put the two together. He was a friend. He was a real friend. What a blessing. What a gift, to have him give that to you. He didn't give it to everybody. It was a hell of an experience and I wondered—why me?"

John O'Neill

On the computer he used in his Westchester County law office, New York attorney John O'Neill had the cover of *Music From Big Pink*, emblazoned with Bob Dylan's artwork, as his desktop wallpaper.

"Most of my colleagues would comment on it and ask me if my daughter Kathleen had done the drawing, in a tone of voice implying, 'I hope that kid has other talents,'" John said.

But one colleague knew it was the *Big Pink* cover.

"I thought to myself, there is someone in this law firm who is not a cultural philistine," John joked.

The co-worker familiar with *Music From Big Pink* was John Risi. He had a cousin named Joe Lore, who was one of Levon's closest friends. And it was through Risi that John O'Neill received an invitation to his first Midnight Ramble.

"I had been a fan of The Band for a long time," John said. "I remember going to the Felt Forum at Madison Square Garden to see them for the first time in late December 1969. I can visualize the event—where the musicians were onstage. I guess that was the beginning of my admiration of their music."

John was thrilled with his invitation to Levon Helm Studios. But he and his wife, Irene, had already made plans for dinner with another couple on that same night.

"I implored her to get us out of the dinner date," he said.

Irene rescheduled the dinner engagement for two weeks later. John attended the Ramble and Joe Lore introduced him to Levon.

"It was the thrill of a lifetime," John said.

To John's delight, John and Irene were invited back for the next Ramble, which was scheduled for two weeks later—the same night as the rescheduled dinner date. Irene told John he would have to reschedule the dinner a second time if he wanted to return to the Ramble.

"I remember sitting at my desk on the Thursday or Friday before the show, attempting to conjure up a plausible excuse for begging off the rescheduled dinner," John said. "I was agonizing over what to say and the phone rings. It was the fellow we were meeting for dinner. And he apologized because they had to cancel."

The lyrics to "Up on Cripple Creek" immediately came to John.

"I remember saying, 'Good luck had just stung me.'"

John and Irene began attending the Midnight Rambles on a regular basis and John became the attorney for Levon Helm Studios. John also began traveling to Ulster County for Levon's other performances, including a gig in nearby Kingston. An RV was brought on site to serve as a dressing room for Levon and the band. And in typical Midnight Ramble fashion, John was enlisted on the spot to help with the day's logistics, despite his lack of experience in the music industry and, perhaps more importantly, security.

"My job was to see that people who didn't belong in the trailer didn't get in the door," he said with a laugh. "The only problem was the only person I recognized was Levon. I wasn't too effective as a gatekeeper, I suppose."

Tom and Cathy Gagliardi

On July 2, 2005, Tom and Cathy Gagliardi were driving around Woodstock. They had left their home in northern New Jersey for a weekend jaunt through the Catskills and on the way up, listened to The Band on their car stereo. The road trip and the music got Tom wondering who from The Band remained in the town where the legendary musicians had left such a huge rock and roll footprint decades earlier. The Gagliardis were making their way around downtown Woodstock when they came upon a poster in a shop that read, quite simply, "Levon Helm: Midnight Ramble with Little Sammy Davis." There was a phone number on the poster, but that was it. There was no website and no street address.

"We asked the owner in the store what it was all about," Tom recalled. "He said, 'Levon just started these things at his house. He calls them Midnight Rambles.'"

They noticed that the next Midnight Ramble was scheduled to take place that night and they set out to find Levon Helm Studios. After being given vague directions, they ended up at The Bear Cafe, on the other side of Woodstock from where they wanted to be.

"There are a handful of people there," Tom recalled. "One local guy says, 'Oh yeah. He's on Plochmann Lane, but I don't know the street number.'"

Tom and Cathy were given directions for Plochmann Lane and, they figured, "We'll follow the directions. We'll see the sign for Levon Helm Studios. We get to Plochmann Lane, drive to the end, turn around and go back—and go back again. We're going back and forth on Plochmann, which is what we heard countless times at the ticket booth, by the way."

Years after setting out in search of Levon Helm Studios on that July evening, Tom and Cathy Gagliardi found themselves running the ticket booth for Levon Helm Studios and welcoming Levon's fans from around the world to the Midnight Ramble. And on May 28, 2011, well into the Gagliardis' ticket-booth tenure, Tom, a longtime drummer, found himself playing drums alongside Levon at a Ramble. A Band fan since high school, Tom that night had a truly once-in-a-lifetime, "Oh my God this is happening" moment.

The previous week, Tom's band had played a pre-Ramble barbecue outside of the studio. On May 28, Tom was sitting on the radiator behind the drums, where staff and guests sat during the Ramble, when Levon turned around and waved him over to a second drum kit. Tom grabbed a pair of drumsticks and double-drummed with Levon on "The Weight."

"He punked me," Tom said with a laugh. "He enjoyed it as much as I did."

But let's not get ahead of ourselves. When last we left the Gagliardis, it was July 2005, they hadn't even paid their first visit to Levon Helm Studios, and they were driving back and forth on Plochmann Lane. On their final run up Plochmann, Tom and Cathy crossed Glasco Turnpike onto Lewis Hollow Road, which climbs Overlook Mountain and offers more isolation, with more trees and fewer houses, as you make your way farther and farther from downtown Woodstock.

"We're in the middle of nowhere and we're like, 'This can't be it.' We start to turn around, hoping for a cell signal. We finally see two bars. I stop. We back up a little bit—'Okay, we've got a signal. Don't move.' We call one last time."

Barbara O'Brien picked up on the other end of the line.

"She said, 'Levon Helm Studios. Can I help you?' I said, 'My name is Tom. I called and left a message.' So she says, 'I'm sorry, but we had to cancel the show because we're doing construction. But please come back some other time.' I said, 'We're right on Plochmann, looking for you.' She said, 'Oh. You're on Plochmann Lane?' I said, 'Well, not right this second. We're up in the woods somewhere.' Barbara responded, 'You're nearby. By the way, do you know anything about computers?'"

At the time, Tom worked for a global networking computer company. So yeah, he knew a few things about computers. Barbara had just gotten the first shipment of Levon's *Midnight Ramble Sessions: Volume One* DVD and was trying to play it on her computer. But she couldn't get the volume to work. So she and Tom continued to speak on the phone.

"I said, 'Did you try this?' and we're breaking up. She said, 'Come on by. We're having a meet and greet because Levon felt bad that the Ramble was canceled and that people had either bought tickets or based their weekend on it. We're having a bite to eat, some drinks. People are hanging out with Levon. Come on by. Let me get this thing going and I'll bring you over to Levon to hang out.' She said, 'Is that okay?' I was like, 'Yeah. That's okay.'"

Armed with Levon's address, Tom and Cathy barreled down Lewis Hollow Road onto Plochmann Lane and pulled into the driveway for Levon Helm Studios. There was a pile of dirt where the ticket booth now stands. They parked their car and found Barbara. Tom solved the issue with the volume on her computer. Barbara asked Tom and Cathy to go down to the pond, where Levon was hanging out with his guests, and bring him back to watch the DVD.

"We float down there and there's the man," Tom said. "He's holding court. He greets me and Cathy like we're old friends."

Tom and Cathy met Levon and the group and then everyone headed back to the studio.

"We're walking back now and Levon was making everyone else feel more important than him," Cathy said. "It seemed at first that he was going out of his way to do that. But we later realized that's just the way he is. He never gave that, 'I'm the star' vibe."

Tom said that experience shaped how he and Cathy managed the ticket booth.

"That welcoming is what we carried to the ticket booth and everywhere else at Levon Helm Studios," he said. "We always had the attitude that these folks whose names we were checking off a list may never have the opportunity that we had, to meet Levon that first day. We're just going to pass on what Levon would have done, as if Levon was running the booth. That was the attitude."

Back at the studio on their first visit, Tom, Cathy, Levon and the group were watching the DVD and Levon slipped away before heading upstairs. Barbara gave Tom the O.K. to follow Levon.

"I figure, I can watch the DVD anytime," Tom said. "So I go upstairs to the studio and Levon is over by the piano. And he says, 'Hey, Tom.' He remembered my name. It's just me and him. He tells me how the construction of The Barn was maximized for sound—the cupola, the wood beams. He's going through it with such pride—'no nails'—telling me the whole story."

Levon brought Tom upstairs to the control room, then out on the deck.

"He's telling me what he went through with cancer and the treatments. He says, 'You know, Tom, you've just got to realize every day is special.'"

The sky in Woodstock was clear that day, with no clouds. And Tom watched as Levon looked upward and closed his eyes for a moment. Then he opened them, turned toward Tom and said, "What a day to be alive."

A couple of hours had passed since the couple from New Jersey had stepped into the land of Levon. Tom was hanging out with Levon. And Cathy is looking for Tom. She finds him and Levon on the deck and they realize it was time to leave. But, Cathy said, Levon turned to them and said, "Hey Tom, Cathy, I'd like y'all to come back tomorrow."

Tom told Levon that he and Cathy were grateful for his hospitality, but they don't want to take advantage of his kindness.

"He said, 'You're not taking advantage. We're just going to be doing this tomorrow—hanging out, having some food and drink.' We look at Barbara. She says, 'If that's what the boss says, come on by.' So we did."

On their way back to Levon Helm Studios the following day, the

Gagliardis stopped and picked up some gourmet dog biscuits for Muddy, Levon's dog, along with an apple pie for Levon and Sandy and a bottle of wine for Barbara. They arrived at the studio, parked and headed for the pond. There was a bonfire going and Levon was feeding the blaze with pieces of old wooden outdoor furniture.

"It was great, though we really didn't talk about music with him that day," Tom said. "We were talking about the pond. We were talking about his trees and how the woodpeckers had made holes all over, from the middle part of the tree to the top. He called it the 'Woodpecker Condominium.' He was telling us all about the fish and the pond and the turtles."

Levon told jokes and everyone watched Muddy chase fish in the shallows of the pond. The hang wound down when Sandy called Levon in for dinner. Tom and Cathy then shared some one-on-one time with Barbara.

"She started telling us what was going on," Tom said. "And we were like, 'What can we do to help?' She was a little cautious at first, and rightfully so. She said the big thing is 'We're trying to raise money. Every week is tenuous. He could lose the house.' We learned how Barbara was leading a small team that had stepped in to help.

"Barbara saw what was going on and was saying, 'We can't let this happen.' I remember her saying, 'Here's this guy, he's not only a famous musician and actor, but he had done so much for the community. How can we let this legend—not only from being a star, but a legend from the town—how can we let this guy down?' She said, 'We're going to do everything we can.' When she said, 'We,' I didn't know who that was. We saw Barbara being the catalyst. We realized what she was doing to get these shows going and make them viable as a source of income for Levon and Sandy to keep their home. That's when she told us, with the house burning down and then he had to rebuild and he was underwater to pay that; then he got the cancer and he couldn't work; he couldn't get the kind of gigs, the income he depended on. That, together with the stories of how he helped the community—we're like, this is a no-brainer."

Tom and Cathy asked Barbara how they could help.

At the time, Tom said, downstairs at the studio, "There was nothing. It was a garage with maybe a couple of foldout tables. To that end, every week, we'd come back and Barbara and Geanine had done something new to the place. We were going up there on Saturdays when there weren't Rambles."

Tom and Cathy installed the track lights in the hallway that connects the garage to the stairway up to the studio, and they helped go through a lot of stuff, coming across a gem in the process.

> Tom: "I'll never forget when we cleared out the storage room. Our daughter, Laura, and son-in-law, John, were there."
> Cathy: "We came across the script for *Coal Miner's Daughter.*"

Thousands of Levon's fans would get to know Tom and Cathy as the folks who ran the ticket booth. But Tom and Cathy didn't start out running the ticket booth. They were simply volunteering their time to help Levon.

> Tom: "In the early days, there were no assignments."
> Cathy: "You did anything that was required."
> Tom: "You showed up and you figured it out. If the garbage needed emptying, you emptied the garbage."
> Cathy: "The work we all did brought the team together like a family."
> Tom: "Everyone just did stuff. There were no departments."
> Cathy: "You just walked around and saw what had to be done."

Barbara also asked Tom and Cathy to see what they could do back home in New Jersey to help spread the word about the Rambles.

"I thought about Fairleigh Dickinson University, near where we live," Tom said. "I went through the WFDU website and I saw a show on the college radio station called, 'Crash on the Levee.' Jerry Treacy has this show 'Crash on the Levee.' I thought, 'Wow, how perfect.'"

"Crash On The Levee (Down in the Flood)" is a Bob Dylan song that appeared on *The Basement Tapes* record by Dylan and The Band.

So Tom gave Jerry a call.

"I told him who I was and that I was trying to help with the Rambles," Tom said. "He was more than gracious to listen and help out. Right from the get-go, he started mentioning the Rambles on the show, playing songs by Ramble guests and musicians. He had Ramble musicians on the show as guests for interviews."

And then, one Saturday, Barbara told Tom and Cathy she needed help with the ticket booth.

"After the first night at the ticket booth, we were invited to hang out a little bit," Tom said. "We were all cleaning up, it was down to four or five of us. Barbara said, 'We're going to meet.' I remember saying to Tony, in front of everybody, 'How did we do?' He said, 'You did good.'"

Tom and Cathy had passed the audition.

At that point, Tom said, "The crowds weren't big but they were growing."

And then the program at Levon Helm Studios, for the volunteers, became a little more organized.

"I'm not sure if it was Barbara, Tony or Geanine who said, 'We need to get things a little more organized,'" Tom said. "We're going to have dedicated responsibilities—security, merchandise and the ticket booth. We got the ticket booth and we loved every second of it."

But, Cathy said, everyone was still responsible for everything.

"If you go inside to see the show, you've got to keep your eyes open. If you see something going on that shouldn't be going on, you become security. If you see garbage, pick it up."

Added Tom, "You were there for one reason and that was to get Levon back on his feet."

And all of this comes back to Barbara O'Brien.

"You could see how committed she was and so determined and just willing to do whatever it took," Cathy said. "I've seen Barbara cleaning bathrooms, sweeping floors, doing whatever it took to keep it going. She set the example for everyone by doing, not just saying."

Once Tom and Cathy were assigned to the ticket booth, their experience at Levon Helm Studios kicked into high gear.

"There were times that Tom and I would work outside at the booth and

Levon would step out on his deck and he would blow kisses our way, or send big waves our way," Cathy said.

And then, of course, there were Levon's fans, who drove from just about everywhere to attend the Midnight Ramble. Their first contact with the land of Levon Helm would be Tom and Cathy at the ticket booth.

"How many anniversaries, birthday parties, bachelor parties—you name it," Tom said. "They'd pull up, maybe in a party van or something, or a limo, whatever. And the driver would roll down the window. Somebody, whoever the guest of honor was, would have this look—'Where am I?'— It's dark. You're in the woods."

Cathy added, "Sometimes we'd say, 'You're at a Barry Manilow concert.'"

Tom continued, "You had to be there to see the facial expression of the person being surprised and the person doing the surprising—the biggest smiles. You never got tired of that. And then there were the virgin Ramblers. You could tell the instant they rolled down the driveway, by the look on their face, whether they were attending their first Ramble. Once they realized where they were, they'd be blown away. And then they'd get out of the car.

"The whole thing by the fire pit next to the ticket booth, that was a meeting point. We wouldn't get to hang out there until everybody was checked in. But we'd hear some great stories—'I remember Toronto, '65. We saw Levon with the Hawks.' They came from all over the world—everywhere in Europe, Japan, Pakistan. Yeah—there were other reasons why they'd come to New York. But they were not leaving until they came for the Ramble."

Added Cathy, "How great it was to be there at the end of the night and a guest would say, 'It was everything you said and then some. We'll definitely be back.' We heard, 'We'll definitely be back,' so many times, and the wonderful thing was they meant it. Not only would they come back, but they'd bring their kids, their mother, their father."

Not everyone, however, played by the rules.

"There were these guys who got lost in the woods trying to sneak into one of the Phil Lesh Rambles," Cathy said. "They got lost in the woods next to Levon's property. Their car was parked somewhere. They were like the guys we had during some shows—they came to buy tickets, learned it was sold out, then you could see them cutting through the woods. These guys, on the night that Phil Lesh played, decided to cut through the woods and they got lost, and I think scared. They ended up calling the police to rescue them. Another one—how many 'cousins' Levon Helm had. Oh my God, he had so many 'cousins,' I can't tell you. 'I'm Levon's cousin. He told me to come here to see him tonight. I can't wait to see him.' We heard every trick in the book. Some of them were very creative, others were hilarious.

"We had this guy pull up with four people in a car once, it was during a Jackson Browne show, which sold out right away. He gave us the name 'Smith,' which wasn't on the list. We asked if it could be another name. 'Jones,' he says. Now we're on to him. You know what, dude, you gave it a good shot.

"One time, I was wearing my studio-issued denim jacket with 'Levon Helm Studios' on it. I was in Saugerties and this guy said, 'Whatever you want for the that jacket.' And it said 'Cathy' on it. He said, 'I can change that.' I said, 'I couldn't sell this. There isn't enough money in the world.'"

As with each member of Team Levon, Tom and Cathy's perspectives on the Midnight Ramble, its beginnings and its evolution, offer a window on an endeavor that transcended live music by a mile.

There was the New Year's Eve Ramble that Tom prepared for by heading to the loft before showtime and taking fishing line, to which a disco ball was attached, and casting it over a beam above the stage. The countdown to midnight arrived, the clock struck 12:00, and the fishing line got stuck before slamming to the stage.

All of this took place center stage, in front of the band, the audience and Levon.

"There was a simplicity to everything in the early days of the Midnight Ramble," Tom said. "Everything had a 'MacGyver' twist to it."

At the 2007 Levon Helm Studios holiday party, members of the band and the staff celebrated in the studio, while Levon and Sandy's dog, Lucy, gave birth to puppies next door in the house. Levon would split his time between the party and the delivery, offering support while in the house and updates while in the studio.

Through it all, musical and non-musical events alike, the Midnight Ramble momentum continued to build.

"I remember Barbara saying, 'We're going to do this, we're going to do that,'" Tom said. "And we're like, 'She's nuts. I think she's lost it.' And things started to happen.

"Week after week, we went from being this single, isolated thing, that was kind of up there in the woods to people saying, 'Wow, what's going on up there?' People would come up to me and say, 'I heard about the Ramble. Do you know anything about that?' And for the Beacon Theatre, that was like, 'Wow. Levon can do this. He is back.' And we know there were people who doubted the viability of the success of this—that it could become something."

Cathy recalled one show at the Beacon that Tony LoBue could not attend because he was ill, and it taught her a lot about Levon.

"Levon had just gotten off the stage and he was very sweaty," Cathy said. "He had the towel around his neck. He comes up to me and says, 'Cathy. Did you hear about Tony?' I said, 'Yes, he's got pneumonia but he's going to be okay.' Levon said, 'I'm glad to hear that.' That said a lot to me and it just reinforced why we were out there in all kinds of weather—the cold, the rain—at the ticket booth, doing what we were doing. For him to walk off after a big show like that and the first thing he said was, 'How is Tony?' I'll never forget that as long as I live."

Tom described the early days of the Ramble as a whirlwind.

"Every week, something else happened, something wonderful. The Beacon shows. The Grammys. The puppies. Being a part of the Midnight Ramble was magical. Of course, it got bigger and better after that, but those early years were special of their own doing. And it all centered around a drummer who captivated everyone by just being himself."

To that, Cathy added, "Levon was what you saw. He was humble and gracious to everyone who entered the Midnight Ramble world. The stories are endless, as are the memories of a wonderful man who let us into his life."

Chris Howe: 'Peeling the Apple'

During the Midnight Ramble era, Ulster County resident and Sheriff's Office Corrections Officer Chris Howe spent a lot of time with Levon. He drove Levon to road shows, escorted him safely to and from the stage, stood nearby during the performance, and got him back home.

Whether it was a road trip to the Beacon Theatre or Terminal 5 in Manhattan; Bank of America Pavilion in Boston; Wellmont Theater in Montclair, N.J.; Gathering of the Vibes in Bridgeport, Connecticut; The Flynn in Burlington, Vermont; Casino Ballroom in Hampton, New Hampshire; or any of the many other Northeast locations the Levon Helm Band played, Chris would make sure Levon, and usually Muddy, got safely to and from the show. In the early days of the Midnight Ramble, he drove an RV to multiple points in the South, with Levon and Little Sammy Davis among those on board. Chris was also with Levon for the filming of *In the Electric Mist* with Tommy Lee Jones. And wherever he drove Levon, Chris, like millions of us, relied on a global positioning system to direct him.

"I got a GPS and we'd go to the weirdest addresses," he said. "I would pull up backstage, amazing myself a lot. The GPS was great. It made things easy."

According to Chris, Levon agreed.

"This makes it a lot easier, knowing where the place is," he'd say.

But The Band, it seems, took a much different approach to finding venues back in the day. In describing their journeys to gigs decades earlier, Levon talked about "peeling the apple."

Back with The Band, Levon told Chris, they would arrive in a town and just keep driving, beginning on the outskirts, completing laps and working their way inward until they found the crowd. Once they found the crowd, they knew they had gotten to the gig.

"They would just drive around until they saw the crowd," Chris said in amazement. "Hey—that's where we're playing."

That was "peeling the apple."

Chris caught word of the Midnight Ramble in the very early days.

"One of the guys I worked with, Timmy McGuire, was doing security up there early on," he said. "Some of the guys working security weren't going to the show one week. He was talking to someone on the phone and when he got done one the phone, I said, 'Whatever you're doing, I'll give you a hand.'"

That brought Chris Howe to his first Ramble.

"It was wintertime, February or March. I'm still not sure who played and, of course, I didn't even know who Levon was. I had no idea. As these people start coming out of the house, I say, 'Who is this guy?' I didn't know who The Band was; or Vivino, Erik Lawrence, Bernstein, Brian Mitchell, Amy, Levon, Larry—I really had no idea who any of these people were. I went up there just to help Tim out. I enjoyed it. It was a lot of fun. I got to say hi to a lot of people I knew. I talked to Barbara the week after that and told her, 'Hey it was a lot of fun. I'll come up and do it anytime.' She said, 'Okay, we'll count you in.' I started going up for every show, setting up chairs, making a fire in the fireplace, making popcorn in the popcorn machine."

Chris started off working security in the loft at Levon Helm Studios. Within six months, he was the gatekeeper at the door that separated that part of the studio where the Rambles were held from the part of the building where Levon and Sandy lived. So if you wanted to get into the house after a Ramble, you had to get past Chris.

Like just about any other member of Team Levon, including Barbara, Chris will tell you that he found himself in some incredible places, in the company of some incredible people, thanks to Levon Helm and the Midnight Ramble.

Chris traveled far and wide with Levon, from backstage at Radio City

Music Hall to the Ryman Auditorium in Nashville to the green room at *Late Night with Conan O'Brien* and *The Late Show with David Letterman*—and hundreds of spots in between.

"I don't know how to describe that man," Chris said. "He was like a neighbor, a friend to everybody, even though he was who he was. He didn't let that affect him. He was sincere about playing music for people and didn't care about all the hype, the Hollywood ass-kissers. Even the guy behind the counter, at some hot shop at four o'clock in the morning—Levon called him 'Sir.' He was polite to him and engaged him in conversation.

"I'm thinking to myself, this guy's been around the world four or five times, he's super famous but doesn't act like it. He acts like your buddy, your neighbor. He talks about college football a lot, and the respect he had for everybody caught me off guard. I'm thinking, 'This is some movie star, some rock and roll star,' but that was before I had a chance to sit down and have sushi with him, or be in a Chinese buffet restaurant with him, or some hot shop at four o'clock in the morning when he was getting pork rinds and chili."

Asked about that which made Levon happy, Chris said good sushi, his friends and musicians in his band.

"After a good show, he would walk a little lighter," Chris said. "He would float on his footsteps, knowing the show went well, that the sound was good, that what he heard and what went out to the audience was good. That made him happy—that and his dogs. Muddy was his best friend in the world."

Added Chris, "Levon was honest. He didn't pull any punches. He said what he was thinking and didn't really care."

The Speight Family

If you want a sharp perspective on Levon Helm during the Midnight Rambles, talk to someone who was 13 years old when he first met the man from Turkey Scratch.

"Growing up, you're a nobody, and in a crowd, he'd be calling my name," said Bill Speight Jr.

"I'm a little kid, running around. I don't even play an instrument. And he's calling my name out. 'Hey Billy, come over here.' He'd shake my hand, give me a hug. And he'd remember everything about you. He was never fake about anything. He was real."

Ask Levon who his close friends were and the Speights of Putnam County, New York, would be at the top of his list. Bill Speight was a retired Yonkers firefighter and for him, the Midnight Ramble was a family outing that involved his wife, Jean; sons Billy Jr. and Charlie; and daughter, Colleen.

Decades earlier, Bill Speight had learned about The Band from a friend who was a Bob Dylan fan. And during the late summer of 1971, Bill experienced Levon live for the first time when he and a bunch of pals drove up to Monticello Raceway in Sullivan County, New York, to see The Band perform with Kris Kristofferson.

That gig took place about 10 miles from Bethel, where Levon and The Band had performed two years earlier, at the Woodstock festival. The stage at the raceway was set up on grass, between the bleachers and the track. Bill at the time considered the $7 ticket price to be "astronomical." And fans outside the venue who didn't want to pay, or couldn't, hopped the fence on the side of the track opposite the stage. Once over the fence, they darted across the grass and hopped a second wall into the bleachers.

During the show, Bill said, "Rick and Levon were laughing, rooting for the kids to get in for free." And this endeavor generated a strong response from security.

"Back then, the guards would be chasing you with nightsticks, running after you," he said.

Bill found The Band's live performance to be compelling.

"The fact that they traded off on the vocals was unique. After a while, you really felt like you knew these guys. They were just on a whole different level."

In 1973, Bill traveled to New York's Finger Lakes region to see The

Band, the Grateful Dead and the Allman Brothers Band perform at Watkins Glen.

"I was just going to see The Band," he said. "And that's how I always was at the Rambles. People would say, 'Anyone special playing tonight?' I always said, 'I'm here to see Levon.'"

Living in south Yonkers years ago, Bill and Jean saw a lot of live music, including Johnny Cash and The Band at the Westchester Premier Theater in nearby Tarrytown. And from Yonkers, live music in Manhattan was a quick, 35-minute drive. There were many good times for Bill and Jean, seeing The Band. And then came The Last Waltz.

"Nobody was happy about it," he said. "We were heartbroken. If you were a Beatles fan, this was like The Beatles breaking up."

But, Bill said, "After The Last Waltz, you'd see Rick and Levon performing at small clubs in New York City. You'd go see them and think, 'This isn't too bad.' I was satisfied. It was better than it was before. You're seeing them in a small environment. We went from seeing them in stadiums to being right in front of them. You'd see them walk past the bar, and stop at the bar, which was amazing. Back then, we used to go see The Who and bands like that. Now you're seeing someone who you think is a big rock star, right over there talking to fans. That was akin to seeing Mick Jagger and Roger Daltrey playing a little club."

At the Rambles, Bill said, "I still felt that way—not that Levon tried to portray that image."

Bill saw the re-formed Band for the first time at the Capitol Theater in Passaic, New Jersey. He was particularly interested to see what Jim Weider could deliver on the guitar.

"I remember looking at Jim Weider, saying to myself, 'I wonder what he can really do.'" Bill said he was glad to see that with the retooled lineup, "It was still The Band."

In 1986, Richard Manuel died and The Band underwent yet another transition. At the Speight home, the kids were getting older, they were becoming Band fans and Bill's dedication to his favorite rock band endured. The Band in its second reincarnation released three albums, *Jericho* in 1993; *High on the Hog* in 1996; and *Jubilation* in 1998.

"Those three albums," Bill said, "they were great."

Rick Danko died in 1999 and Bill and his friends traveled to Woodstock for his memorial service at the Bearsville Theater. That was where Bill first heard that Levon was performing at the Joyous Lake in Woodstock with the Barn Burners on Wednesday nights.

"I was amazed," Bill said. "Levon Helm playing for $10. I would call the firehouse and get my friend Pete McCaffrey on the cell phone. I'd say, 'Pete, listen to this,' and I'd hold up the phone. I'd go back to the firehouse, talk about being up there and say, 'Levon was right over there.' The shows were very crowded. I looked forward to that so much each week."

One Wednesday night, Bill arrived in Woodstock and parked on Mill Hill Road, where the Joyous Lake was situated. A car pulled up in front of him and parked. It was driven by Levon Helm.

"I thought, 'I don't want to get out of the car,'" Bill said.

But Levon and Bill ended up getting out of their vehicles at the same time. Bill said hello to Levon and they walked into the Joyous Lake together.

"I felt like he walked me in," Bill said.

As the two entered the club, Levon had his hand on Bill's shoulder.

"I felt like I knew him over that short walk," Bill said. "And I realized he was trying to get me in so I didn't have to pay the $10. I went out of my way to backtrack and I gave the guy the money."

Bill drove the two hours from Yonkers to Woodstock every Wednesday to see Levon perform with the Barn Burners. He eventually started chatting with Butch Dener, the former road manager for The Band, who was now working with Levon.

"One night, I was up there with a friend," Bill said. "Butch came over and said, 'They're going to be recording over at Levon's. Can you come?' He said, 'You know where he lives.'"

The next day, Bill brought his friend, Mike Lyons, with him to the recording session.

"We pull in and we see this place," Bill said, "and we're like, 'Oh my God.'"

That was Bill's first visit to Levon Helm Studios.

"Butch said to be there at 1:00. We were probably there at one minute to 1:00, being prompt. Levon was down by the pond. He started walking up to us. He knew who we were."

The recording session had yet to start, Levon was the only person around and Bill thought they had arrived too early.

"I told him we would leave and come back. In his hoarse voice, he said, 'No, no.' We spent the whole day up there. Levon was giving us Cokes."

Sometime later, Bill, Jean, Charlie, Billy Jr. and Colleen traveled to Bodles Opera House in Chester, New York, not too far from Woodstock or Yonkers, to see Levon play with the Barn Burners

"After the show, we went upstairs," Bill recalled. "Levon said to us, 'We're going to have a big party at The Barn. We're going to have a rock and roll show. My voice has been coming back.'"

At the time, he was mouthing the words during shows, but had no microphone.

"He talked about a Southern-type rock and roll party with hot dogs and hamburgers. He said, 'Call me in two weeks.' Now I'm having a heart attack. I've got to call him. He wrote his number down for me, upstairs at Bodles. I watched him write it down. He made his fours just like a golf course flag. That's how my father did it, too. Of course, I'm waiting two weeks. I'm not going to call a day before or a day later. I called him up and was on the phone with him for probably 40 minutes. It was the easiest conversation I ever had."

At Levon's invitation, Bill and Jean went up to the studio just for a visit, when there was no music going on. That was the day they met Barbara O'Brien. Bill recalled that, at the first Ramble, the studio was cold, and he said, "You could count the people in the place."

But at Levon Helm Studios, good times were at hand.

"He always included us and a lot of other people," Bill said. "What amazes me was, back then, we really didn't have money for entertainment. Levon provided all that and that's why I loved going up there.

"You want to pay him back. I really wanted to be part of it. I just wanted to do something. Normally, I'm not like that. I don't push myself into situations. But I wanted to help. Levon was the type of guy who would never ask for anything—and for me, that's the type of person that deserves your help. I always told my kids, if you want to know how to treat people, just watch Levon."

Said Jean Speight, "For some reason, Levon took a special interest in us. Spending time with him was the same as being with a close family member—very relaxed and comforting. Our conversations were not only about music, but about everyday family concerns. That's the way he was—a kind, compassionate person."

The Speights did all they could to pay Levon back by volunteering their time.

Jean helped out with checking people in at the Ramble. Bill, Charlie and Billy Jr. volunteered in the ball field, parking cars. Charlie later helped out in the ticket booth. Bill went inside, where he worked security. And Billy served as garbageman.

"I told him he had the best job up there," Bill Speight said.

Billy Speight Jr. said the garbageman gig had its perks.

"That was my excuse for going into the studio, during the show—to empty the garbage. Barbara would invite us to sit on the radiator. You're sitting behind Levon. My dreams aren't even that good. There is not a better experience. It doesn't even feel real. You get up because you don't want to wear out your welcome."

The Midnight Ramble unfolded and the Speight family became a critical component of Team Levon. But nobody could anticipate the direction that the relationship between Levon and the Speights would take in 2011.

One night at home, Billy Jr. slipped into a coma. He was rushed to the hospital and not long after, the Speights got word that Levon was coming to visit. The man from Turkey Scratch was going to bring a boom box because he thought music would help stir Billy Jr. from his coma.

As Billy Jr. lay in the coma, Jean whispered in his ear that Levon would soon be there.

"He's in a coma," Bill Speight said of his son. "And a tear comes out of his eye."

The following morning, Billy emerged from his coma, hours before Levon arrived.

"It's the truth," Bill Speight said.

Mike DuBois

Mike DuBois got to know Levon periodically while attending shows in the 1990s and he spent time at the studio after Levon hired a friend of Mike's to renovate The Barn.

An artist originally from Syracuse, Mike met Brendan McDonough, Brian Parillo, Andrew Shober and the rest of the Apple Picker's Union at a house party held in the vicinity of the nearby Ashokan Reservoir, after the guys had moved to Ulster County.

That's where DuBois learned of Levon's "rent parties." At the time, Mike said, Levon wanted to record a children's album. Mike ended up creating an album cover for the proposed project, with animals playing instruments.

And although that album never materialized, Mike ended up generating all the artwork for Levon Helm Studios, the Rambles and the road shows.

Mike created the "Midnight Ramble Sessions" poster with the mandolin, the tree and The Barn—the one that became an iconic image for all things Midnight Ramble early on—as well as all the other images that transferred the feel and the vibe of the Ramble to posters and t-shirts. All of the artwork that satisfied Levon's fans, because it allowed them to bring the Ramble home with them, all of that was Mike's work.

"Levon loved everything carnival and circus and barkers," Mike said of Levon's vision for the images. "He liked a little bit of edge. He wanted it to be a little crazy."

And then came the album cover for *Electric Dirt*, Levon's follow-up to *Dirt Farmer*, and the winner of the first ever Grammy for Best Americana Album. Levon told Mike that he wanted a shotgun shack, a 1956 John Deere tractor and an outhouse on the cover. Levon called the image's protagonist, a guitarist on the front porch of the shack, "the unambitious farmer." Mike's work evoked R. Crumb and the cotton fields of Turkey

Scratch—and Levon loved it all. If you ever wanted to hear Levon's signature belly laugh, mention Mike's cover for *Electric Dirt*. Mike still has Levon's original drawing for the cover, which features a stick figure and a box for the house.

"He was a real get-to-the-point-kind-of-guy," said Mike, who also worked with Levon to design the cover for *It's Showtime: The Midnight Ramble Sessions Vol. III* CD. "He loved to tell stories. He was an authentic character who would speak his mind. It was fun to roll with him."

Pat Cahill

In February 2000, New York State Assemblyman Kevin Cahill, D-Kingston, introduced Assembly Bill 9629.

This legislation, introduced at the request of the Ulster County Legislature, called for the designation of state Route 209 in Ulster County, beginning at the Sullivan County line and the Town of Wawarsing border and ending at the intersection of Route 209 and Route 9W in the Town of Ulster, as the "Clayton 'Peg Leg' Bates Memorial Highway."

According to the Library of Congress, Bates was born Oct. 11, 1907, in Fountain Inn, South Carolina. He was the son of a laborer named Rufus and a sharecropper and housecleaner named Emma. Bates began dancing at age 5, but at 12 suffered a horrific injury. His left leg was amputated after it had gotten caught in a conveyor belt at the cottonseed gin mill where he was working. But Bates's uncle carved him a wooden peg leg and he kept on dancing.

He imitated the newest rhythm steps showcased by tap shoe dancers and added acrobatic steps. From minstrel shows and carnivals, Bates made it to Vaudeville, breaking the color barrier and dancing on the same bill as Bill "Bojangles" Robinson, Fred Astaire and Gene Kelly. Bates went on to dance in Paris and Harlem nightclubs, including the Cotton Club. He performed on Broadway in the 1930s, reinventing "such popular tap steps as the Shim Sham Shimmy, Susie-Q, and Truckin' by enhancing them with the rhythmic combination of his deep-toned left-leg peg and the high-pitched metallic right-foot tap," according to the Library of Congress website. Bates made his first television appearance in 1949 and went on to appear more than 20 times on *The Ed Sullivan Show*.

In 1951, he took his earnings and with his wife, Alice, bought a turkey farm in Ulster County—Kerhonkson, in fact, not far from Woodstock—and converted it into a resort.

"The Peg Leg Country Club, in Kerhonkson, New York flourished as the largest black-owned-and-operated resort in the country, catering to black clientele and featuring hundreds of jazz musicians and tap dancers," according to the Library of Congress.

Clayton "Peg Leg" Bates died on Dec. 8, 1998. But his legacy lives on in Ulster County thanks to the state law designating Route 209 in his honor. And that recognition played a role in state Route 375, which links the towns of West Hurley and Woodstock, becoming Levon Helm Memorial Boulevard.

Decades after Peg Leg made history in southern Ulster County and around the world, Kevin Cahill's brother, Pat, became head of security at Levon Helm Studios. Pat Cahill had worked for years on his brother's political campaigns, for both Ulster County Legislature and the New York State Assembly. Sometime after Levon's death, the legislation naming Route 209 for Peg Leg Bates gave Pat an idea. He thought re-naming the road Levon lived on, in honor of the man from Turkey Scratch, would be a fitting tribute. Plochmann Lane in Woodstock, however, is a town road and Kevin Cahill was a New York State lawmaker. So Pat kept thinking. And that brought him to Route 375, which is connected to Plochmann Lane by a short stretch of state Route 212.

In the wake of all this, on Feb. 20, 2013, Assemblyman Kevin Cahill introduced bill A05176, "An act to amend the highway law, in relation to designating New York State Route 375 from the intersection of New York State Route 28 in West Hurley to the intersection of New York State Route 212 in Woodstock as the 'Levon Helm Memorial Boulevard.' The bill passed the Assembly on April 29, 2013 and was adopted by the state Senate a month later on May 29. Gov. Andrew Cuomo signed it into law on June 19, 2013.

"Route 375 is now Levon Helm Memorial Boulevard," Pat Cahill said, "What more could you want?"

The son of a Hudson River tugboat deckhand and a mother who served as City Clerk, mayor's secretary and Parking Violations Bureau chief in the City of Kingston, Pat Cahill grew up in the first capital of New York State. As a teenager, he was pretty impressed with his art teacher at J. Watson Bailey Middle School.

One day, the instructor told his students they could each bring in a record album of their choosing to be played during class. And while Pat's classmates were into classic rock—bands like AC/DC and Blue Oyster Cult—the 14-year-old headed in a decidedly different direction and brought in a record that dazzled everybody—*The Best of The Band*.

"I definitely left an impression on the teacher," Pat said.

He had discovered the album in a box full of records that his brother Dennis had left at the family home while moving from one apartment to another.

"I'm going through the records," he said. "I'm pulling out anything that said, 'The Best of' or 'Greatest Hits.' The Grateful Dead. The Allman Brothers—I didn't care. I pull out The Band and was like 'Woah.'"

At the time, Pat didn't know much about The Band.

"I knew they were from Woodstock," he said.

But with a title like *The Best of The Band*, Pat thought the album had to be good.

"It's self-explanatory. I put it on and every song on the album is a hit. I fell in love with The Band."

As Pat got older, he immersed himself in the group's music.

"It was Richard's and Levon's voices more than anything," said Pat, whose brother Dennis got to know Richard Manuel while bartending at the old Sled Hill Café in Woodstock. "Levon and Richard really struck me."

Pat got ahold of Levon's autobiography. He saw Rick Danko perform with his fellow Ulster County resident Jorma Kaukonen of Hot Tuna and Jefferson Airplane fame, at the legendary Uncle Willy's bar on Broadway in Kingston. And Pat couldn't get enough of The Band, Ulster County's very own rock ensemble.

Asked what he liked about the group, Pat said, "I want to say it was probably them being local. Even though not one of them was from here originally, they were local—and accessible. They weren't highfalutin. You'd see Danko riding around in a broken-down Mercedes; looking for a ride home from Uncle Willy's at night. But that was typical Danko. You could walk up to him in a store and not be starstruck. You could have a conversation with him. You could see that they were human."

Years later, Pat would see Levon play with the Barn Burners at the Joyous Lake in Woodstock. And after that, Pat—the man who would eventually become head of security at Levon Helm Studios—gained entry to his first two Midnight Rambles by sneaking in.

"They wanted $100," Pat said. "I'd never be able to afford that. I started having kids. I was a brand-new father. I had a mortgage. I started having all the adult responsibilities. I couldn't imagine paying $100."

Pat and three friends snuck in. Once inside, he saw Chris Howe, who Pat had gotten to know through work, manning the front door. Pat worked for the City of Kingston Department of Public Works. Ulster County was building a new jail adjacent to the city transfer station and Chris was part of the Ulster Sheriff's transition team. The following Monday, Pat saw Chris at work and told him that if Team Levon ever needed a hand, Pat was in.

Sometime later, Pat got the word to come up to the studio. Billy Bob Thornton and The Boxmasters were opening up a Ramble and his help was needed with security. So he reported for duty.

"Chris said, 'You never know who's going to show up here,'" Pat recalled. "I said, 'I like the Black Crowes.' Chris said, 'Oh, those guys pop up here once in a while.' And there goes Chris Robinson walking under the portico. I said, 'You mean like him?'"

After that night, Pat was asked to work on a regular basis. And then he was asked to oversee security. Assuming the role of security chief for the Midnight Ramble meant he would join Chris at the end of each show near the piano as Levon made his way across the stage, raising the arm of each band member in triumph. Chris waited for Levon to make his way to the piano, then escorted him through the crowd to the house.

"One of the proudest days of my life is having them ask me to be head of security," Pat said. "That was my only experience working in the music world, at the studio. And I don't want any other one because how can you top that? It was great. It was the best, probably, four years of my life."

Making the whole endeavor that much sweeter was the support Pat received at home.

"My wife never had a problem with it," he said. "My family completely understood. I turned my family, my kids, my wife, my mother, my neighbors into Levon Helm fans. I've already told my kids, 'At my funeral, you're to play nothing but the Grateful Dead and Levon Helm.'"

And what about Levon Helm, the guy?

"He was never down," Pat said. "No matter what he went through, he was always that same guy. He never changed. Talking to Levon was like talking to your favorite uncle. You hung out, you listened to the stories."

And the fame?

"As sweeping as it was, the impact of his fame on the Hudson Valley was nothing compared to what the Hudson Valley meant to him," Pat said. "He chose Woodstock to make his home. He was just a guy who lived here and that's how he wanted it. It's like Dennis the Menace talking to Mr. Wilson over the fence. He was your neighbor. Bob Dylan could have been his neighbor—Bob Dylan or Pat Cahill; it didn't matter who you were. This was home, just like a home should be."

Added Pat, "It was easy for me to say he was a friend of mine. But to hear him say that I was a friend of his—I'm good."

Walter Turk

In February 2012, Ulster County native Walter Turk found himself driving Levon Helm to Valdosta, Georgia, where the man from Turkey Scratch was headed for a long overdue getaway and some well-earned rest and relaxation.

Levon was on a break from touring, recording and playing Rambles back home in Woodstock. He had selected Valdosta because of its proximity to New Orleans, which Levon was also considering for a visit. And who knows, Levon thought, he just might take a glass-bottom boat ride if he felt like it.

Levon's destination in Valdosta was a Best Western Hotel and at some point, after checking in, he and Walter paid a visit to a local shop that sold Western clothing. Levon had selected items for Amy and her two sons, his grandsons. But while continuing to shop, he didn't appreciate the pressure from a sales clerk, who wanted to know if he was going to buy the items he held in his hands. Levon ended up leaving the merchandise in the store, but returned the next day.

He bought the items he had selected the previous day and treated himself to a new pair of cowboy boots. Once back at the van that Walter had driven south, Levon put the boots on and asked his traveling companion for two bottles of water. According to Walter, Levon poured one bottle in each boot. Then, still wearing the boots, Levon, according to Walter, said, "All right, I'm ready to go."

The two arrived back at the Best Western and hung out at the pool, with Levon still wearing the boots. About a half hour later, Walter said, Levon pulled the boots off, dumped out the water and put them back on his feet before declaring, "That's how you break in a cowboy boot—get 'em wet and they shape to your foot."

As with other members of Team Levon, Walter filled multiple roles at Levon Helm Studios and on the road.

He served as handyman, driver and cook; he worked hospitality for shows; and, in general, was a utility player who responded to situations as they emerged. Walter served often as Levon's personal assistant and driver, and those two roles are what placed him behind the wheel on that trip to Valdosta just weeks before Levon passed away.

Walter speaks fondly of that journey south, during which he and Levon, once set up at the Best Western, took day trips to admire southern live oak trees and their curtains of moss. There were the stops at one of Levon's favorite steakhouses: Ryan's Restaurant; and daily dinner runs Walter made to The Smoking Pit restaurant to get Levon plates of pulled pork, chicken, cornbread, collard greens and a half pound of brisket. That serving was increased to a pound-and-a-half once Muddy made clear that he enjoyed brisket as well.

"Muddy got his own plate," Walter said.

Walter Turk was born in Kingston, grew up there and left high school at age 16 to join his father in the explosives demolition company he operated on construction sites. Walter's father, uncle and aunt were political players in Ulster County and, according to Walter, could get then-Governor, and future Vice President Nelson Rockefeller on the phone to discuss construction work in the Hudson Valley.

Walter's father, Jack Turk, was a member of the International Union of Operating Engineers Local 825. Walter, the second-oldest of four children, was in Laborers' Local 17.

Walter became partners with his father and eventually retired. At the invitation of his friend Jay Collins, Walter arrived at Levon Helm Studios at the end of 2007 to join Team Levon. And he gained plenty of perspective on the man from Turkey Scratch.

"In the presence of others, with all that he had on his shoulders, Levon did not seem burdened," Walter said. "He projected an image of a guy who didn't sweat the small stuff or the big stuff. That wore off on people. I think that's what drew people toward him."

Back in Valdosta, Georgia, at some point during the two-and-a-half-week stay, the son of the eldest Best Western owner—three generations ran it at the time—approached Walter. Despite not letting on, the grandfather, son and grandson running the place knew who Levon was and wanted to respect his privacy. But now they were wondering if they could get a photo with Levon. The man from Turkey Scratch agreed. But after the photo was processed, the family running the hotel approached Walter once again, and asked if Levon could sign it.

"He wrote a whole big 'Thank you' to them for taking such good care of us and not letting people know who he was," Walter said of Levon.

Seven years later, Walter was driving Amy Helm on tour, and the two were passing Valdosta on their way to Texas. At Walter's suggestion, they made a detour and retraced the steps he took with Levon back in 2012. Amy and Walter ate brisket. They went to the Western shop. And they stopped in at the Best Western, where the photo Levon had taken with the owners was proudly displayed in the lobby.

Walter said Amy thanked the owners for the hospitality they showed her father. She gave them a pair of her father's trademark drumsticks, and Walter took a photo of Amy and the owners in front of the original picture.

"It was a full circle thing for me," he said.

CHAPTER TEN

The Grammys

At the 50th Grammy Awards held Feb. 10, 2008, Amy Winehouse's "Rehab" won for Record of the Year, Song of the year and Best Female Pop Vocal Performance. Winehouse also won the Grammy for Best New Artist. Justin Timberlake's "What Goes Around...Comes Around" won the Grammy for Best Male Pop Vocal Performance and his "LoveStoned/I Think She Knows" won the Grammy for Best Dance Recording. Kanye West won a Grammy for Best Rap Solo Performance for "Stronger" and his album *Graduation* won Best Rap Album. Sharing in the Grammy glory with all these musicians that day was Levon Helm, who on February 10, 2008, won the Grammy for Best Traditional Folk Album for *Dirt Farmer*. From near collapse and implosion, Levon had returned in triumph and was firing on all pistons.

Barbara O'Brien, in true fashion, celebrated Grammy day as a triumph even before Levon was declared a winner. She scheduled a "Gramble" for the afternoon of Grammy Day. A "Gramble," of course, is a Grammy Ramble. A sold-out crowd turned up to celebrate, regardless of what the tally might be in Los Angeles.

"The puppies got here right about Christmas 2007, I think, right after Christmas," Levon said. "We had a Ramble on the night of the Grammys, the day after little Lee arrived; it was all there within a couple months of itself."

Little Lee was Lavon Henry Collins, Amy's son and Levon's grandson. Lee was born on a Saturday. *Dirt Farmer* won the Grammy that Sunday. What a weekend for all involved.

"At the time, I was still in the batter's box with my Granddad business," Levon said of the arrival of his first grandchild. "I was really looking forward to it when little Lee was born. I thought, 'I'm not going to bunt. I'm going to take a swing at it for sure.' Little Lee joined us at the Rambles. He went to Tennessee with us. He went to Baltimore. He went to MerleFest. I just loved running off and checking on him and seeing him again. We didn't do much but sit around and stare at each other. But he seemed to enjoy the shows back then. He liked the action—most kids do, though. They love the action. I did feel close to Amy and that baby of hers. My God, that baby—what a feeling."

"The Grammy for *Dirt Farmer* is a wonderful payback for everybody," Levon said. "It took a while to do it. It wasn't like I could money-whip them into working, so they pretty much did it by the skin of their teeth. Having it turn out successful, so I could pay everyone back, was exactly what we needed.

"Don Imus did a lot for us when it came to *Dirt Farmer.* I've known him for a long time. I first knew who he was when we played the Lone Star. And over the years, he's always been good at helping musicians. Sammy started playing with us in the Barn Burners and we started going down there and playing for Imus. He's had us on, hell, a dozen times probably. The 'I-man' and I just kind of buddied up. And he started doing such great things for us—helping us with *Dirt Farmer,* talking the record up on his show, and having us down to play and telling people all about the Rambles and when we would play places like the Beacon Theatre down in the city. Wouldn't it have been for him, that first album might not have got the buzz that we needed for it. I've always admired what he does. I love being a part of that Cattle Ranch for Kids with Cancer. It thrills me to see us all get together and make a million dollars in a night. I love to see that kind of response and be part of it.

"The first time we went down we had that live thing, a DVD—*The Midnight Ramble Sessions Volume One*—and it was a nice package. The

I-Man showed it up and we got a few sold. It got our name back in the deal. That was the first thing I had done in years; it kind of primed the pump for *Dirt Farmer*. Imus encouraged me to come on and do it. I was still a little bit hesitant about it, you know? And the I-Man said, 'Come on, let's go.' We got a great response, particularly through the internet and for the first time we realized what that internet could do for ticket sales and record sales and all that stuff."

Speaking of the Grammy for *Dirt Farmer*, Levon said, "If I hadn't won, I would have had to say, 'Well, it didn't mean anything anyway.' But it does help and I'm happy that I won it. You know, you put that little sticker on the cover, it sells the product so well and it does help. I can't point to anything yet, except *Dirt Farmer* as, you know, working under this, 'have your cake and eat it, too,' kind of policy that we're doing. We didn't run ourselves crazy making it either—we let it find itself. You don't get any more done by rushing. You aggravate yourself. And you make it more like a damn job, just because you're doing it to yourself. It's enough of a job as it is. I believe that's just the only way you can do it—let it get legs under itself.

"But I'll tell you what, the first Grammy was kind of—you could interpret that as half-sympathy. The second one, *Electric Dirt*, I believe was more fun to make than *Dirt Farmer*.

"With all of the horns and stuff it was more of a party album, more of a rock and roll album. 'Growing Trade' is a good Americana kind of story there. There have been days when I didn't have any kind of a song I thought I was interested in to cut. And Amy would say, 'I thought we were going to do "Kingfish."' I'd say, 'Okay baby, let's do "Kingfish,"' and damned if it didn't turn out to be one of the best songs. That's kind of what we've done—is kept the faith with each other and trusted each other and give each other that confidence.

"I really did enjoy the week after winning that second Grammy, for *Electric Dirt*. Every now and then I'd look over at Sandy and say, 'We won that Grammy, you know.' And I said, 'You know what, next year, at this time, we'll still have won it.' Anytime you look back to 2009, by God, we'll have won it. Now all we need is about four or five more of them.

"With *Electric Dirt*, all we did was cut twice as much as we needed and took the best tunes. We never set any deadline on ourselves and it worked out. We never really did push ourselves. You can't have a big clock on the wall. It ain't conducive to music making. I was kind of worried about 'Heaven's Pearls' because it's a hard tune to sing right. But boy, when Amy and Byron put the harmonies on there, and with the horns, it sounds more R&B than it ever has. I don't know how the songs on *Electric Dirt* all found their way—just us listening to each other and keeping the faith. For 'Kingfish,' Amy kept saying, 'It's a good one, you should do that one.' And she was right. It's one of the best songs we've got, with the horns and everything. It's one of those 'picture' songs. And we cut Happy Traum's 'Golden Bird.' Everyone who heard that song said they hear bagpipes. And the game is, can you make them hear it without them? That's what we're getting paid for.

"Most people don't know; they think you go in there and you turn on the recording machines and everyone just plays as good as they can. But it's like building a house—you have to put the foundation in and then you have to stack it up. And if you don't make a mistake—if you don't get shit on there that you don't need once you get it all layered in there, it's complete and it don't sound over-produced. When you get too much, it's no good. It's been the most fun I've ever had with anything like this, because we ain't never won a goddamn thing. So it's all brand-new.

"I never did think much about it back in the old days, because I didn't know what the fucking Grammy was, or anything else. The Band never won a Grammy. But looking back, them motherfuckers should have given us something. Shit—'Best New Bunch of Bastards' or something, you know? The 'Newest Bunch of Sons of Bitches.' They didn't know what to do with us, so they just acted like we weren't around.

"Everything was so goddamn—it was really left of center. What was supposed to be happening—we were supposed to be running around with beads and flower power and all that shit, doing some psychedelic shit. That was the most un-musical shit any of us had ever heard. We didn't even want to talk about it. We didn't care.

"With the Grammys, that was the shame—nobody ever came up to Richard Manuel and said, 'You're the best son of a bitch we've got.' And at one time, by God, he was. There wasn't nobody who could out-sing that son-of-a bitch. Shit. It couldn't be done. Give me somebody who could sing 'Georgia' and turn around and do 'Turn on Your Lovelight'—it's too hard to do. That's too wide a span. And then turn around and get one of them falsetto things, 'Lonesome Suzie.' And you couldn't hear when it would shift—that shift between natural and falsetto. You can't hear it with Richard. You listen to those old records, you can't hear when Richard changes that gear—oh, God love him. But he never got a goddamn thing like a Grammy, you know. Playing with Bob was all right, but Bob just couldn't sing quite as good as Richard could. I'd just rather hear Richard sing."

After *Dirt Farmer* won the Grammy, Levon said, "We started to get calls about using the studio. People like the sound of *Dirt Farmer* and then when they come and see a Ramble, they realize that a lot of it is the studio, the sound of this room. During *Dirt Farmer* we were finally able to get enough good equipment and good machines together that we could make a decent sounding record now. That's been our latest celebration now, is to hear the place not referred to as so white an elephant as it used to be. It still costs a fortune to try and heat it, but it sounds good.

"We got in on a few of the festivals. That was one thing *Dirt Farmer* did for us. It got us invited to Bonnaroo and MerleFest and a lot of the good shows. One of the best was the moe.down festival in upstate New York. Boy that was a lot of fun. I hope we do it next year and you need to go with us if we do. It's a great festival. Up there, it was a whole lot like MerleFest. It had a small-town flavor to it and the people running it were all relaxed and nobody felt like they had to exercise their authority, ordering anyone around or any of that malarkey. It was real peaceful, plenty of good space for people to come out and stuff, just a well-run community festival."

The Mountain Jam music festival in the Catskills welcomed the Levon Helm Band twice, for two memorable performances.

Staged by Radio Woodstock owner Gary Chetkof and Gov't Mule's Warren Haynes, Mountain Jam was held at Hunter Mountain Ski Bowl, in Hunter, Greene County, New York, not far from Woodstock. Many in the Hudson Valley claimed this prime-time festival, held in their backyard, as their own social gathering, an event in which they were heavily invested, on an emotional level. Showcasing live music in the heart of the Catskills for thousands of people, with peaks surrounding the festival site, embodied Levon's spirit in so many ways, and underscored why so many people choose to call the Hudson Valley home.

"That Mountain Jam thing," Levon said, "is a going concern."

Levon first played Mountain Jam in 2008 and took the second-to-last slot on the final day of the festival, preceding Bob Weir of the Grateful Dead and his band RatDog. The culmination of Mountain Jam that year took on an extra shine as Levon joined RatDog on drums for the Bob Dylan song, "She Belongs to Me."

Two years later, Levon closed out Mountain Jam with a "you-had-to-be-there" extravaganza that celebrated his 70th birthday, with an epic show, featuring some true heavy-hitters as guests.

In true Levon style, he worked his hardest to turn his own birthday gala into an experience that focused on his guests, rather than himself. The evening turned into a colossal show that nobody, from the musicians who sat in on stage, to the audience members gathered on the slope, would soon forget.

Steely Dan's Donald Fagen, Levon's Woodstock neighbor and a frequent guest of the Levon Helm Band, led the charge on the Grateful Dead's "Shakedown Street" and The Band's "King Harvest." Bluegrass mandolin player Sam Bush performed on "Up On Cripple Creek."

Alison Krauss joined in on "White Dove." Steve Earle and Allison Moorer were featured on "Sweet Virginia." Warren Haynes performed "The Same Thing" and "Blind Willie McTell. "Across the Great Divide" and "Tears of Rage" featured Ray LaMontagne. Jackie Greene came on board for "Hang Up My Rock And Roll Shoes" and "The W.S. Walcott Medicine Show."

And Patterson Hood gave the mountain a show-stopping, you'll-never-see-this-again version of "Unfaithful Servant." Chetkof outdid himself by having a cake, that replicated The Barn, waiting for Levon and the musicians when they exited the stage.

At the 2012 edition of Mountain Jam, about six weeks after Levon had died, members of the Levon Helm Band joined in with Gov't Mule to deliver a tribute to Levon that rocked the rafters hard. The musical momentum maintained the thrust of a torpedo chasing a cannonball. The impact that Levon had left on Hunter Mountain, Mountain Jam, the Hudson Valley and every musician on that stage resonated loudly that night, which was beyond beautiful but terribly bittersweet.

In a press release announcing the special tribute, Warren Haynes said, "Levon was a musical hero of mine. His 70th birthday celebration at Mountain Jam two years ago was a magical night and a truly inspiring musical performance. So bringing back that incredible band to share in our tribute seemed like a great way to honor his memory."

Released June 30, 2009, *Electric Dirt* won the first Grammy ever awarded in the new category of Best Americana Album. To achieve this honor, Levon beat out some stiff competition—Willie Nelson & Asleep At The Wheel, Wilco, Lucinda Williams and Bob Dylan.

"Americana music is the first thing that's new that we've seen since reggae, as far as I'm concerned, that fits our sensibilities, you know," Levon said. "A lot of this rap stuff, once you get away from Biggie Smalls and Tupac, boy, a lot of the rest of it is just BS. There ain't nothing that you can remember. Vanilla Ice, he had some of that stuff that would get into your ear. You could remember him. You could remember Biggie Smalls. I loved a couple things Biggie did. There was just something about the musical part of it, that just—you knew it was Biggie Smalls. It seems like they started hip-hop and used that 'getting-back-to-basics' as their standard. That's as American as anything. But for a long time they had all that big hair—Poison, White Snake. There wasn't a goddamn thing except reggae—for a long time, that was the only thing that was new and offered anything that you could tap your foot to, Bob Marley, some of them other guys."

The Grammy win for *Dirt Farmer* gave Levon Helm Studios a soaring sense of triumph. The Grammy that followed, for *Electric Dirt*, reminded us all—devoted fans, critics and doubters alike—of how Levon Helm endured.

CHAPTER ELEVEN

Arkansas

In a swamp at the junction of Lee, Monroe and Phillips counties in Arkansas, there is a National Historic Landmark that designates the point at which surveying for the Louisiana Purchase began in 1815.

A dozen years prior, President Thomas Jefferson finalized the Louisiana Purchase, which the Library of Congress describes as "the greatest real estate deal in history."

The United States purchased the Louisiana Territory from France for $15 million, or approximately four cents an acre, according to the Library of Congress website. Upon ratification by the U.S. Senate on October 20, 1803, the Louisiana Purchase treaty doubled the size of the United States and opened up its frontier to expansion of the West.

According to the Arkansas Department of Parks, Heritage and Tourism, a survey party on October 27, 1815, traveled north from the confluence of the Arkansas and Mississippi rivers to establish the north-south line now known as the Fifth Principal Meridian. That same day, a party of explorers traveled west from the junction of the St. Francis and Mississippi rivers to establish an east-west line called the Baseline. The intersection of these two lines in that swamp generated the point from which all surveys of the Louisiana Purchase—a rolling frontier from the Gulf of Mexico to Canada that would eventually include Arkansas and twelve other states—would be conducted.

The St. Francis River empties into the Mississippi River north of Helena, Phillips County, Arkansas. Helena is about 20 miles from Marvell, Arkansas. And Marvell is about eight miles from Turkey Scratch, Arkansas, where Anna Lee Amsden, Mary Cavette and Mark Lavon Helm grew up together as kids and forged friendships that would last a lifetime.

According to the U.S. Census, the population of Phillips County, Arkansas, in 1940, the year Levon was born, was 45,970. In 2015, the Census Bureau estimated the population to be less than half that—19,513. And according to the Central Arkansas Library System, Phillips County in 1990 was ranked by the U.S. Census Bureau as one of the 16 poorest counties in the nation.

"I grew up right down on the river there," Levon said. "They call that the Delta, the Mississippi Delta and it's all cotton country. I grew up on the Arkansas side of the river. There's a little town out in the country there called Marvell—one of those little, wide places in the road, a little wide spot where they roll up the sidewalks every night about 5:30-6:00. Unfortunately, it's one of those little towns that's just about gone. All those little towns down in the Delta have been suffering through these hard times—Marvell and Helena, too. You look down the main streets, there's more stores that are closed than there are that's opened. When I was a kid, you couldn't hardly walk down the street there were so many people, and now those towns are like ghost towns."

Back when Levon, Anna Lee and Mary were kids, Marvell was the place to be on a weekend.

> Anna Lee: "The old Capitol Theater had a pool hall on one side, a theater on the other side and there was the bank building."
> Mary Cavette: "On Saturday, you couldn't even find a parking space. Everyone came to town and everyone would visit around."
> Anna Lee: "The kids would be running wild and the parents would be sitting out."
> Mary Cavette: "We'd come to town in the middle of the afternoon."

Every Saturday afternoon, Anna Lee said, "Everyone would go to town, especially in the fall when we had money. Lavon would get a quarter and he'd go to Anderson's Drug Store. He loved that place. He'd get a Coke float and a bag of peanuts for fifteen cents. He'd have popcorn at the movies.

The movie started at one o'clock and it was continuous—they had the comedy and the serial. At ten o'clock at night we're still waiting for him to get out of the movies to go home. We'd have to drag him out."

The only time anyone had money, Mary said, "was in the fall when it was cotton picking time."

That was in Marvell. Turkey Scratch revolved around A.B. Thompson's Grocery Store.

"Mr. Thompson had a lot of sharecroppers," Anna Lee said. "That store was mostly for his sharecroppers. They did the trade there and everything. He furnished their houses and paid their heating oil and doctor bills. A.B. Thompson's—they were good for sandwich meat. They still have the best bologna sandwiches in town. And they have the best bacon. When we were kids, we'd go to the grocery store once a month to get staples, like flour. Everything else, everyone raised their own food. Everyone had a big garden and a cow and a pig or chickens and they raised everything."

> Mary Cavette: "Diamond [Levon's father] and Daddy used to bring me and Lavon to meet the big yellow bus. It would be muddy. If one of them would bring us, we'd ride a horse—one in front and one behind, and Daddy or Diamond. If we came on the tractor, both of them would come, in case we got stuck. Getting to school was a big deal."
>
> Anna Lee: "At school, we had a wood heater and outdoor bathrooms and a pump house. We had to raise one finger if we had to do number one and two if we had to do number two. It was a two-room school building."

When Levon and Anna Lee and Mary were kids, Mary's mother and Levon's mother, Nell, would make lemon icebox pies.

"They weren't like they are now," Mary said. "I think Nell may have made up the recipe. But it was two cans of Pet milk and you would do this eggbeater thing. We didn't have electricity, so, of course, we didn't have an electric mixer. Every Sunday morning we'd beat this Pet milk up. Nell would make two pies and Momma would make two pies. Once it got fluffed up or whatever you call it, you would put sugar in it and then you would squirt a lemon on it and they cooked it, and it was very lemony. I don't know anyone else who made this pie. Here's the trick: We had to make one for Lavon by himself. He ate the whole pie. He used to be a huge eater. Oh my God, he could put away food that you couldn't believe. He would eat a whole pie. He's always been skinny. Lavon has always been able to eat anything he wanted all his life."

But Levon was as much about the giving as he was about the taking.

"Unfortunately, and he was like this as a child, he would give away his last penny," Mary said. "If he had Coke money and someone else didn't, he'd give it to them. He was always very generous. And we didn't have money. Lavon and I never knew how not to share—and that's not because we're great humanitarians; that was the way we had to live. Everybody had to share, because everybody was so poor."

Mary described their childhood as "wonderful."

"We went swimming in the creek," she said. "We chopped cotton and picked cotton. We just did what country people did. We just thought that's the way it was. Of course, we griped when we had to work, especially Lavon."

> Anna Lee: "Turner Lake—we used to go swimming back there. The mud would be that thick when you'd wade out in the water. That's where everyone from the church was baptized. Chopping cotton for Mary's Daddy, we'd rush just like crazy to get to the end of the road to jump in."
> Mary Cavette: "Lavon had a 4-H Club calf, which he never took care of. We did. I don't know he how talked us into it."
> Anna Lee: "We'd pump water for that thing and haul water and brush it and he sold it and he got all the money."

Diamond Helm, according to Mary Cavette, "was hysterical and did not know it. He did not know he was funny. Diamond would do something like get stuck in the ditch and Lavon would start laughing. He would say, 'It's not funny, this is exactly where I wanted to be.' He would never say, 'I made a mistake.'"

Once, Levon was driving the tractor after the cotton had been planted but had yet to bloom.

"He was driving down the rows," Mary recalled, "He had a portable radio and was slapping and singing."

Diamond, Mary said, told his son, "Levon, let a business thought run through your mind—it will not kill you."

Levon, Mary continued, "never took anything seriously. He had the great ability to make something funny out of any situation."

But he also kept friends first.

"I cried a lot," Mary said. "I was a crybaby. And of course, he always made sure I was taken care of, because I was like his sister."

The Helms, Mary said, "were the first people out in the country to get a television."

This was because Levon and his younger sister, Linda, who had achieved notoriety as a young musical duo, landed a gig on television.

"I think it was in Memphis, they were going to Memphis to be on *Dance Party* or one of those shows," Mary said. "We all gathered up at their house on Saturday because Lavon and Linda were going to be on TV. They had this TV with an antenna on the roof and Diamond went out and was switching it around. Well, we don't see nothing but fuzz. We just see snow. Finally, Lavon and Linda came on. And we can't even see. All we see is an outline and fuzz. And Diamond says, 'Aren't they good?' We couldn't see diddlysquat. But it was fun. During that show, they had an advertisement, it was for ham. The little ham was animated and it would go across the screen. The advertisement came through perfect."

As a young man, Mary Cavette said, Levon slept a lot.

"The bus had to wait on him every day," she said. "Somebody said, 'You ought to get some of that ham. It will wake Lavon up.' Nell said, 'I could cook a whole damn hog and it wouldn't get Lavon out of bed.' It was just one big fun thing after another."

When they all got older, they'd all head to town, together, in Anna Lee's family car.

"There was Lavon and Mutt Cagle—we couldn't go to town unless they went with us because it was dark and it was gravel and if we had a wreck or a flat tire or something, we had to take them along," Anna Lee said. "One time I got grounded because I stayed out too late or something. It was my Sunday afternoon to get the car and I had to stand in my yard and wave at them leaving in our car because I was grounded."

And then came date nights.

But, Anna Lee explained, "Nobody ever went just a boy and a girl on a date. You always had six or seven people."

And then Mark Lavon Helm went and got famous. But he never abandoned his roots.

"We have waited in more lobbies for him than anyone could ever imagine for a human being," Mary Cavette said. "One time, The Band was playing the music festival in Memphis. Of course, it was Memphis in May—it rained every year. They still had it in the mud. Lavon and them were going to play. That's when they were all still together. Lavon said, 'We'll bring our bus. It will be inside the musicians' circle.' I said, 'How am I going to get in there?'

"And we could not get into the gate. We had to buy a ticket to get into the gate. We're walking around; all the buses look exactly alike. Not one of them has a name on it. We are soaking wet and I'm saying, 'I'm never doing this again.' We see this bus and—you know how they have those big windows?—he is in there, laughing. I said, 'Is that Lavon?' He was just dying. We're just cussing and being obnoxious and horrible. We were so mad at him and we didn't know what to do. And my hair had kinked up like a poodle and he says, 'You girls got to get out of the rain.' And of course, we got on the bus and we had a good time and we forgot we were mad at him. That's just another one of our little trips with Lavon."

Years later, Mary and Anna Lee were with Levon in Fayetteville, Arkansas.

"This was when he was really down on his luck," Mary said. "Me and Anna went to Fayetteville to meet him. I don't know how he got to

Fayetteville. We see this dump. We're talking major dump. And it's got his name on the board. And the board had about four lights out, but you can make out 'Levon Helm.' He said, 'See? I always bring you girls to the nicest places.' He could always get humor out of everything. Me and Anna have been everywhere with him—to the worst places you could ever imagine and the best places you could ever imagine. It's been a really happy ride being his friend and being part of his life."

"I grew up on a dirt farm," Levon said. "We had a cotton farm down in Arkansas. I wasn't very good at picking cotton. My job was usually tractor driving in the summertime.

"There's a hell of a rhythm to those engines, like the John Deeres or those old ones that are two-cylinders. They plop-plop-plop-plop and you start giving them acceleration and you can get a hell of a rhythm going. The old Allis-Chalmers had a rhythm too. I took a little Ford to town once to get it worked on and the guy fixed whatever was wrong with it. And I'm sitting up there on the tractor and the guy says, 'Start it up.' I start it up, and he's listening to it and it's idling, and I'm setting there with my foot, and I'm kind of just tapping my foot on the brake of it in time with the engine. And he's listening and listening and he can't find out what it is. I finally notice he was listening to my foot. But that's just being a kid. I couldn't wait for him to give me the green light.

"From there, all the way out to where we lived was probably about five miles, five-and-a-half miles, so that was wide open the whole way. That little thing could do 25-30 mph. You put them in high gear and pull the hammer down on them. That big 9400—that's one of the biggest ones that John Deere makes. That one will pull a disc 60-feet wide and cutting 10 inches deep.

"That tractor we used for the inside of the album cover on *Dirt Farmer*, that's a 1940 model of a John Deere. It don't have lights. That's before they even put lights on them. You weren't supposed to work at night back in those days. No battery. No starter. You throw that flywheel instead of cranking it. You would throw that flywheel and that's the way you started it up. The old ones, you used to start them on gasoline, then switch over to kerosene or tractor fuel and run that damn thing until it got hot. If you look on the inside of the *Dirt Farmer* album cover, we used a picture of that John Deere dashboard and it says 'cold,' 'work' and 'hot.'

"I just loved to drive when I was younger. My dad had a gas station and we would do up the local funeral home's ambulance every now and then, and I'd always be the one who wanted to deliver it back to the place. I couldn't resist—I'd take it down through the quiet part of town and hit the damn siren, and kids and chickens would go jumping every which way.

"My dad, I guess, he had hopes of me being a scholar, so he never forced me to stay out of school. School started, thankfully, just as cotton-picking season started, so as long as I didn't get kicked out of school, I didn't have to stay home and pick cotton. In the summertime, when the cultivating and the planning goes on, that was when I had to be on duty.

"Out on the farm we had a big, long bathtub. I'd fill that thing up at noon, right after I got through eating lunch. I'd fill that thing all the way up and let it sit out in that sunshine, 'til I got through working. I'd come in from the fields and it would be nice and warm.

"When I was a kid, I got scrapes on my head from one end to the other. They'd wrap something around it and that was it. I never broke a bone when I was a kid. My problem was stepping on things, boards and damn things that would cut your feet. I wanted to go barefoot all the time. That was rough around a farm. But you just didn't go to doctors that much back then. They'd pour a pan full of coal oil and you'd stick your foot in there. If you couldn't soak it in coal oil, then you'd rub bacon grease on it—it's better if it's cold, it'd be more like a salve. You could just rub it on there. You'd use the bacon grease if you're going out on a date. It wouldn't be so smelly. She'd be sitting there thinking about gasoline, otherwise.

"One of the old remedies I remember is for a colicky baby: Blow smoke on the bottom of their feet. You've heard of that one? I guess if you've got a baby and they're crying, you'll try anything. That used to be a dangerous thing back in those days. I had a baby sister that died of colic, and I had an older brother that died of colic—Mom and Dad lost two kids. They had six kids and raised four and back then, that was just common mathematics. Somebody was gonna die. It was unusual for somebody not to."

"Every day at school was a carnival to me," Levon said. "With them idiots I was going to school with, it was like a damn circus. I couldn't wait to get out there and get it started. One of my best friends when I was a kid was 'Fireball' Carter. He was always funny, and he was dumb as me. We'd have to read aloud and he'd come to a word and I'd give him the wrong word. It'd be something like 'Mediterranean.' And I'd say, 'Meditation.' In Arkansas, when I got out, all you had to have, I think, was 16 credits to graduate, and I had almost that many. So, that last year, I didn't take but one or two classes. Pat Wooten is one of the girls who, if I hadn't sit beside her, I never would have graduated. She didn't look at her paper as much as I did. I like to remind everybody in our class: She was valedictorian, but they should all remember who she sat next to. We all went to school together—thanks to Pat, we got out.

"There was Mr. Steiner. He'd look at me and he'd say, 'Helm.' And I'd answer back, 'Sir!' And he'd say, 'Helm, if a book falls from heaven, don't think the Lord threw it.' He would say, 'I need a bright young man to explain this next problem for me. Explain, Helm.' He asked me that one day, he asked me what the answer was, and I said, 'Plus.' He said, 'Oh for the love of God.' Then I'd say, 'I mean minus. I mean minus.' He said, 'Equals, you blockhead.' We went and run him crazy. I thought we had him one day when he came back after Mutt. Our desks were all bunched up and we were kicking at each other and laughing and stuff. Mutt said, 'Mr. Steiner, I don't understand it.' He said, 'You don't understand?' He started getting up. 'You don't understand it?' I thought, 'Oh shit, he done flipped.' Then he went on, 'You and Helm!' By that time, he's right in the middle and he's kicking desks and he's pushing people. 'You come in like a bunch of clowns in the circus and you don't understand?'

"There was another teacher, I used to go in and take her clock. She had that clock for speed tests. And I would take that clock and set it to alarm at about five to six minutes after class took up. One of the best places to hide it was in the wastebasket. I'd put it in the wastebasket and that damn thing would go off, and she would just go crazy slamming and looking, and she would finally find it and look up at me and Watkins. She would get mad and glare her eyes over at you.

"We would come in on Monday and she would call the roll, and everybody had to give a bible verse. You didn't answer 'here' or 'present'—hell, 'Jesus wept.' After she would go around and everybody would give their Bible verse, she would say, 'How many of you went to church yesterday?' And everybody would hold up their hand. Shit, I thought you couldn't lie about it. Then she would say, 'How many of you didn't go to church?' Me and Mutt and Fireball and Watkins, we'd hold up our hands. All you had to do is say, 'No, I didn't go.' That took care of the rest of the class. She'd open up that Bible and start reading, and she'd look at me and look at Mutt, and make sure we was paying attention. We didn't have a damn thing to do on Mondays but read the Bible.

"Miss Brown, she drove that little black car, that coupe. She'd come in the morning. We'd all be lined up over by the Future Farmers of America building. We'd be out there on the corner smoking and waiting for school to start and there'd come Miss Brown. We'd all run over—'Miss Brown, Miss Brown'—and she'd be waving and then drive right off into that damn ditch.

"Miss Wilson, one day, she said I had to write a theme or something. I said, 'Well, Miss Wilson, I just don't have time, I have to do this, I have to do that, I just don't have time.' She said, 'Well, I have to give you a spanking.' I said, 'Yes, well, I guess so.' I started thinking to myself, shit, I don't want this little old woman whipping my ass. I was scared to death. And I went up and leaned over her desk and I turned my feet back and I looked back at her and she was lined up with my ass. And that goddamn paddle, she had it like this, like a baseball bat. I said to myself, 'Shit, this ain't gonna work.'"

———◆———

"When I was in school—and I heard Barbara talk about his too, when she was in school—our class raised so much fucking money that we all took a damn high school trip to Washington, D.C.," Levon said. "We paid for the fucking train, bought our own car, our own railroad car and the hotels and all the food and shit, and still had money left over we gave to the library. There was another railroad car, a bunch of kids from Oklahoma. So, a bunch of the girls in our car got stuck on a bunch of those boys. The mistake they made was they left all the peanuts and Ritz crackers at their seats. I went around and ate it all and had crumbs everywhere. I couldn't eat another peanut. Oh God, that was nothing but laughing.

"At school, we had the candy concession; we sold candy in the school every day. We put on shows, we put on plays. We had something going all the fucking time, making money. It's kids—who's going to turn down a kid? That was just par for the course back in my day. There was something like around 50, 55 of us in my class and we paid everyone's way to Washington, D.C., and went out and saw things and had dinner in hotels, shit like that. All of us got out one night on one of those boats, on the Potomac River there. We had a big dance on there with a band playing, cruising up and down the Potomac. It was the senior trip.

"In my senior year, I had a student bus-driver job and I was playing music on weekends. It was one of those big yellow school buses. It was easy, the same as driving a tractor, just up and down the road, and you'd get paid for it. I forget what I was making. I was probably making 50, 75 bucks a month. I'd drive that bus on them away games on Friday night, with the teacher, the coach and players—basketball and football. I finally quit playing and just went straight for the bus-driving job. I'd sit up there and never got cussed out again. I'd sit up there and laugh while that damn football coach chewed everyone else out."

———◆———

"I've been to all day sing-alongs with dinner on the ground," Levon said. "They'd lay out those cotton sheets—a big row of them. And put out a couple of tubs of iced tea at the end of one of them; another tub full of Kool-Aid. And all up and down those cotton sheets would be platters of cold fried chicken and coleslaw and potato salad. My mom would always make chicken salad. I would stand right in front of her chicken salad while the blessing was getting said and I'd attack that first. I'd go up and down the row of sheets, looking for stuff like angel food cake, things I'd never seen before. That angel food cake was something else. That was the wildest damn thing I'd ever chewed on. Anything you could chew on that was cold, they'd have a bunch of it. It was all gospel groups. In the morning part would be the local church and their choir people. Then everybody'd eat dinner, then other churches would bring in their choir. I could eat, fight and raise hell and listen to music all at the same time"

Mary Cavette recalled these events happening on a certain Sunday, possibly the third Sunday in June or the like.

"There'd be all-day singing, dinner on the ground," she said. "Everyone would hitch up the mules. We had no car. We had the wagon. Everyone would bring food and spread it out on the ground. Lavon and Mutt Cagle knocked the toilet down one time."

The holidays were also a special time for Levon, especially when it came to the dining options.

"During the holidays, we would start eating on Christmas Eve. We'd start cutting pies and cakes and turkey and ham, and the food would last all the way through New Year's. We'd put out a bunch of paper plates and, you know, when you're hungry, go eat. We never had a formal dinner. And when somebody'd come by to see you, you invited them to have something to eat. There'd be eight or 10 cakes, and eight or 10 pies. Mom would make icing out of egg whites. It was delicious. And there'd be a goose and maybe a chicken, just more food than a family could eat in a week. Mom used to make extra dressing. She would take a chicken or another turkey, just chop the meat up into bite-sized pieces and put that all through the dressing—make a big damn pan of it. Then, she might make two pans of it out of one bird, then we'd make dressing sandwiches. Oh boy, put it on bread with lettuce and salt and pepper and make dressing sandwiches. Food don't taste like that anymore.

"That was Christmas, boy. Mom would have every kind of a cake and every kind of pie. They'd just be sitting everywhere. You couldn't see where there wasn't a cake or a pie—pecan cake, with the pecans all on top; an orange cake. Mom would cook all the way until Christmas Eve. And at Christmas Eve, at midnight, the paper plates and everything would go on the table and the doors would open. You could start eating at midnight on Christmas Eve and she didn't cook again until after New Year's. She'd have a couple of hams, a country ham and a smoked ham. She'd fix up some other kind of meat like a roast beef or something like that. There'd be like four or five different kinds of meats and all those casseroles and stuff. She'd make a fruit salad, a Christmas fruit salad. She'd cut the grapes, take the seeds out of the grapes, cut them in half. And then oranges—little, bitty pieces—peel them, then peel the inside, where there's none of that stringy stuff. And apples—peel those and cut them in little, bitty pieces and chop pecans. And then she would put in a little bit of pineapple and take that juice and pour that in on the top with the coconut and the pecans. And you could just eat a barrel-ful. It's not too sweet or rich. What a plate. Nobody ate better than we did. It had to be something special for me to eat supper with somebody else. They didn't eat as good as we did—'I'll meet you after supper.'

"We'd go and eat and throw the paper plates away and maybe eat again—just come relax and eat when you can, as often as you can. That was Christmas. I didn't know we were that poor, 'cause nobody had a better plate. Nobody had a better table than we had. There was pride in the fact that whoever came by—neighbors, kinfolk—you bring them in and they have something to eat. Good manners dictate they have to have a bit of something."

"I'll tell you something these butchers don't know anymore is the pully bones," Levon said. "The most expensive plate in a fried chicken restaurant is the pully bone plate. That's the wishbone, and they cut the wishbone off of the breast. And if you order a pully bone plate, you get about six or eight of those damn wishbones—that's good breast meat. You get about six or eight of those and you get slaw or potato salad or whatever goes with it. I bet you can't find five butchers out of a hundred that can make a pully bone plate. Damn, it's great. It's the best part of the whole damn chicken. My mom would cut them chickens up. She would kill them and cut 'em up. She would always do the pully bone separate, and she'd always do the short leg and the drum stick separate.

"My mom loved popcorn and after supper, usually every night, about an hour, hour-and-a-half after supper, something would come on TV that everybody wanted to watch. And she'd go into the kitchen and make a big pan of popcorn. And she had a pan that she used, and she would go in and put that damn pan on the stove and pour the popcorn oil and the popcorn on the damn thing and put the top on it and come back in and sit down. I ain't never seen her shake that son of a bitch yet. And all of a sudden that son of a bitch would start popping. And she'd get up and walk in there to it and take it up off the fire and every bit of it would be popped—not a burned piece; every one of them just bouncing. Then you butter it and salt it. One of the best things you could do then, before you salt it and butter it, is take some sorghum molasses and cook it and make candy out of it, and you're going to make popcorn balls out of it. You've got that candied sorghum molasses and you butter your hand, put butter on your hand and you squeeze that popcorn into a ball and pour that candy molasses over it and push it together and you end up a with popcorn ball and it's like a Cracker Jack—but better of course. And those popcorn balls are the best thing you can get to eat as a kid. Pop some corn, drink some water, that's what Dad used to say. People would tell stories and sing songs and entertain each other.

"Our dads and our moms and them, they didn't think about taking care of themselves back then. Dad finally realized, after he got older, somebody would say something about one of those politicians being so old, like Senator Byrd, and Dad would say, 'The son of a bitch ought to be alright, he never did any damn work. Those politicians always had the best doctors. He never done nothing but have a good doctor look after him.' And by God, he's right a hundred percent. Shit.

"They didn't think about that stuff. They didn't think about not smoking. I could remember, as a kid, and even after I got grown, going over to Memphis to the hospital there, and my Dad or somebody was in there, and about 15 feet up and down every damn floor were fucking ashtrays built right into the wall. You could just stand out in the hall and smoke. That was a different time. Now they're in that place where they'll talk about something that needs to be done; they'll need to have some kind of procedure and they'll wonder if it's worth it. Goddamn—of course it's worth it if you get an extra fucking day out of it. Shit. The only thing they really had going for them was the quality of food back then. They had the best food in the world. That's why I'm as healthy as I am. Shit. I'm old myself, but I had that milk cow to grow up on."

"When I was a kid, you could look out and see your neighbor's house a mile or two down the road," Levon said. "Now you go down there and shit, the population of Phillips County is nothing. It's not like it used to be. There is probably less going on there now than there ever has been.

"Growing up, we went to Little Rock a little bit. That's where the state fair was, the state championship ballgame and the Robertson Auditorium. They could bring in big shows there. Memphis was a little closer to get to for us. Memphis was fun. Memphis always had the musical community going on there. They had Sun Records and a bunch of smaller labels. Then after that, Stax got started. It was 60-65 miles over there. And me with that brand new driver's license and stuff, I was just learning how to kind of get around.

"I saw Elvis a couple times. He was great, especially after DJ Fontana joined up. They had one of the best bands. It was a four-piece, a hell of a band. I was 14-15. Somebody else was on that show, maybe it was Johnny Cash, the Memphis crowd. But Carl Perkins had one of the best bands back then. His band was as good as anyone. They'd play the local high school gymnasium or high school auditorium. Carl Perkins's band, that was the band. Fluke could tear those damn drums up, left-handed and right-footed.

If you listen to 'Blue Suede Shoes,' it's just about perfect, the way he played. You can't think of nothing that could be better."

On an annual basis as kids, Levon and his sister Linda would travel to Fayetteville, in the Ozark Mountains in northwest Arkansas. Fayetteville sat about 120 miles from Tulsa and hosted the annual 4-H Congress, which drew kids from around the state. That's where Levon met Paul Berry. The two remained friends for the rest of their lives.

"They would come to campus at the University of Arkansas at Fayetteville," Paul said. "They would be there for a week. The boys stayed in one place; the girls stayed in another. They had competitions all week long, meetings, seminars, parliamentary procedure, health, tractor driving and talent. I've never been able to carbon date it—it was '52 or '53, one of those two years for sure—I started washing dishes for the food service at the old student union, three meals a day. I served food in the cafeteria line. That's the first time I had seen him. I'd gone over on my breaks, where they were having the preliminary talent competitions. I was so young they made me take a break in the afternoon. Instead of lying down and taking a nap, I'd listen to the music.

"The first time I saw Levon was with him and Linda, my birthday, October 14, that same year. I had seen him in the competition. His sister had a washtub and a broomstick—that was the bass. The range of it was not very great but it did change tones. Levon had an acoustic guitar. My memory is they started with 'No Help Wanted,' an old Carlisle family signature song. The way they sang it, it had a beat. Rock and roll wasn't even in the language. But they were rocking. They did 'Dance with Me, Henry.' I remember the first time I heard an Elvis Presley tune when I was older. But it didn't hit me with any bigger lick than Levon and Linda rocking. With Levon, I was really impressed with him. And here he comes through the line and I'm serving the chicken and getting it and putting it on the plates. You can't turn the crowd loose to serve themselves because you'd be out. I slipped him a couple of breasts; I gave him extra chicken. We acknowledged each other. And that went on. I don't know that we ever had a conversation through that time. I was a fan. It was thumbs-up.

"One of the years, Levon and Linda won first in talent, and he won the tractor driving competition, also. He won two medals in the same deal. We didn't have any of the kind of communications that you do now, but word would travel around. He and his sister were both blond and fair-skinned and good-looking. They looked like they got off a billboard saying, 'Eat Apples' or 'Drink Cokes.' They were, for amateurs, very professional, assured, but you couldn't even get a whiff of self-consciousness. It was so natural. They would go right in there and take no prisoners. It's corny to say electrifying, but they got the audience immediately. And they rocked them.

"By the time he got out of high school, he joined Ronnie Hawkins. Now, Hawk was a local hero. He was born in Huntsville, Arkansas, but came over and went to high school in Fayetteville. I was born in Little Rock and grew up in Fayetteville. Hawk was a hero. He had us all running errands for him on Saturday morning. And he'd let us hang out with him. He had one of those old Ford coupes with a rumble seat and one of those 'AH-OOGA' horns. We'd say, 'Hey, Hawk.' He'd say, 'Come on. What are you boys doin'?' We'd get to ride down Dixon Street with him, go with him to get a haircut. If you got any hang time with Hawk, you were cool, especially if any of your buddies saw you with him, then you were extra-special cool. A bunch of us kids in Fayetteville were familiar faces. We knew him and he knew us.

"Levon was one of the originals who went with him to Canada. They would always come back, my memory was, at least twice a year and play the circuit in Arkansas. They would play Fayetteville, that would be kind of home plate. They would play over in Tulsa, maybe Oklahoma City once in a while, but especially the old 'Rock and Roll Highway' in Arkansas. They would play the Plantation Inn in West Memphis. They'd play the Cotton Club in Truman, Arkansas. They would play Club 70, which is out there in Hazen, and the big one in Newport—Jerry Lee Lewis, Elvis, everybody played that. Ronnie Hawkins and the Hawks were a hot act. Ronnie, when he was a young man, was a real athlete. And fronting a band, I've seen him do a front flip. He's something.

"Music was really important then, and I guess it is now. You had so many more local, good people. Yes, we had a national *Hit Parade* and charts, but you had groups that would play a more regular circuit that were just killers, that the whole country never heard about and were often our favorites. Because we were in a college town, we saw a lot of big-name, popular musicians. But you didn't have to leave the state to hear as good as it got, and the Hawks are a great example of that.

"And then after they left Ronnie, they still played that circuit. They didn't have a record deal but there was always a lot more sizzle about any date that you might be able to get to at any of those clubs to catch them. They would finish a set in Arkansas, last call would be before twelve o'clock and the joint had to close at midnight. Typically, they would chill out a for a little bit and then go out to a place to have breakfast or something and get back to the club at 1:30 or so in the morning and rehearse 'til daylight. They would go over what they heard; or work on new material. They worked so hard. They didn't just get to be good on the bandstand; they got good at rehearsals. The way they set up, the sight lines, they're looking at each other. They're looking and playing and getting that duet down over and over, and the ending. They knew the owner of the club and they had the run of the place.

"There was a motel where they stayed. Robbie and Levon shared a room; Rick and Richard. Garth always had his own room—Garth was Garth. They all had such respect for him and his personality is not easily accessed. You could tell Garth was very special to them.

"They were different. They could play all the stuff everyone else was playing, but it was better. Levon once said to me, 'Most of what we did, you could do with three chords.' But with Garth in the ensemble, Lee has said so many times to me over the years, 'Garth is the leader. It's just that simple.' Garth knew the most music. They gave Garth a whole lot of things and a chance to rock and do things he never would have gotten to do with any other guys. He was a mentor musically and a teacher in a lot of ways."

"My friendship with Levon, and when we started to have hang time, really began when we were both about 18 or 19," Paul said. "He made such a strong impression on me; I wasn't about to forget him. It was just incredible to see him. I had seen him first as a guitar player and a singer. And then, there he is behind the drum kit. How did he learn all that? It was overnight. The truth was that he had been schooling himself. He had the Jungle Bush Beaters. We would hear about things. Porkchop, who became Conway Twitty's drummer, was out of Conway, Arkansas, and he had a band. And we got to hear him. He was great. He could whistle and play drums and he would do a thing called his naso-graph. He would blow like a kazoo sound with his nose. Hell, you couldn't wait for it to come up for that novelty. A lot of people tried to practice that and ruined their laundry.

"Things evolved as Levon came home with the Hawk, and they stayed at the Iris Motel there, on North 71 there in Fayetteville. It is no more. Once you got tight with them—it's one of those things, we didn't have the term groupies, but it was their local fans. And of course, there were things like—where to eat; get this; figure this out; just a lot of little cool stuff. Then Levon's parents, he had moved them up there, just about as quick as he could, to Springdale, Arkansas. There was a group of us—me and a guy named Kirby Penick, Jimmy Watson, Don Tyson, Herman Tuck. Herman and Don were 10 years older than we were. Levon and the Hawk and the others, they spent a reasonable amount of time in Fayetteville each year and so they began to develop a cadre of real friends there. We weren't just fans. We did things together. I spent more personal time and started off a little closer to Robbie than Levon. But Robbie and Levon, if you were around them in those days, they communicated without saying words. They could either go off and have a conversation or communicate without having to say anything. Richard was an absolute delight to get to hang out with. Rick was younger. But Richard Manuel, Robbie Robertson and Levon Helm, if they didn't play music, they could do comedy. Richard, he was brilliant in his own way, both musically and conversationally.

"We all just evolved—a closer relationship, and we stayed in touch. It was long-distance. We would check in as we were doing stuff. I became good friends with Levon's parents, Diamond and Nell. And we liked each other, whether Levon was around or not. And Levon was just great about staying in touch with his mother and father. He's always been proud of where he came from. It's very much a part of him. I knew his folks and it got tighter and tighter over the years. When I got out of school, this, that and the other, it just got closer over the years, whether he was touring or wherever. I can remember, one night they played Wembley Stadium in London, back in the early seventies. He called here to find out what the Razorback game score was. One time, when my first marriage broke up, I was busted. I had to move back home temporarily with my parents and Levon was home for Christmas, and Stax/Volt was really hot, and they were having their Christmas party. One thing I came out of that marriage with was one of those new T-birds that had the four doors and the doors opened backwards. And it had one of the first cartridge players, the old eight-tracks. Hell, it sounded just great compared to what we didn't have back then. I had that and I think 44 bucks cash. And I had to get my stepson a Christmas present out of that—I mean, I was down.

"Levon said, 'Come on and go to Memphis with me. I'm going to the Stax/Volt Christmas party. There's a girl I'll get you a date with over there. Her name is Janis Joplin.' She was in the same stable with Grossman. I said I couldn't go. And Levon had borrowed $500 from me some time before that. And I wasn't really thinking about it until he said, as he's pulling out—and he knew exactly what my status was—in his own Levon way, he looked at me and said, 'Paul, I haven't forgotten about that $500 I owe you. I'm going to lay that on you when you really need it.' And he did, eventually. He didn't do it too quickly, but we got square. We've laughed about it. And he borrowed my car. He took the car. It looked like the kind of car someone of his emerging, evolving status ought to be in. He was a big deal."

"Levon always had a habit, in the studio, when he thought they had a good cut on something, he often, not always, he often called me up and played it over the phone and we'd talk," Paul said.

"He had Neil Young on the phone one time. He was out in California. He had Neil Young singing 'Old Man' over the phone. The first time I ever heard it was on the phone, not the radio. They were having a good time. It was a share-the-wealth, share-the-musical-wealth kind of thing. That's one of the ways he's made so many friends and kept a high percentage. He's very generous with his talents. He's just made that way. And if it popped in his mind and it was cool, wherever he was, he'd say, 'Paul, or whoever, would really dig this.' And of course, I always did. I was very lucky."

CHAPTER TWELVE

Canada: 'It Sounded Like Going to the Moon'

In the mid-1970s, Canadian DJ John Donabie was working at CJFM in Montreal when he started getting calls, on a semi-daily basis, from a woman, a fan of The Band.

"This woman would call in and say, 'Could you play a song from The Band?'" John said. "A few days later, I'd get a call from the same woman—and this went on for a little while. And finally, one day, she says, 'John, I'm the lady who calls you up for The Band. We actually met once. I'm Robbie's mother. Did you know they're going to be playing just across the border in Vermont next week? They're playing an outdoor concert and here's the motel they're staying at.'"

John called in sick to work and drove down with his friend Matthew to the Burlington area.

"We get to the motel at about 3:30 in the afternoon," John said, "and I ask, 'Would Mr. Levon Helm or Mr. Robbie Robertson have checked in?'"

John strikes out and realizes the guys would have been checked in under aliases. He and Matthew wait in the lobby for a couple of hours and, seemingly out of nowhere, The Band walks in. John said the first thing Robbie said to him was, "My mother told you, didn't she?"

Oshawa, Ontario, about 35 miles from Toronto, was John's hometown. As a kid, he rode his bike to the dance halls that Ronnie Hawkins and the Hawks played. He couldn't get in because he was too young. But he stuck around outside and listened closely.

"It was savage," he said. "Robbie's guitar was something we'd never heard before. We never heard someone bend strings like that, play a guitar like that. Robbie was the one who caught the eye of so many people. The sound of the organ and piano—that wasn't done. Bands in those days were three guitars and drums. They might have a piano or they might have an organ, but not a piano and an organ. The coming together of those two instruments, along with bass, guitar and drums, it was one of the most incredible things to ever come out of this neck of the woods."

About 18 months after launching his radio career in Oshawa, John got a job at CHUM-FM in Toronto. Through his work as a DJ, he became close with Ronnie and in 1969 he was backstage at Varsity Stadium in Toronto with the Hawk. The occasion was a concert by The Band and it was the first time John met Levon Helm. The two men would remain close for more than 40 years.

"They came to Toronto in 1969 as The Band for the first time, playing at Varsity Stadium, a giant rock concert," John said. "I was standing with Ronnie on the grounds."

Levon and Albert Grossman made their way over to them.

"I was just such a fan," John said. "But I didn't say anything."

John that day was wearing what he described as, "this amazing suede jacket that I had spent an entire two weeks' salary on."

Ronnie introduced John to Levon. And Levon, according to John, said, "Son, I'll run you a mile for that jacket."

John turned to Grossman and said, "It's an honor to meet you, sir." Grossman's response, according to John, was, "I'm sure it is."

And then, John said, "Ronnie, who's not afraid of anybody, he said, 'Now Albert, he's a friend of mine. Be nice or I'll pull that little piggly-wiggly of yours.'"

"Back in the '50s, Conway Twitty turned us on to that damn southern Ontario circuit that he was playing out here," Levon said. "That's where he changed from Harold Jenkins to Conway Twitty. He would come back to Helena and play out at the Delta Supper Club. And of course, we'd go see him and he started telling Hawk and us about that nightclub circuit there in southern Ontario—Hamilton and London and Toronto. Back then, you could play the rest of your life and never leave that same circuit. We'd go to London and play two weeks, and they'd hold us over for a week or two, and then we'd go to Hamilton and do the same thing and go to Toronto, and it's time to go back to London. That kind of kept us out of Memphis.

"We would go back home in the fall and in the springtime, and we'd play the college dances up at Fayetteville, and go to Norman and Tulsa and play those spring fraternity dances and things. And then, hell, we would head right back on to Toronto and play that nightclub circuit, those clubs that sell those mixed drinks. We'd never have been able to play Mondays and Tuesdays, only on weekends. It was a whole new ballgame for us— good money and playing every night. Hanging out with all them hookers and pimps down on Yonge Street in Toronto—I was having a hell of a time.

"In London, Ontario, one of those clubs we played up there, there were three stage lights—a red one, a blue one and a white one. There was about a foot-and-a-half between our heads and the ceiling. Everyone had on those thin black ties and the mohair suits. We used to have to wear those damn cummerbunds. You'd put that cummerbund around—damn, I'd sit back there and play a couple sets and that damn thing would get soaked from playing. There was a tobacco belt right outside of London—a whole dirt farming region there, where they grew tobacco, of all things, right there in southern Ontario. Danko would talk about when Lake Erie froze in the winter and they'd get out on it in cars, cut donuts and slide. He said it was a hell of a lot of fun. We got up to Canada and fit right in. We played up there for five or six or seven years. It started in 1958 or '59. Conway Twitty turned us on to that, and it sounded like going to the moon—you know, to leave Arkansas and go all the way to Canada."

———

"Jerry Penfound, our sax player, when he joined up with us, Hawk said, 'Can you go on the road, son?'" Levon recalled. "He said, 'I ain't got no obligations. I can leave tomorrow.' The following Saturday, we're getting ready to do the Saturday matinee and this pregnant woman shows up in the lobby looking for Jerry. And when she sees Jerry, she faints. He had to scoop her up and try to get her upstairs—that happened in the afternoon. That was one obligation he had, and he had one coming and he had three more at home. That night, the damn MPs show up from the Canadian Army—that was another obligation he had. He told Hawk, 'I got no obligations.' He was a damn lucky guy. He could play lots of different things. He finally got a damn job in a piano bar. He would sit up there in a goddamn tuxedo and never even pop a sweat.

"That damn guy, he taught himself to fly. He would go down to the island airport in Toronto, to the little-bitty airport that sits right on the lake around Toronto, there. He'd rent himself one of those little Cessna planes and take off and fly.

"He got some tie tacks. And they were either red stones or blue ones. So Jerry got one of them blue ones and took it to a jeweler and had him mount that damn thing in a ring and he gave it to Mazy and told her, 'This is an Alaskan Blue Diamond.'

"After we finally left Hawk and was on our own, we got popped. And I'll tell you what, it hit the papers. Over the weekend, it was in the Toronto papers and that Monday night, down at the club, we had one of the biggest crowds we'd ever had. Shit, it was funny. The funniest part of it was that the people that busted us, damned if they didn't end up being friendly enough with us, and brought their wives down to the club; they hung out with us and shit. They were laughing their asses off. One guy, he'd look up at me every now and then and he'd start laughing and he's shaking his head. He told me, he said the next time you want to smoke, go to the bathroom, sit down on the toilet, smoke it, and when you get through, he said, just drop it between your legs and flush the son of a bitch, and leave. He didn't understand that it's just a sin to throw that butt away. That butt will work just as good as when it was new. I tell you what, you save them butts, and whack them up and roll them up and man—that's one of the strongest joints."

———◆———

"When we first went to Canada, we got up there and, you know, we started playing on a Monday night and, shit, I was broke when we got there, of course," Levon said. "Around about Wednesday or Thursday, I said to Hawk, I said, 'Hawk, ain't you got a few bucks? Loan me five bucks. I'll give it back to you.' He says, 'I ain't got nothing, son. I'm hungry, too.' I said, 'Okay.' And I left and kind of watched out of the corner of my eye. And sure enough, that son of a bitch got up and went on down to the restaurant down the street. I let him get in there and get situated and I walked in. He had ordered two bacon burgers, a big glass of milk. I just sat there and watched him eat it. He couldn't enjoy it. I said, 'It's good, ain't it Hawk?' He says, 'I didn't know I had this; I reached in my pocket.' He's always been like that. He just can't help himself. Since we got the Rambles going, Hawk has called a couple of times. He's all right. He just wanted to do the same old shit again."

———◆———

"Stan Szelest and Rebel Payne and Sandy Konikoff showed up in Toronto back in about '59 or '60, just after we got there with Hawk," Levon said. "They had one of the best bands in Buffalo. Them boys could play and they were like us. You'd hear about somebody, and you'd want to go see them, and the next thing we're all buddies. And the Hawk, true to his nature, when the Hawk would run into somebody—like when he ran into Richard Manuel's band, he just reached in and grabbed Richard, and away we went—he did the same thing with Stan and Rebel Payne. And they played piano and bass with us for a long time. Then, finally, Rebel left and went and got married, but Stan would come and go. The band would quit and Hawk would get Stan back to help him put another one together. Stan was a true bandleader.

"Stan was the best—funny, always; that quiet. We played 'The Wall' concert with Roger Waters in Berlin in 1990 and Stan came with us. We're digging it all. They marched the Russian Army through. It's been everybody from the Russian Army to all the stars—movie stars, actors, musicians. It's going on and on. And later on, Stan and I, we're sitting there. We're backstage and we're kind of over on the side. We can actually see the stage, plus we can see Jerry Hall's dressing room. They had those little huts. So we want to watch her come and go rather than wanting to see what's happening with the show. Finally, Stan leaned over to me and said, 'Sure would be nice to hear a shuffle, wouldn't it?'"

According to John Donabie, Ronnie Hawkins and the Hawks during the 1960s, "were the biggest thing here in Southern Ontario and on the circuit."

He continued, "But you have to remember, it wasn't like it would become when they were The Band. They were a bar band, but they were known as the best bar band. Everybody came to see them. They were really quite a big deal."

And then the Hawks became The Band.

"The Band at Varsity Stadium in 1969—they had a big cult following, *The Brown Album* had just come out. They were very big, but they would get bigger over time."

And through it all, John and Levon remained friends. There was the time that The Band played a gig in Toronto with Crosby, Stills & Nash. John was chatting with Levon near his drum kit as The Band was about to begin, and excused himself. Levon insisted John take a seat behind his drums and a little to the left—and that's the spot from which John watched the show.

In 1976, John was living in Vancouver when he received a phone call from Levon. John learned during that call that The Band was calling it quits. They were doing a final concert at San Francisco's Winterland Ballroom and Levon wanted John to be his guest. John attended all of the rehearsals for The Last Waltz—"Some of which," he said, "were far better than the actual concert."

"One day," John recalled, "it was the middle of the day and they started bringing out a ton of food. Everybody was pretty hungry. There was a fellow who worked for Bill Graham standing here. There's Ronnie. There's Levon. We're standing there and I see these chicken wings. I went and grabbed a chicken wing. The guy who worked for Bill Graham says, 'These are for the musicians. Keep your hands off the food.' Levon didn't miss a beat. Levon said, 'Gee. It'd be really sad if this whole concert didn't have a drummer. You don't tell my friend whether he can eat or not.' To which the guy who worked for Bill Graham responded, 'Yes, Levon. Yes, sir.'"

Levon worked a similar angle at the concert in Burlington, Vermont, that John traveled to after getting the heads-up from Robbie's mother. After Robbie had arrived at the motel and asked John if his mother had told him where The Band was staying, Levon walked into the lobby.

"And he had this lady with him," John said. "They went off to their rooms to get ready. My friend Matthew says, 'Maybe we should leave.' I wanted to stick around for a few minutes, and sure enough, out they come. Again, Levon is the last one of the five. He says, 'Oh, John, by the way, I'd like you meet my girlfriend, this is Sandy.' She was absolutely beautiful, just beautiful. She could have been Miss Virginia. She was just a knockout."

Levon insisted that John attend the concert. John told Levon he didn't have tickets and just really wanted to say hello, as they hadn't seen each other in some time. So Levon and Sandy hopped in John's car. And that got John and Matthew through security and into the show.

The setting for that outdoor performance, John said, was "absolutely beautiful, with a full moon, and Garth is sitting in a position where the moon is behind his head, and he goes into 'Chest Fever.' It was incredibly beautiful. It's like it was yesterday. It's a night I'll never forget."

John said The Band, back in the day, was a harmonious unit.

"Back in those days, everyone was just wonderful with each other," he said. "It was a wonderful time to know them during that period. Levon and Robbie during that time, they were really like brothers."

John and Levon remained close. And John was on hand as Levon's triumphs continued.

"We were in Connecticut one night with Stan Szelest, Jimmy Weider, Randy, Ricky and Garth," he said. "They were doing a concert in connection with the keyboard player from the Young Rascals and a few others."

John and his son Jimmy had driven to Woodstock in a motor home and took Levon and the gang to their show.

"We're driving back and Levon was in a great mood," John recalled. "He said, 'Well, John, it's going to be quite a day tomorrow. I'm going to meet with Ringo Starr. I'm going to be part of this big shows of his. He wants to put an all-star band together. That should be something. Ricky's going too.'"

And John was around for tough times, as well.

"Levon, no matter how much money he had made or lost, he had an inner strength that I certainly don't have, especially when he was fighting cancer," John said. "He and I talked about it one night. He said, 'When they told me to forget about singing, that I could never talk again, I made up my mind, that wasn't going to happen.' In his head, in that brain of his, he wasn't going to have other people tell him, 'You can't do this,' 'This is what's going to happen to you.' It was him in the end; he fought back to where he could put those albums out."

Of the songs on *Dirt Farmer* and *Electric Dirt*, John said, "Yes, the voice had changed, but some of the songs sounded old-timey and the voice kind of went with it. And he could drum sick with cancer better than those healthy as a horse. He would sit down at those drums and before you know it, it would be three or four hours later. He had this inner strength. It was like Popeye taking his spinach. Those drums just did it for him."

CHAPTER THIRTEEN

Woodstock, Saugerties and Ulster County

Sometime in the 1990s, Don LaSala was at a Piermont, New York, club called the Turning Point to see Rick Danko perform.

A sound engineer who toured for years with NRBQ, Don had arrived early with a friend who knew the keyboard player performing with Rick that night. It was sound check and set-up time and Don noticed immediately that there was no soundman for the gig. He stepped in, adjusted Rick's microphone, set the levels on the mixing board and geared up to serve as soundman for the evening. After sound check, Don found himself hanging out with Rick in his RV.

They chatted about music in general and, "We told rock and roll war stories," Don said.

But Don wasn't yet ready to tell Rick about his strong link to The Band—a very strong link. Don and his wife, Sue, owned Big Pink, the famous house near Woodstock where The Band had lived and worked with Bob Dylan decades earlier, writing some of their most iconic songs, generating landmark recordings in the basement and setting the stage for an album that remains one of modern music's milestones. Big Pink the house, of course, was the inspiration for *Music From Big Pink*, The Band's legendary debut album with the cover that features Dylan's artwork. The basement of Big Pink is where Dylan and The Band's infamous *Basement Tapes* collection was recorded.

Back in Piermont, Don's gig on the soundboard with Rick went well.

"Afterward," Don recalled, "we knew each other a little better, and I said, 'You know, Rick, I'm the guy who bought Big Pink.' His face lit up. He launched into Big Pink stories and told me how they had so much fun there. He was just a little kid about it."

Don purchased Big Pink in 1998. A friend of his who lived in Woodstock saw an ad in the *Woodstock Times* that said, "Famous Rock-n-Roll House for sale by owner." Don and his friend saw the house, hit it off with the owner and ended up going to see his band play in New York City. His fate was sealed.

Including the basement, Big Pink encompasses about 1,850-square-feet and sits on four acres in West Saugerties, in the Town of Saugerties, which sits due east of Woodstock, a town with which Don was very familiar. He attended the Woodstock festival in Bethel in 1969. And Don was in town on a regular basis during the late 1970s through the 1980s, when the guys in NRBQ lived in Saugerties; performed regularly at the Joyous Lake; and recorded at Bearsville Studios in Woodstock.

"My wife, when we were first looking at it, she said, 'You only want Big Pink because of Dylan and The Band,'" Don said with a laugh. "And it really wasn't, though I thought that was a kick. I had worked in the music business. I ran a mastering studio out in San Francisco. Out there, every other house is a famous rock and roll-er. Granted, none of them are Big Pink."

Don finds it curious that the road leading to Big Pink is Parnassus Lane. That's because Mount Parnassus, in central Greece, was among the Greek mythology dwelling places of the Muses—the goddesses of literature, science and the arts—and you would be hard pressed to find another road in Ulster County that showcases the majesty of the Catskills better than Parnassus Lane. You really have to work hard to find Parnassus Lane—or you really need to know where you are going. Tree-lined on both sides, Parnassus Road brings you around a bend to greet Overlook Mountain in the distance, with a field laid out before you and the Big Pink driveway to the right.

But for all of its lore, Big Pink's strong attraction for many likely lies in the fact that it's simply a house—and, of course, The Band lived and worked and ate and slept there.

Big Pink was Don and Sue's extended weekend place. They typically spent three days a week there, sometimes more. They owned a home in the New York metropolitan region but wanted a place in the country so their 9-year-old could spend time in a rural setting. Also, Sue had grown up on a backwoods road in the northern Adirondack Mountains and later lived in rural Oregon. Don and Sue eventually bought a second place in Woodstock and now rent out the main floor and converted attic of Big Pink for "Big Pink Residencies." These stays of two or more days allow Band fans, Dylan fans and anyone seeking respite from the city to experience West Saugerties as The Band did, with interior décor that reflects the Big Pink era. Don regularly uses the basement as a music studio and while it's not part of the Big Pink Residency experience, he brings guests down for a visit and discussion of the history of the place.

"I often like to refer to the Basement with a capital 'B'," he said. "It's not an ordinary basement, but 'The Basement.'"

When Don and Sue bought Big Pink, they quickly discovered that the fireplace didn't throw off much heat.

"We would load it up with decent hardwood, but you'd have to sit right in front of it to warm your hands," he said. "We ended up putting a wood stove in."

And they sealed the whole place up—well just about the whole place.

"A lot of country homes have a problem with mice," he said. "We didn't have a problem with mice."

There was one hole in the house that Don never quite got around to sealing. And he and Sue had noticed snakeskins hanging from the ceiling of the basement.

"I thought that was pretty curious," he said.

When they first bought Big Pink, Don and Sue rented out the attic and kept the basement and the main floor for themselves. There was a guy living up in the attic, a sound man who, incidentally, had worked for the second incarnation of The Band. On one occasion, he was sleeping on a futon in the attic. There was a hole in the wall, out of which came a black snake that slithered above his head.

"He called me up and told me what happened," Don recalled. "I said, 'Man, get some spackle and fill the damn hole.'"

Regarding those snakeskins in the basement, Don figured out that when the snakes shed their skin, they'd rub themselves up against the electric conduits. But they were also hunting and catching the mice.

"I was a little weirded out by it at first," he said. "But it was nature's way."

And how about the snakes now?

"That's been remedied," Don said. "No snakes, no mice. Though you do see black snakes around the area."

The history of Big Pink, its acoustics in the basement and easy load-in through a ground-level basement door that offers access from the driveway all encouraged Don to create an environment for making music there with friends.

"I wanted to do music here," he said. "But it couldn't be about the money. A lot of people said, 'Oh, you could charge by the head.' I didn't really like the idea of that. I wanted to keep it on another level. I wanted to keep it a high-minded thing. I thought about it for a year, year-and-a-half and I decided I wanted to do a local thing and bring live music back."

That set the stage for Don and Sue's Big Pink Socials in 1999. There was no advertising, no invitations for the general public and no cover charge. It was just an open mic for about 40-50 people who either knew Don and Sue or knew someone who knew them.

"We had a lot of fun," he said. "I felt like we were bringing music back to the basement. And of course we recorded it all."

The first album Don LaSala ever bought was Bob Dylan's *John Wesley Harding*, released in 1967.

That same year, The Beatles released *Sgt. Pepper's Lonely Hearts Club*

Band and *Magical Mystery Tour* and the Rolling Stones released *Their Satanic Majesties Request*. A year earlier, in 1966, The Beach Boys had released *Pet Sounds*. And in 1968, the Rolling Stones released *Beggars Banquet*.

During this same period, in 1968, The Band released an album that was very different from all of these, an album with a different origin and direction framed by groundbreaking arrangements, instrumentation and writing. That album was *Music From Big Pink*.

"*Music From Big Pink* came out and it was kind of a big deal," Don recalled. "Dylan had three songs. He did the cover. It was a real different sound. Back then, we were dependent on FM radio DJs to tell us what was going on, so we'd heard about him being holed up in the Woodstock area. So the album came out and there it is, there is the house."

As for this thoughts on the record, Don said, "It was kind of mystifying to me."

And what about the pink house in upstate New York around which the entire project seemed to revolve?

"It seemed like they were in awe of the place," he said. "I always thought about that. Why would they be in awe of this kind of strange, not particularly interesting house, from an architectural point of view? Could it just be because they had fun here? Yeah, I've had some fun houses I've lived in. But I don't really think about them that way. Then I realized, it's the natural environment and sense of nowness in this compelling natural space that tips common, everyday experience into inspiration. This ordinary house with pink siding somehow smiles at us while sitting outside, gazing at Overlook Mountain in the afternoon sun. It's an emotionally moving counterpoint to the eternity of the natural forces extant around us."

Don and Sue know plenty about Big Pink's natural surroundings, which likely haven't changed much from when The Band lived there.

Upon arriving for Sue's first trip to Big Pink, the LaSalas were greeted by a luna moth—"as big as a dinner plate," Don said—right next to the basement door. Hawks and eagles regularly circle in the sky above the house. Wild turkeys peck at their reflections in the basement windows. And there was that time, after Don and Sue had purchased Big Pink, that they were in the basement with another couple. Don and a pal were playing guitars together that night and all of a sudden, Sue advised everyone to remain still.

"We look over and a baby deer—not even a fawn, it was smaller than a fawn; it looked a day or two old; it was so tiny, it looked like a toy—it came in and walked right up to where my buddy and I were playing guitar," Don said. "We weren't saying anything and stood still. My wife quietly came over and put her arms below it like a forklift and just very gently picked it up. The thing was not afraid at all. Its little mouth opened and closed. And Sue walked it to the door, where the mom was standing. We all remained quiet. The doe didn't run, she was watching what's going on. Sue put the baby deer down gently, in front of the mom. The mom just turned and walked away and the baby followed."

Don believes the doe was eating the pink roses that grew to the right of the basement door, the door was ajar, and the mother inadvertently knocked it open.

"And the baby deer heard the music and came in to stand with us there," he said.

As for the house and the lore and The Band and Bob Dylan, Don said, "I just really do believe there is a little something about this place that is more than just the sum of the physical parts and the fact that it's convenient to play in. Those guys could find peace here."

Head north from Manhattan on the New York State Thruway and you will come upon exit 19, which offers access to the City of Kingston and the Hudson River to the east and state Route 28, the Catskill Mountains, and Woodstock to the west.

About four miles from the traffic circle in Kingston, you will find state Route 375 in the Town of Hurley. Also called Levon Helm Memorial Boulevard, Route 375 will take you to Route 212 in Woodstock. A right turn takes you to Saugerties, where the Woodstock '94 festival was held and where late-night television star Jimmy Fallon grew up. Turn left and you will drive into downtown Woodstock, passing on your way the latest edition of the Woodstock Playhouse, a previous incarnation of which hosted the recording sessions for The Band's 1970 album, *Stage Fright*. The Woodstock Playhouse is also where Larry Hagman made his professional stage debut. Anne Meara, Dick Van Patten, Diane Keaton, Judd Hirsch, Lee Marvin, Chevy Chase and Angela Lansbury have all graced the stage.

Keep driving and Route 212 becomes Mill Hill Road, which at the crest of a hill and a bend in the road at the Village Green becomes Tinker Street. Make your way through Woodstock, and you will see that—as much as the music and the festival—this municipality is defined by its two hardware stores; its independent bookstore, the Golden Notebook; Bread Alone Bakery; and shops and restaurants that nurture a local economy driven by the arts.

"Woodstock has a long history of accepting people who are different and that's been an important part of artists feeling comfortable in this community," Mike DuBois said. "There is a sense of community here among creative people of all types."

Dawes drummer Griffin Goldsmith described this community another way.

"There is definitely something in the air in Woodstock," he said.

Zero in on just about any decade from the 20th Century and you're likely to unearth some great stories about Woodstock, the famous people who lived and visited there and how celebrity fused with everyday life for the locals.

Offering plenty of insight into Woodstock during the 1990s is Rick Schneider, the morning show host and music director for Red Hook, New York-based radio station WKZE. This Red Hook is in Dutchess County, across the Hudson River from Woodstock, as opposed to the Red Hook in Brooklyn. And WKZE can be found at 98.1 on your FM dial in the Hudson Valley.

Rick during the 1990s booked bands and musicians at the old Tinker Street Cafe in Woodstock, he hosted the open mic and served as sound engineer for the house. Rick spent most evenings at the Tinker Street Café on

Tinker Street, and for one stretch of about 2-3 weeks in 1996 welcomed the guys from Phish, for drinks, around 11 p.m. each night.

Phish recorded their 1996 release, "Billy Breathes," at Bearsville Studios; and band members Trey Anastasio, Mike Gordon, Page McConnell and Jon Fishman headed to the Tinker Street Cafe each night, following work on the album, according to Rick.

"We'd say hello, they'd sit at a corner of the bar and talk shop—albums, songs," Rick said. "They were really polite. But you couldn't get a word in edgewise. I'd go over and bring them another round, they'd say 'Thanks' and, BOOM!—pick up right where they left off. It was pretty intense."

Those recording sessions culminated in a stealth gig that Phish played at the old Joyous Lake, a short walk from the Tinker Street Cafe. The gig was billed as "The Third Ball" and took place on June 6, 1996.

Rick said Joey Ramone performed at The Tinker Street Cafe, with a band he was recording with. The lead singer for The Ramones included three of his own band's tunes, including "Blitzkrieg Bop," during the middle of the show.

Rick said Evan Dando of The Lemonheads played the Tinker Street, and so did Dave Pirner of Soul Asylum. The Dave Matthews Band also performed at the Tinker Street Cafe, while they were in Woodstock recording their breakout album, "Under the Table and Dreaming," at Bearsville Studios.

"Nobody knew who they were," Rick said. "They were just dudes."

Towering above all things Woodstock is Overlook Mountain, which for many in Ulster County defines that point where the Catskill Mountains emerge, providing a relentless sense of place and an enduring identity.

"To understand the one constant in Woodstock's history, we need only to glance upward at the face of Overlook Mountain," reads the website for the Woodstock Chamber of Commerce & the Arts. "There, in its gentle slopes, you will find the beacon that has summoned the creative spirit and the unique individualism that has filled the pages of Woodstock's story throughout the years."

In August 1965, according to *This Wheel's On Fire*, Levon and the Hawks were playing Tony Mart's, a club in Somers Point, New Jersey, on the Jersey Shore. They had moved on from the Hawk. And then came Bob Dylan.

"Mary Martin hooked us up," Levon said. "Mary Martin knew us from Toronto and worked for Albert Grossman and knew that Bob was going to try and put a band together. And she told Bob, she said, 'Hey, they're already together.'"

A month earlier, in July 1965, Dylan had scrambled like eggs the Newport Folk Festival, by playing electric guitar. His backing band included Mike Bloomfield on electric guitar, Al Kooper on electric organ and Barry Goldberg on electric piano.

The crowd booed.

Robbie and Levon joined Kooper on organ and Harvey Brooks on bass for Dylan's show at Forest Hills Tennis Stadium on Aug. 28, 1965. And once again, the crowd booed during their electric set.

Then came a gig at the Hollywood Bowl and with it a much warmer reception. That lineup gave way to Dylan playing with Levon and the Hawks, and the booing continued. On October 1 of the same year, Bob Dylan with Levon and the Hawks played Carnegie Hall in New York City. Recording sessions followed. And in November 1965, the lineup played Minnesota, Ohio and western New York, followed by two nights at the majestic Massey Hall in Toronto and the last show of the month in Washington, D.C. The booing crowds followed them through it all. Bob and the gang flew back to New York, Levon left Bob, the band and the booing behind him, struck out on his own and ended up in New Orleans, working on a lay barge.

"It took about two hours by crew boat to get out there," he said. "I just walked in and said, 'I'm ready to go.' When I told them that I grew up on the farm, driving tractors and shit, that was it. It was right beside the rig, and the front of that lay barge had a big fucking spool and it had like a mile or two of six-inch pipe coiled around that damn big spool, the width of the boat. And the divers would go down and plug that pipe into the rig, and they had a frame they put over the side that sinks down to the bottom and they'd turn it on and it blows air. They'd drag it and it blows out a big trench about four to five feet deep, and the pipe lays right in the trench and the current covered it up; and that was our job, to hook that pipe up.

"I wasn't out there but just two trips. The first trip, I was out there for about two weeks, three weeks, and I went to New Orleans and spent all my money right away and had to go back. You could make about a grand a week. And if you got overtime that second week you're out there, everything doubles up. So when I got off of it the second time, I had, I don't know, I had two, three grand."

Once off the lay barge, Levon headed to Springdale, Arkansas, to see his parents, then to Fayetteville for a visit with his old friend, Paul Berry. Then, according to *This Wheel's On Fire*, it was off to California to hang with Bobby Keys, Leon Russell, Johnnie Cale, Roger Tillotson, Jesse Ed Davis, and Jimmy Markham.

"I played out there with Jimmy Markham some," Levon said. "And we had a booking agent we called 'Felix the Cat.' He had one of them little 'give me the deed to your ranch' kind of mustaches, and he would pay us to play every Sunday night—$10 a piece. Me and Markham and Bobby Keys and a few of the regulars, we would hang around at Leon Russell's place. Leon had put together one of them home studio deals, him and J.J. Cale. Me and Markham and the boys would be hanging around there. Bobby Keys and I were usually in charge of refreshments for everybody. We'd take one of Bobby's saxophones and pawn it, get some capital together and go cop.

"We used to play across from the Roosevelt Hotel. One night, we got Leon to go with us; and we got Johnnie Cale to go with us one night. Otherwise, it was Keys and Jimmy Markham and me, and that big guy who played guitar, Tommy Tripplehorn He's great. Jesse Ed Davis was one of the damn ringleaders. We couldn't get paid the same day. We'd all be standing by, waiting on that $10. Me and Bobby Keys would take our $20, and then we would take one of his horns, he always kept two, and pawn it, and cop. We'd be kicked back by suppertime. I don't ever remember how we got those damn horns back, but we'd always manage to get it back, so we could pawn it again.

"Back then, they had come out with some LSD, and they called it Purple Passion. And we got some of that, too. It was alcohol-based. And you would turn it up and take a little swig and it was just like drinking rubbing alcohol; it was all purple. And in about 40 minutes, the goddamn walls would start dripping.

"The damn walls would turn liquid on you. All of a sudden, it just got too thick. I was about half-scared and I started thinking, the only way out of this, is, I'm going to have to go to the damn hospital, I guess, and check in. Then I immediately thought, well, what the fuck are you going tell them is wrong with you? Well I kicked that idea out. I wasn't going nowhere. Shit. I was pretty safe where I was. There were some other occasions. That was the worst one. Getting to that particular spot and after, I was just going to deal with it. There were some funny spots either side of that scared place. It was a heavy, heavy thing for me. For me, it was just a little bit unpredictable.

"One night, me and Bobby Keys, we got Bruce Channel out of his gourd. We were all just—our heads were like a damn bell. Finally, I guess, we took Bruce home and let him lay down. He needed to lay down. That was just one of those nights where we were giggling about everything. I saw one guy walking down the street and he just looked like the funniest cartoon I'd ever seen in my life."

Levon eventually reunited with Dylan and the guys in Saugerties, where they lived in the house called Big Pink.

"One night we were living out at Big Pink and I had one of those damn dreams," Levon said of a dream he had about UFOs. "There used to be a sleeping porch, and that was Richard's bed, and Richard went home to Canada for the weekend or something, and I ended up sleeping in that room and I had a good one that night. All of sudden, I was on board and it was instant communication, right? And it was just fascinating to me, the formation. There was a bunch of them, a bunch of these spaceships, and they were in the most beautiful, geometrical formations. When you looked at it, you knew it was figured to perfection, minute-to-minute. And I would look at that, then I'd look back over here at what we've done, and boy, it was just embarrassing, just really embarrassing. But that's all that happened, that little sequence, and then the next day, it was one of those weird dreams. That's the only one of those damn things I've ever had. I've always wanted to see one. I'd love to see one. But I'm pretty sure that was just a dream. When you look at the sky on a real bright night and see all those stars, mathematically, there's just got to be something else besides us."

As for the majestic beauty of Ulster County—the Catskills, the sunsets, the swimming holes, the creative spirit and the proximity to Manhattan—Levon said, "We were all country boys for the most part. It was an ideal situation for us. We could travel down to the city for a show and sleep in our own bed that night. We were two hours, hour-and-a-half from the city. You can get away from it and get that country kind of sleep. There is so much electricity in the air, it's hard to sleep in the city. Just as you start to go to sleep, here come the garbage trucks."

Levon began to set his sights on the big time as a kid growing up in Arkansas.

"When I was a kid, we'd be out in that fucking cotton field and the one thing that would get my attention immediately was, just say the words, 'New York,'" Levon said. "Oh shit, I wanted to go to New York—especially after I got old enough to make music. That's where Carnegie Hall is and that's where Madison Square Garden and all that stuff is. Shit, if you're going to call yourself a musician, you've got to be able to go there and not get run off. The first time I got there, it just bowled me over—just so big you couldn't comprehend it all. We went there to see Morris Levy about a recording contract. It wasn't like we were just bums on the street. It was just fantastic. I finally found a place where I could see all the movies I wanted to see—open all night—and that was one of my thrills. I would come to town, we would get here once a year, whatever it was. I would hit 42nd Street and spend two days and nights going to movies until I finally passed out. We played a whole lot in New York City."

During the second incarnation of The Band, Levon said, "We were playing with the Cate Brothers and the whole damn truck was stolen after we played the Lone Star Café one night. They followed us over to the Gramercy Park Hotel and there they were. They lifted the truck, just took it on home. The Cate Brothers had some good guitars. We had those drums. It was an old Ludwig and I found it in a damn pawnshop down there on Santa Monica Boulevard in Los Angeles. Garth found it for me, told me about it. It was the bass drum, the snare drum, two toms and a cymbal for $160. That old floor tom only had one skin on the top. The bottom part didn't even have a head. But it sounded good. It had wood rims on the snare and the bass drum. They just sounded good. The next day, we were over at Manny's Music on West 48th Street, talking to Henry. He's saying, 'Oh, Levon, I just can't treat you like I used to. I can't give you the breaks I used to give you guys. You guys used to come in here and I'd tell you to take the store. I didn't care. But I can't do it anymore.' I'm saying, 'Henry, we've got to play tonight. I can't argue this out with you. We've got to go set up. You know we're good for it.'

"Another night, the damn bus driver got so goddamn drunk that nobody wanted to ride with him. We're right in the middle of Manhattan, we played the Lone Star, and got ready to go and he just, all of sudden, is drunker than a monkey's ass—just goddamn down. He couldn't get away from the curb. And I get up and I'm looking and said, 'What are we doing here? Are we going to sit down here all night?' One of the boys says, 'Willie's in bad shape.' I said, 'Yeah. Now, get out of the way.' So I got behind the wheel and I drove the goddamn bus. I got a broomstick about that long and put it on that gas pedal and put it under the edge of the dashboard. It would run just about 80 mile per hour, 82, you know, right in there. We'd come up to a tollbooth and I'd just kick it out of the way.

"Me and Danko brought that Corvette from Manhattan one night at about 2:30 in the morning and we went from, I think it was the George Washington Bridge, to the Kingston exit, and I think it was like 56 minutes.

We didn't even get in the right lane. We'd just go in that left lane and ZOOM. We were doing 110-115—just as much as it would eat; just rocking right on up. The faster we got, the lower we squatted. I didn't care. You may as well get hung for being a sheep as a lamb."

"I've been in Woodstock ever since I first showed up in the sixties," Levon said. "I'm one of those people who came for the festival and stayed. It fit so good, especially if you're born and raised in the country, like I am. Back then, Mrs. Kirschbaum, she was something. Boy that was good stuff, those crumb buns she used to make. She had two places. She was in Woodstock, right on the left as you pull into town from Bearsville. Then she was in Bearsville, the old schoolhouse, I guess, right across from the Odd Fellows hall, there. She was there for a long time. Louise used to run the sports shop. I'd go in and buy socks and stuff from her. When I lived out on Cold Brook Road, I used to go to the Wittenberg Store a little bit, but I would usually go right on into Mrs. Kirschbaum's and I'd pick up some buns and stuff. Then I'd go over to the Bearsville Market and get a couple of quarts of milk in bottles. Oh, it was great.

"Right there in town there is that one maple tree that sits right in front of where the old post office used to be, on Tinker Street. I swear, in the fall, you could smell the color of that thing it's so bright. It's beautiful. It's about as red as any maple you've ever seen. The other good thing about Woodstock is, there's been so many famous-type star people, that have come and record and one thing or another over the years, that someone famous can come and see us and the town doesn't react objectively, or startlingly, to any of those kinds of occasions. So anyone who comes to Woodstock can feel comfortable."

Built in only 48 days and propelled into the Hudson Valley arts legacy with the June 30, 1938, opening of *Yes, My Darling Daughter*, the Woodstock

Playhouse, in 1968, held the final Sound-Out, a series of local performances that inspired the Woodstock Music and Art Fair, held one year later in Bethel, New York. But fans of The Band know the original Woodstock Playhouse as the place where the ensemble's 1970 album, *Stage Fright*, was recorded.

"It was one of those round-top buildings and the sound was just fucking great," Levon said. "We brought in that truck with all that equipment and hooked it up there and cut that record there on the stage. Sometimes, we would close the curtains and just keep the sound on the stage. And sometimes we would open the curtain and let the sound dissipate in the room. We were able to do all kinds of things like that to accommodate the songs. We didn't set up like a show, we set up pretty much to record.

"We took the name for *Stage Fright* off the song, and that was kind of the feeling at the time. We were playing for some pretty big crowds. Stage fright was one of those things that you had to watch. It can attack your ass. I've never been bothered by that shit, as long as we're going to play some music, or we've got a small idea, because you can always leave, you can always walk the fuck out if it turns ugly. But shit, I kind of enjoy the tickle of it—you know, run out there and see if you can hold them for however long you can hold them."

"The first time I met George Harrison was when he came up to Woodstock," Levon said. "He came up to see Bob, and Bob had everybody over for a dinner for George. He was really the best kind of guy you'd want to meet; the first one to stick his hand out and befriend everybody."

Sometime later, George was working with Ringo on what would be Ringo's self-titled 1973 album release.

"We were out in California, trying to record ourselves and he got ahold of us some way or another, and asked us to play on one of Ringo's tunes and we said 'Sure—great idea, George,'" Levon recalled. "And we ran down to their studio there in Hollywood and got to meet Peter Sellers, which was a big thrill for me. That *Pink Panther,* that's one of the best ones, you know.

George and Peter Sellers had a studio full of beautiful Hollywood starlets and hungry-looking musicians. We had a big time though, it was great. Ain't much not to like about it. Ringo and I have been friends forever. He is the best. I just love him. He's done so much for me. There is nothing not to like about the guy. He's just one of the best people you'll ever see around. He's smart as hell—and he's a drummer. We're going to be on the same page, nine out of 10 times. As far as I'm concerned, there ain't nothing I wouldn't do for the guy. He's been so good to me and my family. I can't think of anything I wouldn't want to do for him. I'd be disappointed if he asked anybody else. And it's just for the satisfaction. I damn sure wouldn't brag about it.

"Me and Danko were on the Ringo tour in 1989 with David Fishof and one night, we got ahold of some fake bottles and the fake blood. We got those bottles that were made out of sugar, they just shatter—they sound like a gun going off when they break. We faked a big fight between me and Joe Walsh.

"People would walk up to David Fishof and say, 'Boy, I don't know what they're into it about, but it's getting rough.' Dr. John would say, 'I just hope this shit don't break bad.' And every time, David says, 'Let me go talk to them—they're big boys, they'll work it out.' Finally, they bring David down, and when they come in you could just hear us out in the hall, yelling—'You son of a bitch!' And we've got paper plates, paper cups and stuff; a couple of chairs turned over, scattered over the room. And we've taken each other's shirts and just pulled the neck, ripped them, and we've got blood in our mouth, in the corner of our mouth and stuff. And we've got the two-part blood—they're both clear until you mix them. We poured half a bottle on Joe's head, down his ear, and down his neck, and poured the other part into a paper plate.

"So at the critical moment, David walks in, and Joe's saying to me, 'I'll tell you what's wrong with this band, there's too many fucking drummers.' And then he turns his back and drops his hand on his hip, and I look around like, 'Boy, now is my chance.' I reach behind and pull out that bottle and he drops up on the edge of that equipment case and lays his hand on it. I come over the top of the case, just going as slow—if you go too fast the camera can't see it. We've already worked it all out. We've placed the shot. Jimmy Keltner's doing the camera.

"We worked it all out, where the action's going to be. All he has to do is turn the camera. David comes in—'Hey you guys! Hey you guys! Hey you guys!' I come down with that bottle and he sees that bottle and he goes, 'NOOOOOOO.' And I hit Joe and that thing just sounded like a pistol. BANG! And Joe just fell, like he was shot. And on his way down he grabbed his ear and it just turned crimson. It looked like I cut his ear off. And then I run up on him, like now's my chance. Instead of kicking him, I just jumped down on the ground with him, and we picked each other up. Oh God, it was funny. David was just, goddamn he was trying to laugh. But he was wondering about how many tickets he'd have to give back. We were about 30 minutes from show time. He was wondering if we could get Joe's ear sewed back on his head. He had to play that show—sew that ear on and give him a shot of something to goof him up a little bit. Give him one of those goof balls—he'll play the show. 'You know Joe, he won't want to not play the show.' That happened down at the Garden State Arts Center, down there in New Jersey. And lo and behold, there's John Candy. So we just grabbed John Candy and got him on the bus with us when we left. We laughed all the way back to New York. I threw a party in my room."

"You gotta hand it to Woodstock," Levon said. "They have stayed this way forever. They ain't let nobody come in here and change the look of it. Goddamn, it feels like itself. Nobody would go to Dunkin' Donuts if they had one here. Hell, we got Bread Alone—we got a real bakery. Those Maverick concerts, that's something that's enjoyable in the summertime. They usually start around three o'clock on Sunday afternoons and they have chamber music. You know, it's not too early. One of their big draws every year is the Tokyo String Quartet. They've got the Maverick Concert Hall—it's an old concert hall and they open that thing up. You can take blankets and set 'em up outside, take a bottle of wine, lay outside on your blanket or go inside the place. It's that beautiful chamber music. They have all those old instruments—harpsichord and violins and things. It's just the sleepiest sounding stuff you've ever heard. It's beautiful stuff. You'd enjoy it. They've been doing that Maverick concert for years and years. And those musicians are just lifelong musicians and they are so accomplished and dedicated; it's fun to hear them. And the way the old place is built, it's very natural stuff.

"And at about 4:00 p.m. every Sunday, when the weather's agreeable, they have the drum circle, right there, down by the flagpole. You all should go down to the Village Green, right in the center of town. There will be about 50-60 drummers around the flagpole. They'll all be beating and banging and dancing; it's quite a show down there. And there are plenty of extra drums, so you can just grab one and go for it. You would love it. You'll see what Woodstock is like. They have every kind of a damn drum you can imagine. They bring a whole boxful of them. You can just pick one up and you're raising hell. We took Amy's boy, my grandson, little Lee, a couple times. He gets right in the middle of it."

Among the many musicians who lived in Woodstock and had arrived there from somewhere else were Happy and Artie Traum, brothers from the Bronx whose imprint on this artistic community has lasted decades and will always resonate a little louder than others.

Happy met Bob Dylan when the man from Minnesota first arrived in New York City from the Midwest. Happy lived on the Upper West Side, performed in Greenwich Village coffeehouses and along the way got to know Bob and musicians such as Tom Paxton, Phil Ochs and Richie Havens. Happy and his wife, Jane, lived in New York City, but they began coming to Woodstock for visits. Happy performed there multiple times. And the couple had friends in Woodstock, including the late folk singer John Herald, who they visited during the summer of 1965.

"He took us swimming in Big Deep," Happy said of the Woodstock swimming hole. "Coming from the middle of New York City, it just kind of blew our minds. In '66 we spent the summer, a long summer, in Bearsville.

That's when we became reacquainted with Bob, right after his motorcycle accident. We had lost touch with him after he skyrocketed to glory. It never occurred to us when we would see him at Gerde's Folk City and the Gaslight and places like that in the Village—we always knew he was special and we always knew he was going to be famous, but we never had any idea how famous."

Happy and Jane heard "Like a Rolling Stone" on their car radio in 1965 while traveling to Woodstock.

"And that completely blew our minds," Happy said. "Then we knew."

Bob, Happy and Jane all ended up in Woodstock during that summer of 1966.

"We somehow let him know we were in Woodstock and he immediately said, 'Come on over,'" Happy recalled. "And he was very reclusive at that point; very, very few people had access to Bob. We spent a lot of time with him in those days. We had kids who were the same age."

Happy and Jane moved to Woodstock permanently in the fall of 1967. As they settled in, they got to know the guys in The Band. Happy and Jane had seen Bob perform with The Band at their 1965 Carnegie Hall show and again when they played that venue in 1968 for the Woody Guthrie tribute performance. Decades later, Happy sat in often at the Ramble. And Happy and Levon remained friends until Levon's death.

"Everybody in Woodstock played with the Traums at one time or another," Levon said. "You could always count on them for a gig or two. If you were a musician, you knew them, boy—you were going to work with them or for them or something. Happy and Artie were always in the right spot. Artie was a real gifted musician. He was almost like a jazz musician. He was a very skilled player."

Millions heard *Music From Big Pink* by The Band on a vinyl LP they purchased at their local record store in 1968. Happy and Artie Traum, on the other hand, heard *Music From Big Pink* on a reel-to-reel tape in Robbie Robertson's Woodstock home, before it was released for public consumption.

"We went up to Robbie's house," Happy said. "I do have this image of being in the living room with Robbie and Garth. Robbie had called, he said, 'Why don't you come over and listen to our new record?' Artie and I were about to make our first record. Robbie and Rick taught us 'Going Down the Road to See Bessie,' so we had that kind of relationship. We recorded that for our first album, in 1969."

For the *Music From Big Pink* listening session, Happy said, "It was a reel-to-reel. It was a big TASCAM. We sit down and we listen to the whole thing, side one and side two, and we had never heard anything like it. It combined our love of acoustic music, which is where we were coming from—big time—and suddenly here was this raucous, hard-rock band that was playing with Dylan. We heard this stuff that had so much roots to it, so much tradition and the elemental American sound and it was also so democratic. You'd hear one voice, then another voice. You'd hear Rick, you'd hear Levon, you'd hear Richard—all this stuff coming in and out. It was a revelation to hear this. And we were immediately dumbstruck."

Like a lot of people, Happy said Levon during the Midnight Ramble era wasn't much different than the Levon of the 1960s.

"He'd tell great stories," Happy said. "He liked a good dirty joke. He was just down-home and easygoing."

And, Happy added, "Because of the way we lived, we didn't see any of the dark stuff."

Happy remembered a "gregarious" Levon from back in the day.

"He was always that warm guy," he said. "He definitely had a tough side and I saw that a few times. But it was never aimed at me, so I never felt it. I always knew him as a generous guy. I never dealt with him professionally, in that I never hired him to be on a record or something like that. I didn't see that part of him. But I did see early on that if you asked him to show up somewhere for a benefit and he was able to do it, he did it."

One of Happy's memories illustrates how Levon effortlessly reconciled his colossal success with his lack of pretension. Happy, Jane and some of Happy's folk-music contemporaries in 1974 were placed on the guest list for the Madison Square Garden performance of Bob Dylan and the Band.

The after-party was held at the Plaza Hotel and, Happy said, "It was such a total star scene."

Rock stars and movie stars were everywhere.

"And who are we?" he said. "A bunch of folk singers. It was crowded and we walked into one of the rooms. I felt like a total fish out of water."

Then Levon spotted Happy and Jane.

"He just said, 'Come this way,'" Happy recalled. "We went into his room. Rick might have been there. It was completely like, 'Yeah. You're welcome here.' That's the kind of thing I think of when I think about Levon and I think about my various associations with him through the years. We were never close, close friends. But that's the kind of thing I was always so grateful for—he saw we were standing there like we were on another planet or something, and he immediately invited us in. Anytime I came to the Ramble, it was the same thing."

Levon, Happy said, "Either liked you or he didn't like you. If he didn't like you, he had no use for you at all. If he liked you, for whatever reason, you were one of the guys; you were equal. He would introduce you to somebody you were in awe of, but as if you're as important as they are. I never felt a big divide. If it was his tractor salesman in Arkansas, he'd probably treat him the same way he'd treat George Harrison. And that's an amazing trait in somebody like that. At the Rambles—packed with people in absolute adulation of him, which he ate up, he loved it. Who wouldn't?—he still talked to people. He shook people's hands. He was gracious to people, no matter who they were. I have to say, it's something I really miss about not seeing him. He was a very democratic guy, in a funny way. He didn't grow up on Fifth Avenue. He was a poor dirt farmer from Arkansas. And he never forgot his upbringing."

Speaking of Levon's magnetic personality, Happy said, "Whatever it was, it wasn't necessarily charisma. You're not necessarily going to have people's heads turn when you walk into a room. But he had a joyful spirit about him, even when he was down. He would always shake your hand and look you in the eye."

For Happy, this represented the Levon Helm of the 1960s all the way through the 2000s.

"I saw the changes in him, his fortunes went up and down," Happy said. "But he never changed."

———•———

Happy is known the world over for his company, Homespun Tapes, which he co-founded more than 50 years ago with Jane, his wife and partner. Homespun features well-known musicians—including Levon—offering music instruction in a wide variety of genres. Happy felt Levon's enthusiasm for working with Homespun underscored the trust the two men shared and Levon's generous spirit in sharing his craft and technique.

Look no further than *Electric Dirt* to see how highly Levon regarded Happy. Levon's 2009 Grammy-winning album included Happy's song, "Golden Bird."

Happy has known *Electric Dirt* producer and Levon Helm Band music director Larry Campbell since the 1970s, when Larry would perform in Woodstock with Happy and John Herald in the Woodstock Mountain Revue. Happy is in regular touch with Larry and knew that, as plans were laid for *Electric Dirt,* Larry and Levon were looking for songs for the new record. Talk turned to one of Happy's tunes, "Golden Bird."

"I was pushing Artie's songs," Happy recalled. "Larry said, 'Send "Golden Bird," too.' That song has been covered a few times. Eric Andersen did it. But to me, having Levon do it was a pinnacle. It's an affirmation of our friendship in a way."

———•———

Ulster County, New York native and Gov't Mule multi-instrumentalist Danny Louis saw the original Band play once, in 1974, at the Orpheum Theatre in Boston. But prior to the performance starting, the PA system had blown. Attempts were made on repairs but they were unsuccessful, so the guys turned their monitor speakers around to face the audience and performed with a very different approach.

Monitor speakers are typically pointed directly at a musician so they can hear themselves sing and play their instrument. The crowd typically listens through the PA, or public address system.

At this gig though, it was the monitors that were providing the juice for the crowd. The Band, Danny said, played softly enough where the musicians and audience alike could hear everything clearly, gently and sweetly, vocals and instruments alike.

"It was one of the greatest concerts I ever heard, the singing and the playing, and it wasn't coming through a giant PA, so it didn't numb you with the intensity of it all," Danny said. "It was like listening to them play in a living room."

More than 30 years later, Danny was performing with Levon, for all intents and purposes, in the man from Turkey Scratch's very own living room. Technically, it was inside the studio at Levon's home, during the Midnight Ramble. And that experience changed Danny Louis forever.

"The whole tradition of the house party and what they called juke joints in the South, that was all part of the Ramble," Danny said. "It was a party at Levon's house. The fact that he wasn't maybe ever going to sing again and now he is singing again—that's big, big stuff."

Over the three decades that elapsed between that Band show in Boston and the Midnight Ramble, Danny had forged multiple friendships that would intersect at The Barn.

Danny and Jimmy Vivino first met in the 1970s at the old New York City club Tracks. Vivino later enlisted Danny for his very first Manhattan gig—playing keyboards with Vivino and drummer Steve Holley, of Wings fame, at the Bitter End in Greenwich Village on Sunday nights.

And Danny's business partner in NY Noise, a Manhattan music house that specialized in television and film music, was in a band with Brian Mitchell.

"There were a bunch of Rambles were I wasn't specifically involved but was asked to sit in," Danny said. "I was later asked to sub for Brian and by then, after a half dozen experiences, Levon and I were on a cordial talking basis. He seemed to be pleased with what I was doing and I was pleased as hell to be there."

Danny has a long history with Weider, from when both played around

Ulster County in the Johnny Average Band. And Danny was longtime friends with Randy Ciarlante.

"I first heard Randy play with The Kids," Danny said. "Randy was the singing drummer dude."

Danny was underage at the time but able to access the local bar scene thanks in large part to "Uncle" Willy Guldy, the renowned club owner in Ulster County. He was also helped along by a note he had from his principal at Rondout Valley High School, which allowed him to drive a car past the 9 p.m. restriction that came with a junior license in New York State.

Danny was issued the note because of his musical prowess on the trumpet in high school musical ensembles. The note, however, was not always used for its intended purpose.

"I needed that permission because, more often than not, I was visiting another school and playing after hours," he said.

Danny years later would play in a band with Randy. And during the 1980s Danny was in the room to witness a gig that featured Randy and Jimmy playing with Levon at the Lone Star Café in Manhattan with the Woodstock All-Stars. On that particular evening, Steve Winwood and Ted Nugent both sat in on guitar.

"I don't remember a gosh darn note that they played because it was so long ago, but conceptually it was mind-blowing," Danny said. "Ted played some cool blues guitar that night which really surprised me."

The Rambles later emerged, not far from Danny's own Ulster County home. They left a broad impact on him for many reasons, including the fact that they were a "lifeline" when he would come off the road from a tour with Gov't Mule.

"When I would come home, I would go through a little bit of culture shock," he said. "I wasn't playing out in any of the bars or anything. This was a way to get me out of the house and co-mingle with, not only my peers, but with historically-significant music figures that were in and out of that place routinely, especially the host.

"It was a lifeline to staying in it instead of just being home and wondering what to do next after coming off the road. It's kind of shocking when you tour at the level that Mule does, five-to-six nights a week, and it stops.

Where's the jam? That ongoing musical conversation that I have with Mule is, other than my family, the most fulfilling interaction I can possibly have. When that's gone there is a lot missing.

"Levon was a lifeline for me and he kind of knew it. 'Let's get Danny out of the house.'"

Danny also played on the road with the Levon Helm Band and Wilco's 2011 Solid Sound Festival at MASS MoCA—the Massachusetts Museum of Contemporary Art—in North Adams, Massachusetts, was particularly meaningful.

"The quote I heard from Levon was, 'I thought you could use a night's work,'" Danny said with a laugh.

Much of the allure that Woodstock held for Levon came by way of Arkansas.

"Woodstock reminds me of Arkansas, especially around Hurley Mountain Road," Levon said. "That's the prettiest road in New York. Once you get to the end, you go over the Esopus Creek and you're 100 yards from Marbletown Park. The creek runs by it and they got on the bank of that creek and dumped ten truckloads of sand and made a beach. You gotta go there. They got a soccer field and a basketball court. They got family-size burners. You can bring a bag of charcoal, do yourself up a burger and have a lunch. It's a nice little park.

"When I see those cornfields on Hurley Mountain Road and all that dirt farming going on, the brand of music and just the way people are—upstate New York in general is just beautiful. It's just one touch football field after another. In the summertime, it's just right. The sunshine around here, you can take your shirt off and stand around all day long and you won't hardly get burned. The sun is just that much more milder up here than it is in Arkansas.

"I just crave that sunshine. I don't know what it is. I dodged the sunshine after I got off the farm. And after I took those radiation treatments, boy, I just started craving it. I don't know why. If the sun's shining, I like to get out in it and take my shirt off and just stand around. I've been promising myself I'm gonna load up and get in a damn van or a motor home or something and just head south and go until it gets hot and then stop and get out and sit in the sunshine—just get in a motor home and chase the sunshine. When I started getting those radiation treatments, I just trusted my instincts and I just started craving the sunshine. It proves that those animal instincts are correct. You just want that sunshine. There is a healing power to it. I just couldn't be happy unless I was in it. There wasn't nothing else to look for. And all I would have to do was keep it off my neck. I would sit in a certain way so that it wouldn't hit my neck. And man I just lived in there. I know it was one of the things that helped me over. I can really get dark, too. I've got that redneck skin. After a while, it will get really brown. Up here in Woodstock, the sunshine is so mild that you can't hardly get a sunburn. Growing up down in Arkansas, you can cook your ass—and I have. I have cooked before. It's like a little piece of Arkansas up here in the Catskill Mountains. These southern Catskills right here look just like the Ozarks. And the people are so damn close to the same. It's a really good place. I tell you what, come on up and I'll hide you out."

CHAPTER FOURTEEN

The Second Coming of The Band

Twenty-eight years before the launch of the Midnight Ramble, an advertisement in the *Woodstock Times* beckoned readers to "Levon's 'Saturday Night Get Down,'" a gig at The Getaway Country Inn in Saugerties, featuring Levon Helm and the Woodstock All Stars.

"Levon's inevitable midnight Jam Out," set for January 26, 1985, featured Frank "Lay it in there" Campbell on bass, Jimmy "Kid tough" Weider on guitar, Cindy "Va voom the looker" Cashdollar on Dobro, Stan "The man" Szelest on piano, Randall "March 'em Son" Ciarlante on drums, and Levon "Home boy love-in" Helm on drums and anything goes.

The cover charge was $7. One hundred advance tickets guaranteed a seat in the "show room." The ad concluded with the promise that, "You Don't Have to Go away to Getaway."

Two years prior, The Band had reunited without Robbie Robertson. Also in 1983, Artie Traum had invited Jimmy Weider to perform with him, Campbell, Cashdollar, Rick Danko and Levon Helm in the rotating lineup of the Woodstock All Stars. Weider's first couple of gigs with that ensemble were at the Joyous Lake in Woodstock and the Lone Star Café in New York City.

Jimmy at the time was also playing with Ciarlante in a country band called the Stetson Brothers. The name was a goof on Stetson cologne and Levon sat in on occasion. Richard Manuel would also sit in on these gigs, which were held at The Getaway. Levon returned the favor by asking Randy to sit in with the Woodstock All Stars, with whom Levon was playing a lot of mandolin and harmonica, in addition to his drumming and singing.

During the 1980s, The Getaway, located on Route 212, just over the Woodstock town border, was a musical epicenter. And The Band was back.

———

Jimmy Weider met Levon in the late 1960s, not long after the man from Turkey Scratch arrived in Woodstock. Jimmy, a fan of The Band, was working at the Sound-In, a stereo shop in downtown Woodstock frequented by musicians.

"I met Levon in, probably, '68," Weider said. "I was working for Kermit Schwartz—a tremendous, tremendous guy. He smoked three cigarettes at the same time, had a big Maalox ring around his lips, and all the guys and all the bands loved him.

"He had the best stuff—Revox, McIntosh. Everyone had credit. David Sanborn would come in. Levon and The Band would come in. They all had budgets. They were all making records. They'd all bring in their latest cut. When The Band cut a record—*Stage Fright, Cahoots*— they'd bring it in. Kermit would put it on full blast. Those guys loved him. He was so nuts. He was a real character. That was where I met Levon."

As far as live music was concerned, Woodstock in the late 1960s and early 1970s, according to Ciarlante, was "popping." Randy would often see bands at the old Café Espresso, where Bob Dylan at one time rented an upstairs room.

"It was rocking," Randy said. "As kids in high school, we'd hitch a ride to town, sneak into the clubs and watch all this really good music. Because of Albert Grossman and Bearsville Studios, a lot of musicians infiltrated Woodstock. On nights off from tracking, they would sit in or form their own combos. Butterfield had those cats from Chicago, and the scene was the Elephant, the Espresso, and numerous other clubs around town, so there was music in Woodstock six to seven nights a week. On a Wednesday night, you could see Van Morrison's band. All those guys were living in Woodstock. Woodstock was popping back then. It was unbelievable. You saw everyone come through town. Charlie Mingus came through, salsa music came through, Richard Bell was in town playing with Janis Joplin."

And years later, Richard Bell played in the second incarnation of The Band.

"Once in a while Rick would sit in, Rick and Richard sometimes," Weider said. "Levon always kind of kept a low profile. I never saw him sit in around town."

Randy had met Levon in 1978 or 1979. He was playing with Eric Andersen at Town Hall in Manhattan, opening for Levon and the Cate Brothers. The next time Randy met him was through Weider, in Ulster County. Randy joined the second incarnation of The Band as second drummer in 1990.

> Randy: "For the most part, I think the veteran Band fan's attitude was 'How come they don't have Eric Clapton and Steve Winwood?' and 'What do they need two drummers for?' Lavon was trying to build a band; hard to do if you have a crew of iconic stars on board. That's fun in the short term, but I'm not sure those types of ensembles have a long shelf life. Lavon had spent years with us playing in small clubs, when there were 75 to 150 people in the place. We were having fun playing all types of music—and he knew he could trust us."
>
> Weider: "Levon knew how to build a band. You build a band by playing a lot and everyone listening. It's like Danko always said, 'You've got to listen.' And he's really right. If you're not listening, you're not playing with each other. That's a big part of being a band. You're not on your own when you're in a band and Levon was really about making a band sound. And he ended up building the Levon Helm Band, which was so phenomenal. I was so happy for him."
>
> Randy: "There is a definite dark side that permeates the music business and when you've seen it rear its ugly head as many times as Lavon had, you learn to nip it in the bud before it bites you. In a working ensemble you spend more time with your bandmates than your family, so a fundamental step in being successful in that

communal process is building trust and understanding. Lavon had fine-tuned his extrasensory perception—or his sixth sense if you will—and he was extremely proficient at weeding out folks who had an agenda. He wanted to build a team. The total unit was more important than its individual components. It was a premise the original Band built its brand around and our effort was an extension of that concept."

As a young guitar player growing up in Woodstock, Weider often covered Band tunes with his fellow aspiring musicians, while jamming in his apartment. On his becoming a member of The Band years later, he said, "Who knew that fate would have it?"

When Randy signed on, he and Levon double-drummed together. And, Weider said, "When Levon would play harmonica or mandolin, Randy would hold the fort down and play the drums. Levon loved it. They had a tight, two-drum thing happening."

Randy had been playing drums professionally since he was 15.

"I had played in bar bands for many years," he said.

But, he continued, "You've got all these signature drum parts that Lavon created and his fan base wanted to see and hear that. They didn't quite understand why there were two drums in the mix. But Lavon wanted to change things up and he also wanted to play other instruments. Richard Manuel played a lot of drums on The Band records, so this was an extension of that concept.

"I had to first understand what The Band music was all about. Somehow, I had to come up with counterparts to what the main drum arrangements were. I think Lavon trusted me and I was the first to be told if it was rubbing the wrong way. He trusted that I wouldn't try to jump on top of the music, or take it in the wrong direction, and he liked the fact that I adjusted my parts quickly. The song was served first—it was always a matter of making the music feel right.

"The Band tunes were strict arrangements. His roots music arrangements were a little more open-ended. In The Band, for the most part, we stuck to the song's road map—if it ain't broke, don't break it. We didn't extend sections or improvise much at all. It wasn't a jamband. We were trying to make the well-thought-out and crafted parts swing.

"Lavon, he was really happy playing rootsy, Americana-type pieces. I think that's one of the reasons why the *Dirt Farmer* stuff was so successful. He was so connected to it.

"I think the main reason it all worked was, I knew how to build the arrangements with him. But, more important, I knew how to stay out of the way."

Playing with Levon, Randy said, "was a lot of fun. He had a great sense of humor. And he had music flowing through him. Lavon's main purpose in that era was to have fun working with an ensemble. We did a lot of laughing."

> Weider: "Levon had this deep pocket. With his backbeat and kick drum, he could really drive a group. What a feel."
>
> Randy: "You can't explain it. You could write down what he was doing, you could see what he was playing, you could break it down by the beat, but you just couldn't make it feel the way he did—his gift, our pleasure."
>
> Weider: "He felt it. He had a feeling. You could feel it. It didn't just flow by you. He had a touch, a feel—like a great guitarist. And Levon always had your back. He didn't care about rock-star stuff. He cared about his guys. He didn't kiss ass to nobody. He didn't care about anyone throwing out some appetizers. This is the way he wanted it, and he was running a band. He wanted respect for everyone he knew and trusted."
>
> Randy: "When The Band dissolved, he went right back to his roots. That whole thing with The Getaway and what he did with the *Dirt Farmer* music, from my vantage point, that's his roots. Larry and the crew helped bring that together and they were right on the money. And I'm sure having Amy with him was special. When we started playing with him, he covered a lot of roots-rock and roll tunes—New Orleans and Memphis kind of stuff—but with his own feel and take on the tunes. The joy coming out of this guy when he

was playing that music was amazing. I've never seen someone play roots-rock drums like that. It was pretty incredible. It was his true love. I'll always feel that was the flavor he was inserting into what The Band was writing."

Weider: "When he brought me and Randy down to play the Helena Blues Festival, you knew you were in a whole new territory, and that's where it all came from. All that stuff just came right from where Levon grew up. That was embedded in him."

So what was it like to play in a band, with original members of The Band?

Weider: "They heard everything and if you were really messing up or you weren't playing the right part, they'd call you on it. They were really intuitive and very musical, all of them—heavy musicianship. They didn't miss a lick. It was all about trying to get the feel. Nobody can ever play like them. But if you can capture the feel, people will feel the songs. And then you're doing something to preserve the music and, basically, that's the most you can ever want."

Randy: "Rick and Levon really taught me how to sing. They explained to us what you need to do, what you need to hear, how you need to end your notes. They didn't miss a beat. At the time, I didn't know how they had developed songs. I did sense they wanted to change direction. Musicians sometimes get tired of playing the same songs, and they understandably wanted to play something a bit different. So we weren't pushy about it. We never pushed anything. We were always prepared. We wrote our charts or memorized arrangements. I remember the first time going in with 'Carnival.' Once we blew the dust and rust off some of this great music, the fan base enjoyed it and the fellas really enjoyed working through the tunes with us. For me, that's when school was in session. They'd take you back to how they cut the songs and reasons why certain arrangements were chosen. We ended up playing a bunch of the 'chestnuts;' not as many as we wanted, but enough to stay satisfied as we slowly worked those tunes into the set. I never knew why we didn't play 'The Night They Drove Old Dixie Down.' I never asked, and if I would inquire, Rick was quick to say, 'Don't confuse the issue.'"

The final era of The Band included 1993's *Jericho*, *High on the Hog* from 1996, and *Jubilation* from 1998.

"Lavon became sick halfway through the *Jubilation* album," Randy said of the onset of Levon's cancer. "We had to get through it and we had to deliver on the contract. We had to get that project finished, and we barely completed it before Lavon's voice became too weak to sing. I'm not sure if he was ever happy with it, but I certainly hope he felt we tried our best to come up with a good album."

Weider joined the Levon Helm Band in 2009, after Jimmy Vivino headed to California with Conan O'Brien. And Randy began playing drums alongside Levon, in the Levon Helm Band, toward the end of the ensemble's enduring run.

"You watch Lavon after The Band, he seemed to be very happy," Randy said. "I always felt he was happiest playing his roots music. He was doing what he grew up doing, what came natural to him. "The music we played with him in that era was just flowing out of him. When you watched him play—with Jimmy and myself; with the fellas in the Woodstock All Stars; with Jimmy Vivino and the Barn Burners; with the Ramble band crew—there he was, back to the roots. "And I think *Dirt Farmer* and the records that came after, he would have carried that on for a long time. Unfortunately, he's too soon gone. He could have made another ten records and been just as successful. He had a tremendous comeback. It took a while, he fought very hard, but he was back."

CHAPTER FIFTEEN

The Movies

The fireplace in the studio had been lit, the rocking chair was in place, and director Jacob Hatley and producer Mary Posatko were gearing up to film a pivotal scene for the 2010 documentary, *Ain't In It For My Health: A Film About Levon Helm*.

At the time, the outlook for the documentary was bright and the crew had hit its stride.

"We're getting the Ramble stuff, we're getting the B-roll, we're pulling our pieces together for the film," Mary said.

For this critical interview, Jacob had compiled a list of questions he planned to ask Levon, and he and Mary staged the shot with a rocking chair in front of the fireplace. Levon sits down, the camera is rolling, Jacob asks two questions—and Levon stands up and walks away.

"We all just looked at each other," Mary said of the crew. "At the time, we got a little panicked."

Everyone agreed, Mary said, that "this one wasn't going to go by the book."

Ask Mary about Levon Helm, the man and the musician, and her response will speak to how he approached making the documentary that the *Hollywood Reporter* called, "A captivating look at a musician hanging onto his art for dear life, even when he's too weary to perform."

"Levon," Mary said, "did it on his terms."

Ain't In It For My Health offered insight into Levon's creative process, his collaborations, and his approach to performing live and recording. The documentary examined Levon's health struggles, his complicated relationship with The Band and the recording industry, his love of Ulster County, and his command of storytelling.

The film also captured, in fine form, a pivotal piece of the Rambles to which the public was not privy—the post-Ramble hang that Levon hosted around his kitchen table, with band members, musical guests, friends and members of Team Levon.

Underscoring everything in *Ain't In It For My Health* was Levon's passion for storytelling and his ability to charm an entire room, in a very simple, straightforward manner. The man who starred in *Coal Miner's Daughter* and *The Right Stuff* considered acting as big a part of his legacy as his music. And *Ain't In It For My Health* gave him his final bow on the silver screen. Making it all happen on the production side were Mary, Jacob and their crew, who worked hard to earn the trust of, not just Levon, but everyone at 160 Plochmann Lane.

"The Rambles felt like a family and we needed to make sure that we did okay in that family and that we fit in," Mary said.

The film can trace its roots to a Shawn Mullins music video.

Known for his hit song "Lullaby," Mullins made a music video for his song "Beautiful Wreck" that was directed by a student at the University of Southern California School of Cinematic Arts named Jacob Hatley. Shawn Mullins recorded for Vanguard Records, Levon's record label at the time, and Jacob landed the music video gig through contacts he had there. Jacob hired several of his USC classmates to serve as the crew. The video was a success, and Vanguard asked Jacob if he wanted to travel to Woodstock—to make a music video for Levon Helm.

"They said, 'Go shoot what you can with this amount of money in Woodstock,'" Jacob recalled. "It was just a dream gig."

Being a filmmaker, Jacob knew of Levon more as an actor than a musician. Of course, Jacob was familiar with *The Last Waltz*. But Levon's landmark performance as a blind man in *The Three Burials of Melquiades Estrada,* which featured Tommy Lee Jones as director and star, left a bigger impression on him.

Mary came at this project from a completely different angle.

"I was a Bob Dylan fanatic as a young person," she said. "I came to it from that side. I remember Jacob giving me the *Dirt Farmer* CD and saying, 'Do you want to do this?'"

Jacob and Mary both graduated from USC's School of Cinematic Arts and he got her name from a mutual colleague they both knew from college. Jacob called Mary out of the blue. She looked into Jacob's credentials, learned he was highly regarded and she was in.

"Honest to God," she said, "it seemed like an amazing adventure. I was sold."

Now a professor at USC, Mary said that, for the Levon project, she and Jacob "cobbled together a rag-tag bunch of recent USC grads who Jacob said were hungry and willing to work for very little, who we knew would be really good."

That turned out to be cinematographer Emily Topper, sound engineer Phil Davis and producer Ken Segna.

The plan was to be in and out of Ulster County in a few days. The objective was a narrative documentary/music video hybrid. The result was a 21-minute, seamless amalgamation of fiction and non-fiction, dramatic performance and musical showcase that featured Levon Helm, the actor, and Levon Helm, the roots and rock star. It aired on RFD TV.

The video was called *Only Halfway Home.* The title was taken from lyrics in the Buddy Miller song, "Wide River to Cross," the final song on *Dirt Farmer.* The tune summed up the striving that framed much of Levon's life.

"We had such a good time, but we felt like Levon, of all people, is not the kind of person to be captured in a music video," Jacob said. "It's the last approach someone should take to Levon, given his charisma and everything else, and I think he agreed. It's not that we didn't enjoy making a music video, we all did."

But, Jacob continued, "something just fit" about proceeding with a documentary.

"And the record label seemed game to give us a little more money to come back," he said. "We didn't quite put a name on it. We just kept shooting without defining what it was right away."

Mary remembers things coming together while she was at Snyder's

Tavern, in West Shokan, not far from Woodstock, where the musical performances were filmed. When things had wrapped for the day, she said, speaking of Levon and Barbara, "I felt like, at that moment, with Levon driving away in his car with a huge smile on his face, I felt like they thought there was a huge chemistry between everyone. I remember Barbara turning to me and saying, 'This is happening.'"

And what did Jacob take away from the experience of directing *Ain't In It For My Health?*

"If I learned anything, it's that you have to open yourself up to what's there, not what you want to be there," he said. "That was a two-year lesson. You went in with a plan. I was naïve and idiotic enough to draw shot lists and storyboards—'Levon will walk here at this moment'—that's how naïve I was. If you let go of that—which is a very hard thing to do, let go of it altogether—then it becomes something that you wouldn't have expected and it can surprise you in ways that are as rewarding as anything else.

"Yes, it was totally frustrating. I wanted to shoot this scene, or I wanted Levon to talk about this, but then I was totally grateful and surprised that he was talking about something else—and it was better than the idea I had in the first place. It was cool."

And there was that scene in the film with Academy Award-winner Billy Bob Thornton. Levon and Billy—both actors, musicians, drummers and vocalists from Arkansas—sat at Levon's kitchen table following the Ramble in which Billy's band, The Boxmasters, kicked off the night's festivities.

"I am eternally grateful to Billy Bob Thornton," Jacob said. "We thought, 'This guy's going to agree to be in our movie,' and that was enough for us. And once we were rolling, he was game. We had two cameras for that, which was rare. We knew there was going to be a moment where everyone in the room was going to try and clear out, and they were going to catch up. The scene in my mind was going to be a really great scene because it was going to be about this place that they came from—Arkansas—that really doesn't exist anymore. It was going to be a nice, bittersweet scene about home and the notion of home and all that. And it became about The Band and the breakup and everything. When we shot that scene, we were lucky because we had a second camera there, so we had a camera for Levon and a camera for Billy Bob. And that really helped. You could cut it like a traditional narrative scene."

And overall, what did Mary take away from the experience?

"In Levon's presence, at The Barn, oh man did it feel good to be there. You felt lucky—and I still feel that way."

On April 9, 1959—Levon would have been 18-years-old—NASA introduced its first astronaut class, the Mercury 7, which included Walter M. Schirra Jr., Donald K. "Deke" Clayton, John H. Glenn Jr., M. Scott Carpenter, Alan B. Shepard, Jr., Virgil I. "Gus" Grissom and L. Gordon Cooper Jr.

According to the NASA website, "The press and public soon adopted them as heroes, embodying the new spirit of space exploration...During the five-year life of the project, six human-tended flights and eight automated flights were completed, proving that human spaceflight was possible. These missions paved the way for the Gemini and Apollo programs as well as for all further human spaceflight."

In 1979, 10 years after the moon landing and 20 years after NASA introduced the Mercury 7 astronauts, Tom Wolfe's book, *The Right Stuff*, was published. Adapted for the silver screen, the film *The Right Stuff* was released in 1983. It starred Ed Harris as John Glenn, Dennis Quaid as Gordon Cooper and Sam Shepherd as test pilot Chuck Yeager, who on Oct. 14, 1947, broke the sound barrier in the Bell X-1 aircraft.

A pivotal character in the book and the movie was Captain Jack Ridley, who Levon portrayed in the film, as character and narrator.

One of the pleasures of filming *The Right Stuff,* Levon said, was that he got to "work with people like Royal Dano, and Kim Stanley—just to get to go to work every day and ride with Royal and Kim, and then come home at night and get to hear them talk and tell stories. That was just the best, you know? It's like getting to meet Muddy Waters. It was a great show to get to be a part of.

"Phil Kaufman, the director, he took everyone out to the desert there, out in Southern California, and I don't think there was ever a cuss fight. The most amazing part of it—we were right there at Edwards Air Force Base, and at the end of the day, after these pilots trained in these jet planes, they'd come in and they'd practice touch-and-go. That's where they come in and land and roll a little ways, and then come back up and they go around and they do it again, over and over, and they practiced landing. There were usually three or four of them and here they come, right? And they set down and they roll for 50 yards, and right back up again. And there is another bunch behind them. And we're out there trying to do lines back and forth. How they cleaned up the audio, I don't know. We were there yelling at each other with these damn airplanes in the background. I kept thinking, 'I don't know how they're going to use this tape.'"

General Chuck Yeager was the technical advisor on *The Right Stuff,* so, Levon said, "We'd get to see him every day and get to eat lunch with him and hear all those stories. He does everything with both hands and when he talks, he talks with his hands. His fingers are very nimble and he's always twisting and turning them when he talks. He would tell us great, wonderful stories."

"There was this guy, from Fort Smith, Arkansas, that worked on Channel 5. He was the weather guy and he was an actor guy; a local guy who had been in a couple of things and was always trying to get into something," Levon said. "And of course, when I got into movies, he just couldn't stand it, and he used to call Dad all the time and he'd want me to come down to the TV station and stuff like that. And Dad loved it. Dad had him take us out to dinner and every night, he'd come on with the news and the weather. And Dad would say, 'He's the urologist for Channel 5.' I said, 'I believe he's a meteorologist.' He'd say, 'No. He's a urologist.' Yeah, he's the urologist over at Channel 5.

"Another time, when we were playing with Bob, I sent Dad an itinerary, and one of the Cate brothers called him to find out where we were. He got out the itinerary and he said, 'Dillard and the boys, tonight,' he said, 'They're playing in the Colatorium, in South Bend, India.' We had made it—all the way to South Bend, India."

"Playing music and acting, it's a lot the same for me, because it's all that 'combo' kind of thing, you know," Levon said. "Acting is that same kind of harmony singing, sort of an intimacy you have with other people and I try to substitute the director for the producer and when they holler 'action,' try and give it to 'em. It's a lot of fun. You get a lot of directors, most of them will want to do a scene two or three times so you've got two or three shots at it, of getting it. A lot of times, they want you to stretch it out and be a little different each time with it, and that's what makes it fun. It's very much akin to playing music for me. I acted as a kid when we would have little school plays and things. I would usually participate. I always enjoyed it. I never was bothered with stage fright or anything like that.

"It really is fun to watch the people make those movies and to get to know them. With all the prop people, the wardrobe people—they're the ones who make that movie. It's an army of people and without them, it wouldn't be much of a show. I try and just go along with it and make each day brand new and just do the lines; do the lines and trust the wardrobe and the prop people and the lighting people to make it look good, and the director is going to help you with it, too. So I never worry about it. I just do it until they're satisfied with it. I enjoy each take, so it doesn't bother me to do it wrong or in a way that the director don't want. I don't mind changing it around—if I'm saying it the wrong way, if the tempo is a little too quick or something, you just change it around.

"I usually ended up with the 'daddy' parts with the kids in my lap, and that's okay. But I loved that dumber, greener-than-grass-part, like that guy who was in *End of the Line*. When they get to Chicago in the *End of the Line* and they get them in the television commercial and dress them up like pilots, and Leo, my character—he's having a pretty good time. There are plenty of doughnuts and coffee and stuff. Those kinds of characters, I love those the best."

One of Levon's most compelling cinematic adventures brought him to Morocco.

"I went down there when I was in Spain, working on a damn movie deal. Oh, I tell you, Morocco is really—that's Africa. That's another kind of country. I loved their music. That music was fantastic. Morocco was really interesting and exciting and a little bit half-spooky, a little bit edgy—maybe it was just me. But all of them places, man, even Japan—and the food is as good as it is in France—but hell, you're there two or three weeks, you want to go home.

"We went over to Morocco just for an afternoon trip and went to a big hotel and had some food and went to a show with some dancers and musicians and stuff and walked around and gawked. They were doing a movie there, in the south of France. It was a Canadian-Spanish production. Because it was in two languages, when they'd get ready to shoot it, the direction would have to be in two languages. Tony Lucibello, the first assistant director, would say, 'All right, let's keep it quiet and still in the back please.' And then the Spanish guy would be, 'Silencio! Silencio, por favor.' And John Trent, the director, would say, "ACTION!' And this guy would say, 'Accion, accion.' And everybody would start from their first position.

"All those Spanish towns have got a gypsy town and that's where all the nightclubs are, and the action is. So we had all those gypsies up there as extras in the movie. This one kid was getting us some of the best damn hash. And it came like a piece of gum—thin, like a stick of gum and wrapped up in paper, and just about the same size. You'd take that thing and open it, take about a third of it, and start chewing on it. You could eat that whole thing within 15 minutes or so.

"I ate two of those things on the way to another town. By the time we got to the other town, I went out to this little hamburger deal out by the swimming pool and ate a bunch of hamburgers—I must have ate 10 of them.

"One day, one of the goddamn donkeys—that son of a bitch—bowed his back up at one point and broke wind. It was the funniest goddamn thing, and that just got him started. All of a sudden, he bowed up his back again and he done it again. And he kept doing it. Fuck, I'm laughing. I can't even talk. He must have cut up like that for 10 goddamn minutes. We had a fuckin' ball."

―――◆―――

"I got to meet Billy Bob Thornton a few years back," Levon said. "He's a big Little Feat fan, and Little Feat did a concert down in the D.C. area there, and a bunch of us ended up going to it and being on the show. And Billy Bob was there that night; he was part of the show. We'd run across each other. We hit if off great. He started putting his band together and we ended up playing the same damn joints. We'd go down to Arkansas, and he'd have just come through there the week before—Juanita's there in Little Rock, and a joint or two up in Fayetteville. I was surprised, to tell you the truth, when I first heard him, that he was as musical as he is. I thought he might have been one of those guys who, you know, plays the guitar on the side. But he's a musician. He's one of those guys who can do both of them—act and play music. William Robert and myself are on the same label, we are both with Vanguard Records, so that kind makes it cozy and we are both from Arkansas and we are both drummers and we both work hard to be actors and he's a damn good one, too. We hit it off great. The more we're around each other, the more fun we have, and the more alike we seem to be in our upbringing and with what makes us laugh."

―――◆―――

"I learned to act just watching the movies," Levon said. "I've just always kind of learned that way. I've always enjoyed that part of it, especially with music. There is nothing like it. I know there's something to doing it right. I've always loved the movies and I've watched them since I was a kid. There was a plantation south of Elaine, and it was 5-10,000 acres of cotton ground and a big-ass cotton gin, a company store and a big-ass tractor shop. My uncle used to work down there; he was one of their mechanics. On Saturday nights, they would show movies in the tractor shed. They'd clean it up and put up some folding chairs out and the local people would come, and they'd show a movie. I got to go and see *Abbot and Costello.* And it was the one where they got the gorilla. That gorilla come on and people started screaming. So there we all are, sitting in the tractor shop, all the tractors moved out, folding chairs, people digging that movie. It was a weekly thing, on Saturday nights.

"I'd go to the movies in Marvell on Saturday. I would leave when they would make me. My folks would finally come and get me. I wanted to watch the movies at least twice. Even if it was just a terrible movie, you would stay and see the comedy again. You'd stay at least that long. And of course, you'd have the serial, the comedy, the previews and the main feature. You'd even see the one where the guy had one of these welder's helmets and the rocket on the back of him—*Rocket Man*. He'd just fly through the air. I would go to Marvell on a Saturday to the Capitol Theatre and watch Johnny Mack Brown and *The Durango Kid* and 'Lash' LaRue. They would have *The Three Stooges.* They were one of the best. They would have Leon Errol—he was another one. But *The Three Stooges* were my main deal. When they got Shemp, that was my favorite three right there, that was the trio for me.

"It cost 10 cents to get in. They would give away calendars with the names of the movies on them. They had little prize things. They would have drawings on maybe Tuesday nights and Wednesday nights to get the crowd up in the middle of the week. Every now and then they would have a music show come to town and play. But usually it was the Saturday Western, the black-and-white Western. And Sunday, they would have the Sunday Western. That would be when they would go to the Randolph Scott, full cinemascope color, and it would be a little bit more of a show on Sunday. I tried to go every Saturday, and then, when I got older, I would go Saturday and Sunday, see it at least once or twice. They would usually come and drag me out; tell me it was time to come home."

On March 31, 1981, according to the Internet Movie Database, boxer Jake LaMotta was inside the Dorothy Chandler Pavilion, in Los Angeles, when Robert DeNiro accepted the Academy Award for Best Actor for portraying LaMotta in Raging Bull. Also at the 53rd Academy Awards that night was country music star Loretta Lynn, who was on hand when Sissy Spacek received the Oscar for Best Actress for portraying Lynn in *Coal Miner's Daughter*.

The 1980 film based on Lynn's autobiography and directed by Michael Apted also received Oscar nominations for Best Picture; Best Writing, Screenplay Based on Material from Another Medium; Best Cinematography; Best Art Direction-Set Direction; Best Sound; and Best Film Editing. *Coal Miner's Daughter* starred Tommy Lee Jones as Lynn's husband, Doolittle Lynn; Beverly D'Angelo as Patsy Cline; and in the role that one could argue was second in importance only to Lynn herself, Levon Helm portrayed Loretta Lynn's father, Ted Webb—the coal miner of *Coal Miner's Daughter*.

"He called me one time and he said, 'I went down to New York the other day and read for this English director for this movie they're going to make about Loretta Lynn,'" Levon's old friend Paul Berry said. "He said, 'There won't be anything to it—but I gave them your name as my agent.' I was working at Union National Bank here in Little Rock. I had a title; I was a senior vice-president. I looked good on paper. Levon and Sandy were with her folks in the D.C. area. They were snowed in. One of the producer's people calls and says, 'Mr. Helm left your name.' I said, 'Oh yes, I'm familiar with the project and, incidentally, Levon is up for the project.' I said, 'He's spending the holidays with his wife's family in the D.C. area.' And they say, 'He needs to be in Nashville,' and so and so and so and so. 'He's got the part.' I said, 'We need to talk about billing.'

"I called Levon and I told him. He got to Nashville and he told me I had to get over there. We go to the Spence Manor hotel—a smaller hotel, but it was the hotel of choice right then in Nashville. Everybody is there and we go down to talk about this thing. I didn't have a script. I didn't have anything. I had no idea how big this role was. So at the airport, *Coal Miner's Daughter* was in paperback. I bought it and read it. I was trying to see how big 'Daddy's' part was. They wanted to pay him 30 grand or something like that, which was a nice number and was okay, but they didn't get us country boys on the first go-around. I think we got it up to 40, 45, maybe 50 tops. I knew enough. I said, 'I understand he won't be above the title, but where is he?' 'Oh,' they said, 'We'll have him right up there, first or second below the title.'

"You know who suggested him for the role? Brad Dourif. Brad Dourif lived in Woodstock and he was a fan. Tommy Lee Jones and Brad Dourif are friends. Tommy Lee comes to Woodstock and Brad Dourif was the connector of the two. He became a fan, and it became a friendship with Levon. They can't cast the role of Loretta's dad, Ted Webb, they can't do that, and Tommy Lee says, 'I know who can play that part—Levon Helm.' They got him in and the rest, as they say, is history."

"I met Tommy Lee through Brad Dourif, my friend who had a place up in Woodstock," Levon said. "He and Tommy Lee were longtime friends and they were doing the *Eyes of Laura Mars* together, so Brad brought Tommy Lee over for a Band show. We got to hang out a little bit, and then later on, he got me into *Coal Miner's Daughter.* When I see someone like Tommy Lee, you can't do it any better than that. You study someone like that, and you try and be as relaxed and as-for-real about those things as he is. I've always admired Tommy Lee's work and he's been really helpful to me. He's had me in some of his shows. I love to watch him work. I guess he's just a natural—his smartness and his honesty, his character. He's a real cowboy. He's got that Western spirit, that Western character.

"Tommy Lee gave me some good advice, too, you know, about how to develop a little set sense; how to kind of whistle while you work; have your cake and eat it, too; who to pay attention to; and who you didn't have to worry about. The worst thing you can do as an actor is to leave the hotel and not tell anybody where you are. When you get the call sheet and your part says, 'will call,' that means you don't have to get there at all; but be ready. They might call you. As long as you've got one eye on the first assistant director and the other kind of wandering around, you can sit around and play cards or shoot the breeze, play the guitar, take a nap. There's a lot of waiting, a lot of hurry up and wait. The people who make the movies are always great people to hang with. There's always something fun to talk about or do, or stories to hear.

"When we were making Tommy Lee's *Electric Mist,* I portrayed General John Bell Hood, and it took three people in the prop department to get me dressed, with all those damn swords and sashes and stuff. And they had the old boots and the pants, and the thing around the heels, where you keep your pants down in your boot. But to get dressed, it would take three of us, people pulling—like harnessing a horse. Boy, they knew what they were doing making that movie. They hung that big, 12-foot diameter balloon over that damn swamp there, man, and it looked like the most beautiful full moon. It was white, and they hung it just about 150 feet out over that damn crawfish pond—God it was just blazing—and through the camera it looked like one of those harvest moons. It felt like a good movie. They really were doing it right. That's what Tommy Lee's character staggers into. He has his truck wreck. He sees this light through the bayou and starts going toward it and walks into this Civil War camp. He starts scratching his head, right? Then the camera follows him around and there are people getting their leg sawed off, and all kinds of things going on in that camp there. I'll tell you, they had those campfires built and lanterns hanging around, and it felt like 1863. All that stuff—the rifles, they had them stacked the way they were stacked; and all those uniforms.

"Muddy got in a scene with us in *Electric Mist.* We took his collar off and made him the camp dog. And we're all posing for this picture with him right there in the front. And all of a sudden, he had to sit there while they adjusted some stuff. Everyone had to hold their positions. It was hot, and Muddy, all of a sudden—he knew what the deal was—he jumped up and dug himself a nice cool spot and turned around and got down in it himself and was waiting. And on the set they had two pens, and one had raccoons and one of them had damn rabbits in there or something. And Muddy would be laying there. I'd say, 'No, no, boy.' It was funny. He did a pretty good job."

Levon's cinematic endeavors, however, brought with them pitfalls.

"When Sissy Spacek won that damn Oscar for *Coal Miner's Daughter*, she got up there and picked that damn thing up, and she thanked her mother and her father, and the driver, her mother's uncle, the makeup-lady's boyfriend—everybody that she could thank, she thanked them and never mentioned my name," he said. "It was just shocking to me, because me and the Cate brothers and Fred Carter had gone out to California—she came to Arkansas first—and we worked on music with her. The Cate Brothers wrecked their van, driving back and forth trying to rehearse with her. Then we went out to do *The Midnight Special* TV show and took her out there to make her fucking look good and done all that shit.

"And the ceremony started and she thanked the producers and director and all the other cast members and still, I thought, boy, she's really going to throw a nice bouquet at me and the Cate boys, because she lived there in Arkansas with us for about two weeks. And I'll be goddamned. It kind of bothered me because it was almost like, I must have got drunk and insulted the shit out of her, or done something really fucking stupid for her not to even mention my name—'and I want to thank the guy that played my Daddy.' We worked on the music together, did all that shit. She never mentioned my fucking name. I don't know how people took it. I know one thing, I thought I really fucked up. I must have really got drunk and tried to pinch her on the ass and laughed about it in front of my friends or something stupid, and she just fixed my wagon, by God. Someday, I'm going to ask her, 'What did I do?' And I'm going to apologize with all my heart, because I just don't remember what I did. I don't remember what I did, but damn, I'm sorry."

CHAPTER SIXTEEN

Muddy

Before a sold-out crowd at the Midnight Ramble on December 3, 2005, Levon strolled out of the house and into the studio, picked up a mandolin and sat down on a stool. Unbeknownst to him, his dog Muddy had followed him out of the house. Just as Levon sat down, Muddy jumped up and placed his paws square in his master's lap. Then, Muddy turned and looked at the audience.

As if on cue, as though it had been rehearsed, the hundreds in attendance, all at once, let out a collective "Awwwwwwwww."

Levon and Muddy had a relationship like none other.

"That was his shadow," said Chris Howe. "Muddy was at Levon's heel the whole time, all the time. Wherever he went, that dog went—inside the house, out in the studio. If we were going on a trip, he went—in the RV, with a moving blanket on the dashboard, just so Muddy could get up there. We're in New York City stop-and-go traffic and Muddy is on all fours, standing on the dashboard in the RV, looking at people on the street. Levon and Muddy got along great and with no leash for most of the time. I had him on a leash a couple of times. He didn't like that. But Muddy knew what was going on.

"That dog would talk to Levon. When Muddy didn't go to a show, Sandy would open the door to the house when Levon got back home, and the dogs would run out to the French doors in the studio, and Muddy would be talking to him—'Glad you're back. What took you so long?'

"Muddy could tell when the Ramble was going to be over. Muddy wouldn't be around. I'd run into the house if someone needed lyrics or something and he was never around. I'll be damned. I'd walk the boss off the stage and into the house and open the door and who's standing right there? Muddy was waiting for him. Those two had something for sure. They were fast friends."

"Just before Muddy showed up here at the studio, we had a beautiful black Lab named Baby May that we lost," Levon said. "Baby May passed away and Momma was just sick, and me too, for a long time. Brian Parillo showed up one day with Muddy. Muddy was about five weeks, four weeks old. I brought him up to the house and set him up in the bed. Sandy was asleep. I set him in the middle of the bed, and she woke up, and there's Mudrick, looking at her. He was a little bundle of energy. I think Sandy named him. It was an instant healing, just an instant healing for her. She got so busy looking after him and checking on him that she didn't have time to feel sad anymore.

"We bought Baby May. Sandy looked up a Labrador, from a lady that had a kennel. Her name was Mavis. We named her Mavis and of course that got shortened down to May-May and Baby May. She came out of the great hunting dog named Copper Buckshot—I guess that was her grandfather. I took one of my shotguns down to the creek and shot it, and Baby May would walk over and lick that shotgun. She loved to hear it pop.

"Baby May, she came from a line of retrievers. And honest to God, I'd pull that old shotgun out and we'd go out there in the back and I'd shoot it two or three times and she would love it. It wouldn't scare her at all. She would just wait for it. And when I would shoot, she would take off. I wasn't shooting nothing; she just wanted to retrieve something. I'd pick up that gun and her tail would start wagging, just like we were going on a hunt. Yeah, boy—she was bred for it.

"Muddy is so damn anti-fireworks. He don't like fireworks, gunshots, or anything like that. We usually get in the car and go somewhere and Muddy likes to take in the breeze. He looks out the window and lays his chin on the mirror. And he's gotten pretty good at working those electric windows. He could just about get that window down. He knows how to push that button. He don't know how to put it up, but he can put it down. It's like opening them doors in the house. He can open all of them. And when we're in the studio recording, if he really wants to mess the session up, he'll open the door to the house and let all the other dogs out."

After Muddy came Lucy May, who Levon met during the production of the 2009 Tommy Lee Jones film, *In the Electric Mist.*

"The makeup girl almost ran her over," Levon said. "We think she had been abandoned. She took her onto the set, and Muddy and I show up about 15 minutes later, and it's love at first sight. She was named Lucy for Louisiana, where *Electric Mist* was filmed, and May for Baby May and my birthday in May. Muddy fell in love on that movie set. You'd look around for Muddy, and you'd peek down, and look down that row at the makeup trailer. He'd be on that first step, looking in the window. You'd call him and he'd look at you like, 'Yeah, in a minute.'

"We brought Lucy home and the puppies got here right about Christmas 2007. Lucy just decided to have them and had them. Sandy played midwife. And she had seven beautiful puppies, and we celebrated, and about an hour later she had Butter Bean. He's the one who broke his leg. He was the biggest one and the last one born. We kept two. Sandy wanted to keep all of them. We still got Butter Bean and Baby Lou. Boo and Butterbeans, the one with the tail about that long, they came out of the first litter. Then we had another litter, and Fannie Mae, the little fuzzy one, the little fat one, she came out of the second litter.

"Lucy had eight the first time, and nine the second time. This was puppy heaven. We were giving them away. And it all happened in less than a year. Every time you'd turn around, there'd be another one. I'll wake up in the morning and I'll have one with her head on my leg. I'll have another one up under this arm. Muddy, he'll lay there beside the bed, even when he was a baby, and he'll growl like that, and I'll look down at him, and he'll throw his leg up."

"When I was a kid, we had farm animals and we usually had dogs," Levon said. "We had one little dog one time named Cinder. The local grocer had Cinder, who was one of those real highbred Cocker Spaniels—solid black, a beautiful dog. He was bred from one of those hunting families and Mr. Thompson had given a lot of money for him.

"But Cinder just wasn't a town dog. I think he bit the mailman. He bit two or three neighbors. And people were scared of him. So he had to get rid of him. He gave him to me so we could take him out to the country and he was the best dog we ever had. I was probably 12, maybe 14.

"Cinder was right there and my mom would have chickens, a yard full of chickens. It would come Sunday chicken time and mom would come out and she would pick out maybe two sometimes, or three if we were having company. Cinder would watch her, and Mom would point—'That chicken right there.' There'd be 50 or 60 chickens and Cinder would nail that chicken and bring it right to her. Then, she would point at this one and point at that one. He was a smart dog.

"And he ran with Bully, who was a big bulldog that lived down the road and belonged to my uncle. Bully was a snake dog. He wouldn't walk down the road; he would walk in the ditch. And if the huntin' wasn't good, he'd come out and go on the other side, go in the other ditch. And he got bit so many times, he got halfway immune to it. He would get bit by one of those moccasins, and it would swell up for a couple of days, and Aunt Mays would feed him eggs and cream and stuff. And Bully would get back on his feet and the hunt was on again."

"Muddy—he's the best" Levon said. "He throws a little fit every now and then, acts like he's just got nothing but troubles. And every now and then, he'll decide he wants to make an appearance. We bring him to shows. Sometimes he'll come out and take a bow. You should hear the crowd. It's just fun to take him. Everybody picks at him and knows him and everybody babies him and everything. It's just fun to have him along.

"I think he probably just tolerates the music in the studio. He don't mind the recording part. He can stick around longer for that. When the crowd starts getting into it, that's when he'd rather be somewhere else, I think. If we're recording, a lot of times he'll come over and lay down—hang out a bit.

"You get a laugh or two a day out of Muddy. It just elevates your mood. It really does. And he does enjoy his ice cream."

"Mr. Waller, he's the guy that had the dog that Muddy was going and dog-sitting with," Levon said. "He had a dog that died. The dog had cancer and over the last year of its life, we just never knew about it, but Muddy would take off and run around and the guy, Mr. Waller, told us that Muddy would come up there and go into the house. He'd let Muddy in, and Muddy would sit with his dog, and they would lay there for a while. He said Muddy done it 'til he died. We didn't know he was doing that.

"Oh, the things we found out that Muddy did. Muddy would take off and go down and see Jake. And he'd talk Jake into going over to the bank with him because with Sandy, he'd be at that drive-in window, waiting for that bone. We got a call from the bank one morning about 9:30 that Jake and Muddy were waiting there, trying to get a bone. Muddy showed Jake how to do it. Back then, I was more nervous about him. After two or three hours, I'd start looking for him. I'd catch him over at Jake's or somewhere up and down the road.

"One day, I caught him right downtown, between Bread Alone and the shoe store. He's coming up on the sidewalk—'This land is your land/This land is my land.' I'd been looking all morning for him. I saw him and pulled in there by Bread Alone and rolled down the window and said, 'Muddy!' And he looked at me like, 'What are you doing down here?' He come over and jumped in the car."

"I had this metal trough, and the deer would come up and they would take off and you would see that big momma bear walking right out across the yard," Levon said. "She'd get up there and eat. Then she would stop eating and lay down and two cubs would just get on and nurse. They would do it every morning, just about daylight. I watched them for a good while, then Amy and everyone else got scared and the deer couldn't eat. The bear was coming here more than the deer were, so we finally stopped feeding them.

"One time, that big, goddamn momma bear came through that goddamn doggy door in the kitchen. She came right in here and Muddy was going crazy. Muddy was upstairs and ran right down, and she ran right on in through the kitchen and ran into the big room. I saw her go by the door. I ran back upstairs and grabbed my pistol. I was scared to shoot it. I watched that thing run right through the kitchen door. I looked in, and she was in by the big glass doors and she went BAM! She could see her reflection and Muddy, how smart he is, he ran out and ran around and got on the outside and was barking her back this way. So she turned. As she turned around, she dumped a pile this big and as soon as she got through, she ran right on through the kitchen. By then, I'm behind the other door. I ran right to the refrigerator and grabbed some hot dogs. I was going to flip her some hot dogs.

"I didn't know what she was going to do, if I was going to shoot her in the nose. If she got ahold of me, I was going to do something. She ran right out there and got down and went through that damn doggy door, wiggled right through there. They're just like a damn mouse. They can just swallow their bones one way or another—snake their way out.

"On some nights, she couldn't get all the way in. Another time, she pushed that window over the sink. We had to change the security over there. One of them used to just show up out in the ball field and he'd get over behind the garbage pen. We'd be over doing up the hamburgers on the barbecue. You know that big damn dumpster that they have to have a truck to pick it up? This damn bear took it right in the front parking lot, pulled it all the way out into the middle of the field, and tore the hell out of it. It had one of those heavy plastic tops. He shredded that damn thing, man, like a cigarette paper. It was just so easy for him. We told them, we got to have something with a metal door. How he got that damn thing up, and got it all the way out, I just don't know.

"When the momma would come by, she would have those cubs with her. She would come across the yard and she was slapping the ground. I didn't know what she was doing. I thought maybe she stepped on a damn wasp's nest or a hornet's nest. But she was trying to scare everybody. She's slapping the ground like that, ran right up to those big windows there in the big room in the studio, and slapped the window and turned around and ran back. We were all standing and watching and laughing and everything. She didn't like that. She ran back to the woods. She won't get far from those cubs. The cubs will run up the tree. Muddy will tree them, and she'll stand at the bottom, and they'll cuss at each other. It was a show, boy."

A FINAL WORD:

From Red Rocks to Turkey Scratch

With its demands, its deadlines and its dollar-driven despair, life can be so—predictable.

It's so easy to forget that piling into a car and jumping on an interstate highway will never lose its edge, its allure, its seductive draw, that feeling of invincibility when you are literally in middle-of-nowhere America with nothing but the horizon between you and tomorrow. Dusty dirt roads and anonymous side streets can whisk you through someone else's everyday, allowing you to soak it all in before simply moving on down the highway.

That was the life Levon Helm lived for so many years. And that's the life I caught a glimpse of between 2004 and 2012, on numerous road trips that stretched between Levon Helm Band shows—including the eight-hour drive from the Ryman Auditorium in Nashville to the Arkansas Music Pavilion in Fayetteville; and the seven hours from the Orpheum Theatre in Memphis to the Verizon Theatre at Grand Prairie in Texas, passing through Texarkana, Arkansas, and Fate, Texas, along the way.

You drive for hours, stop at a truck stop for gas and get back on the road. That's all that mattered. It was just you and the open road with plenty of time for thinking, laughing, crying, freaking out, calming yourself back down, confronting your own bullshit, and surrendering to open road romance framed by broken white lines, pavement, and oncoming headlights that pass through your world for just a few seconds.

I came across a lot of compelling situations while attending Levon Helm Band shows out on the road, back home in Woodstock, and many, many places in between.

There was the time after one of Levon's shows at The Beacon Theatre in Manhattan, when Chris Howe and Levon had pulled away from the stage door in their SUV and stopped at a red light at West 75th Street and Broadway. Levon opened the window to say goodnight to Pat Cahill, a member of the Levon Helm Studios security team who was keeping watch on the corner. As Levon and Pat are chatting, a fan comes up with a record for Levon to sign and Pat ran interference. The guy complained loudly, saying, "Come on, man. I came all the way from out of town." Pat looks at the guy, motions toward Levon and says, "So did he." With that, Levon's window went up and Chris took off toward the West Side Drive, en route back to Woodstock.

One mind-bender of a night took place in August 2008, at Saratoga Performing Arts Center in New York, north of Albany.

The Levon Helm Band shared the bill at the Saratoga Music Festival with Bob Dylan, Steve Earle and Allison Moorer, Gillian Welch and Dave Rawlings, Conor Oberst and the Mystic Valley Band, and The Swell Season with Glen Hansard from The Frames.

At some point during the early part of the day, musicians who weren't performing were relaxing on a grassy slope off of stage left that was off limits but visible to the public. They were simply watching whoever was playing. I think I might have seen Hansard watching Earle, Oberst watching Hansard. You get the idea.

The last two acts were the Levon Helm Band, followed by Dylan. During Levon's set, I walked over to where I had seen the performers taking in the show earlier in the day, just to see who was watching Levon play. I thought I might find Steve Earle over there. But when I arrived, I found Dylan, standing, wearing a hooded sweatshirt, and paying close attention to the Levon Helm Band delivering a driving "Rag Mama Rag."

Dylan's face was unshaven, and I kept talking myself out of the fact that it was him, standing just feet from unsuspecting thousands, and just feet from me, where I could take about six steps and touch him. Oblivious passersby walked right past him. I only stopped trying to talk myself out of it when I saw a white stripe down the side of Dylan's pant leg—he was wearing those cowboy pants he so loves. And there he was, Bob Dylan, so close I could toss a slice of watermelon to him. And for part of "Rag Mama Rag" that night, for a few minutes, he was just like me, one of thousands inside Saratoga Performing Arts Center paying close attention to the man from Turkey Scratch, Arkansas, watching every move he made. "Rag Mama Rag" ended and Dylan, accompanied by a very big bodyguard, walked off into the darkness and boarded a tour bus.

On July 31, 2010, Chelsea Clinton—whose father, of course, was governor of Arkansas before he became president of the United States—got married about a half-hour away from Woodstock, in Rhinebeck, N.Y.

The wedding took place at Astor Courts in Rhinebeck, the history of which can be traced back to John Jacob Astor IV. He had been, more than a century ago, one of the wealthiest men in the nation. Unfortunately for Astor, however, he was neither a woman nor a child when, on April 15, 1912, he found himself on the deck of the *Titanic* in the North Atlantic Ocean shortly after it hit an iceberg. On the same day that President Bill Clinton gave away his daughter in Rhinebeck, Phil Lesh from the Grateful Dead was at Levon Helm Studios in Woodstock, having quite the day with his two sons, Grahame and Brian. Joined by Larry and Teresa, with Justin Guip on drums, Phil and his boys performed at the Midnight Ramble that night.

During the Levon Helm Band portion of the evening, which included Donald Fagen of Steely Dan on keyboards and piano, Phil sat on the radiator behind Levon's drum kit and sang along as the Levon Helm Band performed "Deep Elem Blues," a traditional song that the Grateful Dead had once included in their repertoire. Lesh also sat in with the Levon Helm Band on "Shakedown Street," a staple of the Grateful Dead's live concerts for decades that featured Fagen on lead vocals. When the song concluded, Larry said something to the effect of, "Shakedown Street, with Phil Lesh on bass and Donald Fagen on piano and vocals—and you heard it right here."

Mike Gordon from Phish was in the audience that night. So was Academy Award-nominated actress Catherine Keener and an old friend of Levon's, two-time Academy Award-winning actress Jane Fonda. Keener and Fonda were in town filming a movie, *Peace, Love & Misunderstanding.* Levon and Jane had worked together on the 1984 television movie *The Dollmaker* and had known each other for years.

Mike Gordon had attended previous Rambles over the years. At one of them, he was joined by Phish drummer Jon Fishman, who I approached and asked if he was having a good time. Fishman responded by smiling and saying, "OH-MY-GOD."

For part of the night years earlier, Fishman watched from that section of the loft that offered a view of Levon at the drum kit, from directly above. Fishman was so engaged, you might have thought he was a first-year art student on a field trip to the Louvre, studying the *Mona Lisa.* Another time, Gordon returned to the Ramble by himself and sat in on electric bass on "Chest Fever" by The Band.

Back on that infamous Saturday when Lesh was playing at the Ramble on the day Chelsea Clinton got married, I was inside the portion of Levon Helm Studios where Levon and his wife Sandy lived, in between sets.

There I was, being a fly on the wall in the kitchen while Levon chatted with Jane Fonda. A few minutes later, Levon came over to the refrigerator to get some ice for his Coke—he loved to drink Coca-Cola with pure cane sugar in those old-times bottles, the caps on which he popped off with a pair of scissors—and he said to me, "John, let me introduce you to Jane Fonda."

Levon grabbed me by the arm, walked me over to Jane Fonda and said, "Jane, let me introduce you to a friend of mine."

For a brief moment, I wasn't standing next to a rock star and a movie star. I was in the presence of two old friends standing around a kitchen table, talking about old times. Levon had a very gentle way of diffusing any notion of celebrity. He wouldn't take anything away from anyone's achievements, by any means. He just reinforced the human side of it all.

Meeting Jane Fonda in Levon Helm's kitchen that night left me—for the second time in four days—thinking about my late father, a retired New York City Police captain. Dear old Dad did not like Jane Fonda because of her opposition to the Vietnam War.

I hadn't thought about my father much in the years between his death in 2006 and that evening in Levon Helm's kitchen. But I had thought about him a lot three days earlier, when Levon and the gang performed at Radio City Music Hall in Manhattan, on a bill with Willie Nelson.

When I was a kid, I loved hearing my Dad tell the story of how he worked as an usher at Radio City Music Hall when he was, probably, 19-20-years-old. He was responsible for escorting the night's headliner, the star, from their dressing room to the stage. He spoke of an elevator he took up several flights to the star's dressing room. Oh, to imagine my father taking that elevator up and then knocking on the door and saying, "Five minutes, Miss Merman," or "Five minutes Mr. Berle," or "Five minutes, Mr. Sinatra."

The funniest was hearing my Dad describe how Ethel Merman was as loud and obnoxious in person as she was in many of the roles she played in the movies. She used to yell at everyone, my father said. I can't help but think of old Ethel in *It's a Mad, Mad, Mad, Mad World* screaming loudly as that crazy band of people—Buddy Hackett, Phil Silvers and Milton Berle— drive around looking for buried money. And I always remembered my Dad mentioning that elevator he took up to the star's dressing room.

So at about 3 p.m. on July 28, 2010, I walked in the stage door at Radio City Music Hall as a member of Levon's entourage. I checked in and, yup, you guessed it, made my way into an elevator and up several flights to where the Levon Helm Band had a string of dressing rooms. Was it the very same elevator? I like to think so. And how could it not be?

After the show at Radio City, I was in the production office and a blonde woman walked down the hallway outside the door. Some of us commented on how much she looked like Jessica Simpson, the actress. Barbara O'Brien, who always had a grip on reality—regardless of the situation that happened to be emerging or collapsing around the Levon Helm

Band entourage at the moment—said something to the effect of, "Hello— that *was* Jessica Simpson."

The next thing I know, Jessica Simpson is in the production office and people are crowding to get into pictures with her. We all surmised that Simpson was at the show because she and Willie both appeared in the motion-picture version of *The Dukes of Hazzard*. Simpson played Daisy Duke and Willie was Uncle Jessie.

So the buzz continued around us all, and I got a hug and a peck on the cheek from Simpson and she was saying, "Goodbye," Goodbye," "Goodbye" to everyone. As she headed back into the hallway, I got a laugh out of Barbara by calling out, "See ya later, Jess."

Another epic adventure unfolded in June 2009, when I flew out to Denver, rented a car and drove to see the Levon Helm Band play a show with John Prine at Red Rocks Amphitheatre in Morrison, Colorado.

The American frontier, the vast abandon of the West, and the riptide of rock and roll all crystallize at Red Rocks in suburban Denver.

Imagine God or mother nature or the universe or grand design or whichever devotion you subscribe to crafting skyscrapers out of nothing more than highly concentrated sand, then dipping it all in the crimson cry of the finest sunset to ever singe your eyelashes. Then, a viewing platform with benches is installed, and the finest musicians in the land are invited in to share their art. That, my friends, is Red Rocks.

"The whole thing looks like it has got rouge on it—them rocks, all that stuff," Levon said. "It looks like somebody painted it with someone's rouge, makeup. And when the sun gets in there about five o'clock, six o'clock, the whole damn thing is like an orange light comes on. It's just amazing. The way it's built in there, that natural kind of amphitheater, it's like playing on the water. It just naturally sounds good."

Opened on June 15, 1941, six months before the bombing of Pearl Harbor triggered U.S. involvement in World War II, Red Rocks stands today as a monument to live music, the American spirit, and the legacy of Franklin D. Roosevelt, the 32nd president of the United States.

Like Levon, FDR lived and is buried in New York's Hudson Valley. Roosevelt was also born there, and his entire life—including his presidency—revolved around the Town of Hyde Park, which is located in Dutchess County, a twenty-seven-mile drive from Woodstock that will take you southeast, across the Hudson River.

According to www.redrocksonline.com, the federal government on May 9, 1936, gave the City of Denver the green light to use the Civilian Conservation Corps to build Red Rocks Amphitheatre.

According to the Franklin D. Roosevelt Presidential Library and Museum in Hyde Park, the CCC during its nine-year existence employed nearly three million young men, ages 17-24, many from urban areas, to work on conservation projects in rural environments. Designed to provide employment during the Great Depression, the CCC planted more than two billion trees; fought forest fires; built trails, campgrounds and reservoirs; aided with soil conservation programs; and built Red Rocks Amphitheatre. CCC enrollees included Robert Mitchum, Raymond Burr and Walter Matthau, who went on to become Hollywood actors; and Stan Musial, who later played professional baseball for the St. Louis Cardinals. CCC enrollees also included U.S. Air Force Brigadier General Chuck Yeager, who Levon got to know during the filming of *The Right Stuff*.

New York City has Madison Square Garden. The Wild West has Red Rocks.

The Irish rock band U2 performed and recorded an iconic concert at Red Rocks, on June 5, 1983.

Jimi Hendrix played Red Rocks on September 1, 1968. The Beatles played Red Rocks on August 26, 1964. The Grateful Dead performed there 20 times between 1978 and 1987.

The Levon Helm Band performed there on June 13, 2009, and it was a grand day for a grand gig. But the altitude—6,400 feet above sea level—took its toll on Levon's voice. Two nights later, at Cain's Ballroom in Tulsa, Oklahoma, Levon's voice gave out as he sang the first lines of the first song of the night, "Ophelia." The rest of the band members, over the course of that evening, stepped up to fill the gaping hole that emerged.

And as you can see in the documentary *Ain't In It for My Health,* things did not get better as Levon and the gang continued that run of shows in Fayetteville and Little Rock, Arkansas.

The day after the show at Red Rocks, I returned my rental car and traveled overnight to Kansas City, Missouri, by Amtrak.

There is a lot to be said for sitting in one of those double-decker train cars with the glass in the ceilings as the sun is going down and you're pulling out of Denver into a stretch of the country that most of us only fly over to get somewhere else—America seemed so big.

After sunrise, the train stopped for a few minutes in Ottumwa, Iowa, the home of Corporal Radar O'Reilly in the television sitcom *M*A*S*H.* Looking at Ottumwa from the train station, I was reminded of those little towns along the New York State Thruway west of Albany, not that far from Woodstock, like Gloversville and Canajoharie—places you might have only ever passed on the highway, when you wonder for just a few minutes about the people who live there, and then, in an instant, you never care or think about them again. I switched trains in Galesburg, Illinois, where Pulitzer Prize-winning poet and author Carl Sandburg grew up, and it was onward to Kansas City. My plan was to catch an overnight bus from Kansas City to Tulsa, Oklahoma, and Cain's Ballroom.

But Cain's and Tulsa and the hottest day I would ever experience in my life—outside of my trip to Turkey Scratch later that week—was still two days away.

With all the traveling I was doing that week, from little towns to big cities, in cars, on planes and trains, the 90 minutes or so I spent in Union Station in Kansas City, Missouri, where my Amtrak trip ended, provided me with some of my biggest adventures. Having wandered through Grand Central Station in Manhattan countless times, at all hours of the day and night, I wasn't really worried about any nefarious incident that might await me late at night, inside the cavernous halls of Union Station in Kansas City. We were in Missouri after all.

As I left my train, there were dozens of people in line waiting to board a departing train. There were a few clerks behind the counter and plenty of folks around.

I paid a visit to the men's room and returned to the main hall. That's when I noticed that everything had gotten awfully quiet. Somehow, in an instant, all of the people I had seen upon arriving here were gone—the passengers, the clerks, everyone. I guess that last train of the evening had come and gone. It very quickly became apparent that everyone seemed to have left, except for a tall, skinny, strung-out guy dressed in jeans and a white t-shirt, who looked like he had been up for days.

It must have been my lucky day. Despite the dozens of empty seats in the vacant and cavernous Union Station, this guy sat down next to me.

I turned to him. He turned to me. And then, out of the blue, as though we were philosophizing together, he asked me, "How can you tell when someone is lying?" I didn't answer, but got up and ventured around the station. I now realized that this guy and I were the only two people in the entire station—or so it seemed. The lights were dim, the hour was late and I was getting a little nervous. All of a sudden, it seemed like I was the only person in Missouri—aside from my new friend. Luckily, I saw two guys standing just outside the station, under a big awning. Ah, I thought, safety in numbers. So I ventured outside.

And then it occurred to me, as rain fell, thunder rumbled and lightning lit up the late-night sky, that I had no idea at which entrance to this monstrosity of a dark, cavernous cave of a train station, and there were many entrances, my bus to Tulsa would be arriving. So, I ambled up to the two guys waiting under the awning and asked them if they were waiting for the bus to Tulsa. No, they said. They had just been released from prison several hours earlier, and were waiting for a van that would take them to a halfway house. And then I looked at them and noticed that they had several cardboard boxes between them, and clear, plastic bags filled with belongings, including clothes. One of them asked to borrow my cell phone so he could call the driver of the van he was waiting for, to see when it would arrive.

And then, in the middle of this thunderstorm, with rain pounding, the lawn sprinklers went on. And the guy who looked like he had been up for days returned, seemingly from out of nowhere.

As I was attempting to piece all of this together, wondering if I would ever catch my bus to Tulsa, or remain forever in Kansas City—or live to see the dawn for that matter—a security guard appeared. He was completely uninterested in the two guys just hours out of prison. And he was equally uninterested in the guy who looked like he had been up for days and who was probably just a few hours away from being behind bars himself. Nope. The man who, thankfully, was the only one armed in this group, looked directly at me with a scowl, as if to say, "What kind of person are you, that you would be hanging out with these three?"

Okay, I thought, "Welcome to Kansas City, Mr. Barry."

Well, I made it to Tulsa, attended the show at Cain's Ballroom and took a Greyhound bus at about 2:00 a.m. to Joplin, Missouri. Lord knows when we arrived, but it was before sunrise, and—I guess to make sure folks don't sleep in the bus stations—they shut them down for a few hours right around dawn. So there I was, in Joplin, Missouri, shortly before dawn, with about four hours to kill until my bus to Fayetteville, Arkansas, arrived. So I bundled up and curled up against my backpack and suitcase and had me a nap, right there on the sidewalk. I slept like a baby for about two hours and miraculously wasn't bothered by anyone—no muggers and no cops.

My next stop was Arkansas, the 25th state, the birthplace of Johnny Cash, the land of Levon Helm.

Just as it can be hard to find the words to describe Levon Helm, I remain at a loss for words to describe Turkey Scratch, Arkansas, where Levon grew up. As someone who grew up in the New York City suburbs, just the words "Turkey Scratch" launch me into outer space. Paved roads turn into gravel. Pieces of farming equipment that would tower above a small cottage dot the landscape.

On my visits to Turkey Scratch, I found temperatures that topped 100 degrees, a lush, tropical climate, farms that consumed the landscape and MoonPie dessert items for sale in A.B. Thompson's store.

Also on my visits to Turkey Scratch, I was able to venture deep into the heart of the American South, and for a kid who grew up in the New York City suburbs, to quote Levon, that was like "going to the moon." Visiting the South for many means a trip to Nashville, or Charleston, or Savannah or New Orleans. But I'll take Turkey Scratch any day, where I felt a rush of national pride just as I do when I visit the Herb Brooks Arena in Lake Placid, New York, where the U.S. Men's Olympic Hockey Team defeated the Soviet Union in 1980 on their way to winning the gold medal.

When I think of Turkey Scratch, Arkansas, and the late Levon Helm, I think of something that Bono, the lead singer of the Irish rock band U2, has said from the stage during concerts.

"America is not just a country, it's an idea."

Well, after visiting Turkey Scratch, Arkansas, twice, I can tell you that Turkey Scratch is not just a community where people work and farm and live and die—Turkey Scratch is an idea. It's an idea built around hard work, results, simplicity that ignites big thinking, nurturing one's self-worth, taking pride in being fair to others, compassion and hustling hard to generate a fair deal for buyer and seller alike.

And yes, you could say all of these very same things about the Midnight Ramble as well.

———

A year after my first visit to Turkey Scratch, while traveling in 2010 from a Levon Helm Band show at the Orpheum Theatre in Memphis to a show at the Verizon Theatre in Grand Prairie, Texas, I realized I could swing through Dallas and scope out Dealey Plaza, where President John F. Kennedy was assassinated on November 22, 1963.

Talk of the Kennedy assassination got Levon going like little else.

"...Hit him, hit Kennedy in a couple spots, and then it turned around and came back and blew half of his head on the back of the trunk," Levon said. "It done a 360 and moved like that. It was so goddamn obvious that someone had stepped out from up in that overpass there and clipped him. It hit him and just sprayed. I saw it. I was watching it. Who was that asshole who said, 'What, you think America had a coup d'état?' Yeah. That's what you call it.

"At the time, we were playing in Canada. So I'm watching it on television. I'm watching the parade on television. I saw it. I haven't seen that film since. He gets in office, names his brother attorney general, and the first thing he does is declare war on everybody, open warfare on everybody. What is wrong with him? I'm gonna tell you the truth. Them boys might have went to Harvard and all that, and I loved them, but goddammit, they had no common sense at all. You just don't do shit like that. Karma will get your ass. Especially with folks like that. You can't run over folks like that."

Hearing Levon talk about the Kennedy assassination, and then seeing him appear in the Mark Wahlberg film, *Shooter*, taught me one thing loud and clear. There is no separating Levon the actor from Levon the man. He wasn't acting. He was just being himself.

Speaking about the Kennedy assassination in *Shooter*, Levon, playing the character Mr. Rate, tells Wahlberg, "Them boys on the grassy knoll, they were dead within three hours—buried in the damn desert; unmarked graves out past Terlingua."

Actor Michael Peña's character, Nick Memphis, asks, "And you know this for a fact?" The response from Levon's character: "I still got the shovel."

I had a similar experience of life imitating art—or vice versa—early on in my time at Levon Helm Studios. Levon asked me if I'd like a stick of chewing gum. I said, "Sure," and he handed me a piece of Beemans. That, of course, made the hair on the back of my neck stand up, because I had seen Levon in *The Right Stuff* many times.

"Hey Ridley, ya got any Beemans?" Sam Shepard's character, Gen. Chuck Yeager, asks Levon's character, Capt. Jack Ridley, throughout the movie. Levon responds, "Yeah. I think I got a stick."

Every time, Shepard says, "Loan me some, will you? I'll pay you back later." And every time, Ridley answers, "Fair enough."

Just as with acting, there was no separating Levon the musician from Levon the man.

Watch him play the drums or watch him appear on the silver screen—it's just Levon being Levon, in his signature, effortless manner. I'm sure he never thought twice about it. He just went out there and was himself, whether he was acting in a movie or playing in a band. I think it was all the same to him. Give the crowd—from the Joyous Lake in Woodstock to Madison Square Garden—the best you've got, and send them home feeling like they got more than their money's worth, because they usually did.

For all of my adventures on the road, there were many nights when the world and all its wonder, on so many levels, came to Woodstock.

In December 2010, none other than Chad Smith, drummer for the Red Hot Chili Peppers, attended the Midnight Ramble.

While watching the Levon Helm Band perform, he clapped along to "Ophelia" and nodded in approval during "When I Go Away."

Smith sat in with the Levon Helm Band on two songs—"Mardi Gras Day" and "The Weight"—playing Levon's cocktail drum kit. At Levon's insistence, Smith moved the cocktail kit closer to his drum set.

"He said to move in closer," Smith said to the crowd. "I'm coming in."

During an interview with the *Poughkeepsie Journal* moments after the show ended, Smith declared the experience, "A dream come true. Such an honor and a privilege. I just didn't want to screw up."

Smith was interested to learn that he played the same cocktail kit that Jack DeJohnette, a Bearsville resident and former drummer for Miles Davis, played while he sat in at a Ramble several years earlier. Smith also said that while he grew up listening to bands like Black Sabbath and Led Zeppelin, particularly as a teenage drummer, he grew to appreciate The Band.

"That's just true, original American rock music," he said.

Before picking up the drumsticks for "Mardi Gras Day," Smith bowed twice in front of Helm and looked at the crowd, raised his arms and pointed both fingers at the man from Turkey Scratch. Smith played the drums with a ferocity and passion that was complemented nicely by timing that accentuated Helm's playing.

Smith at several points seemed to take cues from Helm's playing and at the end of each song, in a very funny, affectionate move, leaned over and played Helm's drum kit for several seconds.

Moments after the performance ended, Smith said he and his wife had recently moved to New York and attended the Midnight Ramble at the suggestion of friends. When asked if the Red Hot Chili Peppers might ever play a Ramble, he paused and thought for a few seconds.

"That's a good question," said Smith, who wore black pants and a black t-shirt with Mickey Mouse on the front. "That's a good question. We play small places, and the energy is just so different, which is so great because it is so immediate, and there is something that is really great about that. I don't know if we're Ramblers—I mean, we can Ramble. We don't need small places to Ramble. We can Ramble at a festival, no problem. I'm going to tell them about it, of course. I can't wait. Flea is going to be stoked."

There was also the night that the band Dawes played the Ramble, on Dec. 3, 2011, and was joined by Jackson Browne.

"My memory of that night is something like, 'I can't believe I did that, was that real?'" said Dawes drummer Griffin Goldsmith. "To say it was an honor is an understatement. It definitely felt like a barn. There was a grit to it. Levon couldn't have been cooler. The whole experience embodied what music should be. It was collaborative in an easy way. Nobody seemed stressed despite the stakes, and despite the fact that some of the greats of all time were in the room. Elation is an adjective that comes to mind."

Browne offered his own take on the evening, while on stage with Dawes.

"I've been hearing a lot about this, but I don't think there's any way it can be described," Browne said. "This is a thrill. This is hallowed ground for those us from California. We've been hearing about this for a long time."

Jimmy Vivino and Garth Hudson were also on the bill that night, performing songs of The Band. During their set, I was in the house, where Jackson Browne was hanging out with members of the Levon Helm Band.

I was sitting in the rocking chair near the fireplace and noticed Levon, by himself, over by the door that leads out to the studio, where the performance was going on. He had opened the door just a bit and was listening very closely to Jimmy sing The Band song "Stage Fright."

The look on Levon's face didn't reveal much about all that might have been running through his mind at that moment, but he was listening with the focus of someone studying the details of a painting, or ruminating over a mathematical equation. It was one of the most poignant moments I ever witnessed up at Levon Helm Studios. It only lasted a minute or two. But I'll never forget it as long as I live.

You can learn a lot about someone you know by watching him take the stage in front of thousands of people, as I saw Levon Helm do at Red Rocks Amphitheatre, in Morrison, Colorado, on June 13, 2010. This is the guy admired by millions. He was a rock star, after all.

You watch this guy, who you have come to know, inspire thousands. He sings "The Weight" and complete strangers thrust their arms in the air in triumph. It's not as if they were simply watching their hometown pitcher win the World Series with a called-strike three in the ninth inning. This was as though *they* had just won the World Series by pitching a called strike three in the ninth inning.

During "The Weight"—always the last song to end a Levon Helm Band show—a sense of triumph consumed the room, radiating from the guy behind the drum kit as strongly as it did from the fans in the audience. Everyone shared in all that Levon had accomplished, with The Band and beyond. And that communal sense of belonging and giving and taking is what drove all those Levon Helm Band shows—at the Midnight Ramble in Woodstock and on the road. That sense of community also framed Levon's comeback.

You look at him up onstage, projected in the image of a celebrity by so many, and at the same time, you see the guy who simply loves to hear a good story as much as he loves to tell one. He's also the guy who, while traveling home from Gotham Hall in New York City on May 5, 2010, after being honored by WFUV in the Bronx, snapped his last toothpick in two and handed me half when he realized there was only one left.

You learn a lot about a guy from watching him strike up a conversation with strangers who are left speechless—physically dumbstruck—in his presence. And you can learn a lot about this guy by traveling to his hometown of Turkey Scratch, Arkansas, and seeing firsthand the unpaved roads and silos and shacks and fields of black soil, all of which testify to the commanding authority of an album called *Dirt Farmer.*

It all leaves you pondering the manner in which this poor kid from cotton country burst onto the world stage, won it all, lost it, then got it all back again. Levon's life was stitched together with a fraying patchwork of triumphant climbs, steep drops, sharp turns, near misses, and head-on collisions. But the secret to Levon's success was that he always bounced back. He always got back in the game for another swing. He never quit.

You can learn a lot about a person from the things that bring them fulfillment—a roaring fire, the bark of a dog, the strike of a stick on a drum, the strum of a mandolin, a horn section or a good joke.

You can learn a lot about someone by retracing his steps through the crowds and the concerts, the struggles and the sold-out shows, the loneliness and the laughter, the desperation and the drama. Likewise, you can learn a lot by retracing their steps along the highways and dusty dirt roads, the red carpets and creaky floorboards—all of which set out a path, over the course of a lifetime, from Little Rock to Toronto, from Woodstock to Broadway, from Red Rocks to Turkey Scratch.

ACKNOWLEDGEMENTS

The author would like to thank Radio Woodstock (WDST/100.1 FM) and owner Gary Chetkof for granting permission to use the following quotes, from an October 2008 Radio Woodstock interview, in this book.

Page 111: "Each band plays at least an hour and we probably play two hours. By the time we quit, which is between 11:30 and midnight, they've had four-to-five hours of music and that's just about enough in one day. You really can lose the outside world and all those aggravations."

Page 112: "There is no pressure around here. When you play, you can start pretty much and finish when you want to and play what you want to. We try to leave it that way, let it be what it wants to be."

Page 150: "Just playing here in the studio for a couple hundred people is as much fun as playing Madison Square Garden. It's actually more fun. It sounds better and it's a lot easier."

Page 151: "We play Road Rambles, down to the Beacon Theater in the city."

Page 234: "It fit so good, especially if you're born and raised in the country, like I am."

Page 185: "The Grammy for *Dirt Farmer* is a wonderful payback for everybody—all of us who worked on *Dirt Farmer*. It took a while to do it. It wasn't like I could money-whip them into working, so they pretty much did it by the skin of their teeth. Having it turn out successful, so I could pay everyone back, was exactly what we needed."

Page 186: "If I hadn't won, I would have had to say, 'Well, it didn't mean anything anyway.' But it does help and I'm happy that I won it. You know you put that little sticker on the cover, it sells the product so well and it does help."

Page 188: "We started to get calls about using the studio. People like the sound of *Dirt Farmer* and then when they come and see a Ramble, they realize that a lot of it is the studio, the sound of this room. During *Dirt Farmer* we were finally able to get enough good equipment and good machines together that we could make a decent sounding record now. That's been our latest celebration now, is to hear the place not referred to as so white an elephant as it used to be. It still costs a fortune to try and heat it, but it sounds good."

Page 188: "We got in on a few of the festivals. That was one thing *Dirt Farmer* did for us. It got us invited to Bonnaroo and MerleFest and a lot of the good shows. One of the best was the moe.down festival in upstate New York. Boy that was a lot of fun. I hope we do it next year and you need to go with us if we do. It's a great festival. Up there, it was a whole lot like MerleFest. It had a small-town flavor to it and the people running it were all relaxed and nobody felt like they had to exercise their authority, ordering anyone around or any of that malarkey. It was real peaceful, plenty of good space for people to come out and stuff, just a well-run community festival."

Page 198: "We had a cotton farm down in Arkansas. I wasn't very good at picking cotton."

Page 199: "My dad, I guess he had hopes of me being a scholar, so he never forced me to stay out of school. School started, thankfully, just as cotton-picking season started, so as long as I didn't get kicked out of school, I didn't have to stay home and pick cotton. In the summertime, when the cultivating and the planning goes on, that was when I had to be on duty."

Page 232: "We were all country boys for the most part. It was an ideal situation for us. We could travel down to the city for a show and sleep in our own bed that night. We were two hours, hour-and-a-half from the city. You can get away from it and get that country kind of sleep. There is so much electricity in the air, it's hard to sleep in the city. Just as you start to go to sleep, here come the garbage trucks."

Page 234: "The other good thing about Woodstock is, there's been so many famous-type star people, that have come and record and one thing or another over the years, that someone famous can come and see us and the town doesn't react objectively, or startlingly, to any of those kinds of occasions. So anyone who comes to Woodstock can feel comfortable."

Page 259: "We'd get to see him every day and get to eat lunch with him and hear all those stories. He does everything with both hands and when he talks, he talks with his hands. His fingers are very nimble and he's always twisting and turning them when he talks. He would tell us great, wonderful stories."

Page 260: "Acting is that same kind of harmony singing, sort of an intimacy you have with other people and I try to substitute the director for the producer and when they holler 'action,' try and give it to 'em. It's a lot of fun."

Page 262: "William Robert and myself are on the same label, we are both with Vanguard Records, so that kind makes it cozy and we are both from Arkansas and we are both drummers and we both work hard to be actors and he's a damn good one, too. We hit it off great. The more we're around each other, the more fun we have, and the more alike we seem to be in our upbringing and with what makes us laugh."

MORE ACKNOWLEDGEMENTS

Preface: "The British viewed New York City...As the years passed Kingston slowly rebuilt..." Nps.gov/nr/travel/kingston/revolt.htm.

Page 254: "A captivating look at a musician hanging onto his art for dear life, even when he's too weary to perform." Hollywoodreporter.com/movies/movie-reviews/aint-it-my-health-film-29421. October 14, 2010.

Page 32: "According to msbluestrail.org...played guitar on records by Chuck Berry and Willie Dixon." msbluestrail.org/blues-trail-markers/hubert-sumlin

Page 32: According to *Rolling Stone* magazine, The Rolling Stones paid for Sumlin's funeral when he died in 2011. Rollingstone.com/music/music-news/mick-jagger-and-keith-richards-will-pay-hubert-sum-   lins-funeral-expenses-2-232027/

Page 229: "In August 1965, according to *This Wheel's On Fire*, Levon and the Hawks were playing Tony Mart's, a club in Somers Point, New Jersey, on the Jersey Shore. They had moved on from the Hawk. And then came Bob Dylan. *This Wheel's On Fire: Levon Helm and The Story of The Band,* by Levon Helm with Stephen Davis.

Page 229: "A month earlier, in July 1965...They all flew back to New York and Levon left Bob and the band." *This Wheel's On Fire: Levon Helm and The Story of The Band,* by Levon Helm with Stephen Davis.

Page 115: Mumford & Sons opened a Ramble in March 2012. "We're going to try and do justice to this hallowed room... we'll certainly try." PoughkeepsieJournal.com, March 12, 2012.

Page 287: In December 2010, none other than Chad Smith, drummer for the Red Hot Chili Peppers, attended the Midnight Ramble...Flea is going to be stoked." Poughkeepsie *Journal.com,* December 5, 2010.

Page 288: "I've been hearing a lot about this but I don't think there's any way it can be described," Browne said. "This is a thrill. This is hallowed ground for those us from California. We've been hearing about this for a long time." PoughkeepsieJournal.com, December 4, 2011.

Page 84: "The explosion of blues...fearful they might miss one note of singing." Poughkeepsie Journal, December 6, 2005.

All Non-Band history of the Woodstock Playhouse: www.woodstockplayhouse.org.

Howard Johnson biographical information: www.hojotuba.com.

LEVON HELM STUDIOS

Levon Helm Studios in Woodstock, New York, where Levon launched and held the Midnight Ramble, continues to host live music on a regular basis.

Visit Levonhelm.com for information about performances, purchasing tickets and more.

LEVON HELM MEMORIAL SCHOLARSHIP FUND

Levon's memory, his passion for music, his passion for local agriculture and the enduring love he had for his hometown Ulster County and Hudson Valley, New York, are all celebrated in the Levon Helm Memorial Scholarship Fund.

Each year, a music-bound student from Levon's community receives a $250 gift; and if there's another student pursuing a career in agriculture, they are also awarded a $250 gift.

If you feel so inclined, you can send a donation in the form of a check to: Onteora High School, 4166 SR 28, Boiceville, NY 12412, Attn: L. Casey. Please write "Levon Helm Scholarship" in the memo portion of the check. Thank you!

THANK YOU

Eternal thanks to Levon Helm.

Eternal thanks to my beautiful wife, Amy Day, and my siblings, Eileen Kalukin, Donald Barry, Jeanmarie Cahill and Maureen Carroll.

Eternal thanks to Sandy Helm and Amy Helm. Thank you so much for your warm hospitality at The Barn.

Eternal thanks and the gratitude of a lifetime to Barbara O'Brien, Tony LoBue and Geanine Kane. Thank you. Thank you. Thank you. A very special thanks to Tony LoBue for the design and execution of the website for this book, rockrollramble.com.

A very special thanks to Mike Dubois for designing the book cover. Thank you Dino Perrucci for the cover photo and thank you Chris Howe for the back cover photo.

Eternal thanks and gratitude to Larry Campbell, Jimmy Vivino, Teresa Williams, Byron Isaacs, Jim Weider, Anna Lee Amsden, Mary Cavette, Paul Berry, Mary Berry, Barbara C. O'Brien, Randy Ciarlante, Erik Lawrence, Elizabeth Freund, Dawn LoBue, Tom Gagliardi, Cathy Gagliardi, John O'Neill, Don Pecora, Jack Kane, Chris Howe, Pat Cahill, Walter Turk, Brendan McDonough, Justin Guip, Mary Guip, Brian Parillo, Andrew Shober, Julia Shober, Chris Edwards, Paul Schmitz, Chandler Thompson, Perry Gallo, John Scurti, Jean Douglas, Jeff Stephenson, John Peck, Mike Sheehan, Bill Speight, Brian Mitchell, Steven Bernstein, Jay Collins, Clark Gayton, Howard Johnson, Mike Merritt, Mark McKenna, Curt Ramm, Allen Won, Bob Brinkman, Doug Sawicki, Regina Sawicki, Connor Milton, Margaret Stewart, Mike Manfredonio, Deb Manfredonio, Steve Farrell, Dolores Farrell, Fran Prendergast, Connor Kennedy, Mindy Kennedy, Mike Kennedy, Tony Leone, Fiona McBain, Ahron Foster, Paul LaRaia, Dr. Alexandra Ramsahai, Jason Desmarais, Jochen Wilms, Carl Carlton, Kathy Gillis, Richard Bockelmann, Paul Van Blarcum,

Kelly DuBois, Amy Berson-Sayers, Pete Genzer, Rob Miraldi, Howard Good, Mike Burkert, Ken Seitel, Gregg Navins, Henry Sirakovsky, Mihir Goswami, Dennis Kastanis, Patrick Heaphy, Mike Donoghue, W.B. "Brad" King and WBKING LLC, Steve Kaplan, Ed Felton, Steve Bohn, Ken Simpson, Peter Berkowitz, Frank Barry, Kevin Barry, Rennie Pincus, Jerry Treacy, John Penney, Dugan Radwin, Meg Downey, Stu Shinske, Rich Kleban, John Nelson, Tony Davenport, Mike Benischek, Tom Tripicco, Patrick Oehler, Robert Brum, Steve Lieberman, Greg Clary, Nancy Cutler, Camille Cooper, Amy Vernon, Cliff Laube, Jean Speight, Colleen Speight, Billy Speight Jr., Charlie Speight, Happy Traum, Jane Traum, Mike Pinsky, James Monroe, Jon Dupee, Small Batch Books, Trish Thompson, Madeline Levin, Holly George-Warren, Robert Burke Warren and Adam Caplan.

Eternal thanks to the Levon Helm Studios team, past and present.

Eternal thanks to Radio Woodstock (WDST/100.1 FM) owner and Mountain Jam founder Gary Chetkof; Radio Woodstock Program Director Greg Gattine; Radio Woodstock team members Richard Fusco, Assa Sacko Zarcone, Lenny Bloch and Justin Foy; and past Radio Woodstock team members Brett Pasternak, Carmel Holt, Franz Kaisik and Noel Nelson.

Eternal thanks to Radio Kingston Executive Director Jimmy Buff and WKZE (98.1 FM)'s Paul Higgins and Rick Schneider.

Eternal thanks to Bardavon 1869 Opera House Executive Director Chris Silva, Bardavon Managing Director of Theatre Production Stephen LaMarca and the entire staff of the Bardavon in Poughkeepsie and Broadway Theater at Ulster Performing Arts Center in Kingston, New York.

And there are no words, anywhere, anyhow, any day to truly express my gratitude to Ringo Starr, Roger Waters, Graham Nash, Warren Haynes and Danny Louis. Thank you, thank you, thank you so much, from the bottom to the top of my very grateful heart.

www.ingramcontent.com/pod-product-compliance
Lightning Source LLC
Chambersburg PA
CBHW022035290426
44109CB00014B/866